Our L...
by Kevin Flyn...

"Being the opening day for hunting season, could it be an accident? Not likely. So who would want to murder Danny? The secrets in this little town will absolutely astonish readers. *Our Little Secret* is destined to be on this year's top ten true crime list. So be sure it's on YOUR reading list!"
—*True Crime Book Reviews*

"It may be hard to imagine keeping murder a secret for two decades. But in *Our Little Secret,* Kevin Flynn and Rebecca Lavoie examine the inner workings of small-town life in the story of Daniel Paquette's death in 1985."
—NewHampshire.com

"A suspenseful read even if you already know the story. The authors have developed names and facts in police reports into characters and plots." —*Concord Monitor*

"A true crime book that delves into every twist and turn in the case." —*New Hampshire Villager*

"The team brings alive the anxiety, fear, and loathing that surrounded the case . . . The book reads like a real whodunit, especially for those readers who know nothing of the case."
—*New Hampshire Magazine*

"A compelling tale and an in-depth look at this complicated subject." —*The Hooksett Banner*

continued . . .

"The book has a reality that is fascinating . . . Truth is always stranger than fiction, and this book portrays that beautifully." —*The Springfield (MA) Republican*

"Kevin Flynn and Rebecca Lavoie tell an extraordinary story with great restraint, skill, and detail . . . How the crime came to be solved is as unexpected as the way it was hidden. This is a great story, skillfully told." —*Dancing with Skeletons*

LEGALLY
DEAD

Kevin Flynn and Rebecca Lavoie

BERKLEY BOOKS, NEW YORK

THE BERKLEY PUBLISHING GROUP
Published by the Penguin Group
Penguin Group (USA) Inc.
375 Hudson Street, New York, New York 10014, USA
Penguin Group (Canada), 90 Eglinton Avenue East, Suite 700, Toronto, Ontario M4P 2Y3, Canada
(a division of Pearson Penguin Canada Inc.)
Penguin Books Ltd., 80 Strand, London WC2R 0RL, England
Penguin Group Ireland, 25 St. Stephen's Green, Dublin 2, Ireland (a division of Penguin Books Ltd.)
Penguin Group (Australia), 250 Camberwell Road, Camberwell, Victoria 3124, Australia
(a division of Pearson Australia Group Pty. Ltd.)
Penguin Books India Pvt. Ltd., 11 Community Centre, Panchsheel Park, New Delhi—110 017, India
Penguin Group (NZ), 67 Apollo Drive, Rosedale, Auckland 0632, New Zealand
(a division of Pearson New Zealand Ltd.)
Penguin Books (South Africa) (Pty.) Ltd., 24 Sturdee Avenue, Rosebank, Johannesburg 2196,
South Africa

Penguin Books Ltd., Registered Offices: 80 Strand, London WC2R 0RL, England

The publisher does not have any control over and does not assume any responsibility for authors' or
third-party websites or their content.

LEGALLY DEAD

A Berkley Book / published by arrangement with the authors

PRINTING HISTORY
Berkley premium edition / October 2011

Copyright © 2011 by Kevin Flynn and Rebecca Lavoie.
Cover design by MNStudios.

All rights reserved.
No part of this book may be reproduced, scanned, or distributed in any printed or electronic form
without permission. Please do not participate in or encourage piracy of copyrighted materials in
violation of the authors' rights. Purchase only authorized editions.
For information, address: The Berkley Publishing Group,
a division of Penguin Group (USA) Inc.,
375 Hudson Street, New York, New York 10014.

ISBN: 978-0-425-24366-4

BERKLEY®
Berkley Books are published by The Berkley Publishing Group,
a division of Penguin Group (USA) Inc.,
375 Hudson Street, New York, New York 10014.
BERKLEY® is a registered trademark of Penguin Group (USA) Inc.
The "B" design is a trademark of Penguin Group (USA) Inc.

PRINTED IN THE UNITED STATES OF AMERICA

10 9 8 7 6 5 4 3 2 1

If you purchased this book without a cover, you should be aware that this book is stolen property. It
was reported as "unsold and destroyed" to the publisher, and neither the authors nor the publisher has
received any payment for this "stripped book."

Most Berkley Books are available at special quantity discounts for bulk purchases for sales, promo-
tions, premiums, fund-raising, or educational use. Special books, or book excerpts, can also be created
to fit specific needs.

For details, write: Special Markets, The Berkley Publishing Group, 375 Hudson Street, New York,
New York 10014.

To Henry and Teddy:
follow examples of goodness and you will become men.
—KF

To the great friends we've made our family,
you make everything better.
—RL

Acknowledgments

The authors would like to thank the many people who contributed—in ways big and small—to the writing of this book. We are immensely grateful for your support.

First, thank you to the many people who shared their recollections that made up the narrative of this story. They include Joseph Bader, Lois Stewart, John Kacavas, Joseph Laplante, Mark Sisti, Paul Twomey, Richard Kane, Rick Kelly, Heidi Boyack Barba, Barbara Taylor, and Michael Cormier. Additional assistance was provided by Sandro Stuto, Sebastian Caradonna, Matt Buzby, Ivan Eaton, Yvonne Vissing, Andrew Livernois, Michael Delaney, Jim Boffetti, Richard Mitchell, Kim Roberts, Dick Campbell, Audrey Cox, Paul Falco, Jeff Lyons, Dan Wise, Kris Neilsen, Jim Cole, Jeff Strelzin, and Will Delker. Also, this book greatly benefited from the cooperation of Seth Bader; the authors are thankful for his correspondence.

Researching a case from the pre-Internet age can be daunting, so we'd like to recognize those who helped with "just the facts." They include Mary Searles of the New

Hampshire Law Library and Ann Rice, Joan Bissonnette, and Rachel Scott of the New Hampshire Department of Justice.

We wish to thank the many friends and family who've allowed us to stand them up at parties, skip nights on the town, bring criminal records on vacation and laptops to happy hour, and otherwise be temporarily absent from their lives while writing and rewriting this book. We would also like to thank those who supported us in our work by providing us the space and resources to do it, namely Jennifer and Joshua Rubenstein, whose Manhattan apartment always inspires quality output, and Marianne and Robert Fleischman, who are consistent in their valuable feedback about our work as it develops and in their insistence on celebrating when any milestone is reached. Thanks also to Rebecca's colleagues at New Hampshire Public Radio, where the telling of stories is not only supported, but is actively encouraged.

Lastly, the authors would like to thank all those who labored for months to bring this project from an idea to the book you hold in your hands. Thanks to our agent, Sharlene Martin, and her staff at Martin Literary Management, and to the consummate and patient professionals at The Berkley Publishing Group and Penguin Group. They include Meredith Rees, John Pelosi, and Marianne Grace. The authors also extend a most heartfelt "thank you" to our trusted editor, Shannon Jamieson Vazquez, whose judgment is always spot-on.

Contents

x **CONTENTS**

Prologue

The two men got out of the Jeep in the quiet woods of
Maine. It was a hot summer day in 1996, and they had
been driving for nearly two hours.

The passenger had slept for most of the ride, slacking
on his presumed duty as navigator. He wasn't sure exactly
how they'd gotten to this place, even though the location
was marked on the map by an X with a circle around it.
He remembered passing the New Hampshire State Police
barracks in Epping before dozing off, and he hadn't
woken up until the driver shook him, telling him they
were finally in Waterboro. He saw a tiny, ancient graveyard
and a trailer park pass outside his window before the Jeep
made a turn off the main road onto the dirt path. A street

sign—for what could only very generously be called a street—said they were on McLucas Road.

The unpaved road soon came to a fork. The Jeep had idled for a moment in neutral as the driver assessed which path to take. The road to the left looked smoother, more traveled upon. He put the Jeep in gear and drove the other way. The wheels slammed into rocks large enough to toss the vehicle's occupants in their seats. It seemed this road was traversed almost exclusively by hikers.

After the odometer ticked off a tenth of a mile from the fork, the driver stopped. He wrote ".1" on the map next to the X. "This is a good spot," he said.

They could see a large brown fire tower in the distance. They couldn't know for sure, but it didn't look like the warden was in the tower, searching the forested horizon for columns of smoke from careless campers or lightning strikes from summer thunderstorms. When the driver cut the motor, the quiet of the woods enveloped them. Other than the rustle of leaves and the calls of small birds, the forest was silent. They were alone.

The driver went around to the back and swung open the hatch. The passenger got out and leaned against the Jeep's door, jumping a little when his companion slammed the hatch closed with a report that echoed throughout the woods.

"Let's go this way," the driver said, clearly in charge. The pair trekked off to the right of the path for about fifty feet. There was a bit of a clearing there, a place where the sun pierced the tree canopy and a small patch of wild grass grew.

The driver looked around at the plot of land and nodded, satisfied with what he saw. He handed the passenger the item he'd retrieved from the rear of the Jeep: a small shovel.

"Start digging here."

The passenger took the tool and stabbed it at the unblemished ground. It was difficult getting below the surface, as the pointed tip needed to slice its way through roots from the nearby trees and vegetation. He didn't know exactly how deep or wide he was supposed to go.

He just knew it had to be big enough to hold a body.

While the first clumps of loam and rooted sod were accumulating in a ragged pile, the driver walked back to the Jeep. He started the engine and drove deeper into the woods, just far enough out of sight to find a place to turn around and point the vehicle's nose back down the rocky path.

This location was not the pair's first choice for their undertaking. The day before they had driven until they reached another circled X on the map, but when they'd arrived, the driver had been dismayed to see how close it was to a main road. The drone of distant 18-wheelers hung in the air, like the threat of approaching thunder. They'd gotten back in the Jeep and had decided to try again, finally finding the spot where the hole was now being dug, one small shovelful at a time.

After turning the vehicle around, the driver walked to the clearing and stood over the man doing the digging. The driver had packed only the one shovel and did not offer to get into the hole, did not offer to take a turn sculpting the grave. He stood over the passenger, arms folded.

"Don't stop now. Make it wider. Go down deeper."

It took close to two hours to complete the grave to the driver's satisfaction. It became harder for the passenger to shovel dirt up and out onto the growing piles of earth around the hole. Finally feeling the size was about right, and taking advantage of his overseer's silence, the passenger put the shovel down. The driver examined the hole and tacitly gave his approval by reaching in to pull his partner out.

The driver directed the passenger to collect some sticks and branches to cover the gaping hole. It would look very much like a grave to anyone who happened to walk up to it, but from the rocky trail, it would easily pass for yet another patch of undisturbed nature.

The driver took the shovel and put it back in the Jeep. There was no body in the vehicle with them. There was no victim—yet. The grave had been prepared in anticipation of a victim who was still very much alive, still very much unaware of her fate.

Murder itself is often a reckless, uncalculated act. Killing is relatively easy. But making a body vanish is hard, and often done sloppily, and in haste. It's the element of the act that often seals the fate of the killer. Even for premeditated killings, disposing of the evidence is not typically part of homicidal thoughts or deadly daydreams. It's not as satisfying to the culprit as the fantasy of the deed itself. But in this case, the detail of how to dispose of the future victim's body, to tilt the odds of permanent concealment in their favor, had been dealt with.

As a matter of practicality, there is no homicide without a body. There are occasional exceptions, of course; instances where enough proof can be found without a corpse—blood evidence, or the discovery of brain tissue, for example. But those cases are exceedingly rare. Any lawyer will say that the longer a body is missing, the harder it is for the government to make its case, even if enough time has passed to declare a person *legally* dead.

The driver had put himself in a position to get away with it, to commit a perfect crime. He would not make the same foolish mistakes of evidence that so many others had. He considered himself far smarter than that. The only wild card would be whether he could keep his co-conspirators—and there were far too many for his liking at this point—from breaking their silence.

PART ONE

Dirty Deeds

And 'tis not done.
The attempt and not the deed confounds us.

—WILLIAM SHAKESPEARE, *MACBETH*

ONE

Cause for Alarm

Lieutenant Richard Kane and his partner, Detective Kimberly Roberts, arrived at the scene on Patricia Avenue minutes after getting the call. It was Monday, March 11, 1996, and although it had been well below freezing in the morning, with snow better than a foot deep on lawns and sidewalks, the afternoon sun made it almost comfortable to stand outside. The sound of snowmelt running into the storm drains along the curbs echoed in the stillness of the street.

Kane, who was in charge of the Exeter detective bureau, had been busy trying to tame the paperwork that accompanied his job when they got the call from the patrol division requesting that a detective come to the scene. The casework of a patrolman is fundamentally different than an investigator's. Most of the time, when a uniformed cop rolls onto a scene, his job is reactionary: he's trying to defuse a situation, pulling people apart from one another, ascertaining who threw the first punch or which driver in an accident was at fault. Detective work, on the other hand, requires drilling down deeper. Some cops chase bad guys; others seek to find out why they're running.

"Okay," Kane asked the two patrolmen already on scene. "Whaddya got?"

The patrolmen said there was some kind of metal device on the ground under the mailbox. The homeowner was inside and talking to the police over the phone. "She says she took it out of the mailbox, then dropped it in the snow when she figured out what it was."

"And what is it?"

"It's a metal pipe, capped at both ends. There's a red string coming out of a hole in the top that's secured with masking tape. It looks like a fuse."

Kane checked for an ETA on the state police bomb unit. The dispatcher said they were coming from Manchester and should arrive in Exeter in about thirty minutes. *Fifteen years on the job in this town and not one of these things ever turns out to be dangerous*, he thought. *Probably some kid's idea of a joke.*

"What's the homeowner's name?"

"Vicki Bader," the cop said. Kane got in his vehicle and, using the car phone, rang the number the patrolman had given him.

"Hello?" a panicked voice squeaked.

"Mrs. Bader? This is Lieutenant Richard Kane of the Exeter Police Department. Everything is going to be all right."

The woman was breathing heavily. Kane asked her whether she would leave her residence if he sent a police officer to her back door. Vicki agreed, and she walked with the officer along the farthest side of her plowed driveway to get to the street.

"It won't go off," the woman told the patrolman escorting her to safety. "The fuse isn't lit. It won't go off."

The cop brought her to Kane. "Are you all right, ma'am?"

"Yes," she said, but her shaking hands and voice said otherwise.

"Do we have permission to go into your house and look for other suspicious devices?"

Again her voice cracked as she told the police to do whatever was necessary.

Detective Roberts drove Vicki back to the police station to calm her down and get a statement. In the meantime, more police cruisers arrived to block off the street. Officers went door-to-door telling people to stay in their houses and away from their windows.

Two patrolmen entered Vicki Bader's red-sided house through the back door, cautiously examining the contents of her kitchen and hallway. The cops moved more like burglars, quietly passing from room to room. They lingered in the bedrooms, pointing their flashlights under beds and in closets. A cat scampered by but otherwise left the patrolmen to their task. Finally satisfied there were no other explosives in the house, they left, carefully closing the back door behind them.

"Nothing," said one of the cops to Kane. Referring to the way the fuse was secured to the bomb, the other officer noted, "But she did have some masking tape in there."

At 4:00 P.M., Corporal Jack Meaney of the New Hampshire State Police Bomb Disposal Team arrived, just ahead of the TV crews tipped off by neighbors now trapped in their homes. Kane gave him a rundown of what they knew about the device, saying they really weren't sure if it was a bomb or a hoax.

Meaney put on his metal-armored explosive-ordnance suit, which made him look more like an astronaut than a state trooper. The suit weighed more than fifty pounds, covering his legs, chest, throat, and head. He marched gingerly to the mailbox with a Polaroid camera in his hands. He wanted to examine the device but also to minimize the length of time he needed to stand over it. He took a single picture, turned around, and pulled the print out as he paced back to his cruiser.

"Well?" Kane asked when Meaney removed his helmet.

Meaney pointed to some of the distinctive features of the device in the developing photo. "I think this *is* a pipe bomb," he said. "And I think it should be removed as soon as possible."

Any hope this was just a kid's prank was gone. Meaney ordered the New Hampshire State Police's bomb disposal truck to come from Concord. It would take them about an hour to get to Exeter.

"We're going to need a place to take this device and deactivate it," Meaney said.

"How about the town's transfer station?" Kane offered. The transfer station was a polite euphemism for the local dump. "It's not that far from here." Meaney agreed, and Kane made arrangements to have everyone cleared out of the dump before they arrived.

While they waited for the truck, Detective Kim Roberts returned with Vicki Bader. Kane asked Vicki if they could take a few items from her home, including the masking tape the patrolman had noticed. She agreed and went inside with one of the other cops to get them.

With Vicki out of earshot, Roberts pulled Kane aside and told him that Vicki reported she'd come home just before 3:00, pulled into her driveway, and then had gone to the mailbox. She'd pulled out the mail, which was lying on top of the pipe, then took out the device. Vicki had instantly recognized it as a bomb and dropped it in the snow before running into the house.

"She says she's seen her ex-husband make bombs like this before, and that we should talk to him," said Roberts.

"All right," Kane agreed. "Got his name?"

Detective Roberts nodded before continuing.

"There's more to this," she said. "There have been a couple of calls to this address in the past couple of months.

Some vandalism. Her tires slashed, her windows shot out with BBs."

"Hmm." Kane furrowed his brow.

"And something else," Roberts went on. "Someone broke into her house and killed all of her pet birds."

Taken separately, each incident was a troublesome crime. *Put these all together*, Kane thought, *and there's something very disturbing going on here.*

"Find me the mailman," Kane said. "We might be able to narrow down a time the bomb was placed in the box."

The forest green ambulance-sized van that rumbled onto Patricia Avenue wouldn't have looked particularly special were it not for the yellow lettering on the side labeling it "Explosives Disposal Unit." Meaney and the driver conferred about the best way to handle the situation, and Meaney put his bomb suit back on again. The trooper walked over to the pipe bomb and placed it in a blast container before carrying it to the truck and setting it gingerly in the back. Kane and some of the other officers followed the truck down to the Exeter transfer station.

Defusing a bomb in the real world is not like it is in the movies, where someone sweats over the choice to clip the red wire or the blue wire. In the real world, the device is typically just a container of chemicals at rest, ready to explode with the proper stimulation. Many of the hows and whys of rendering a bomb inert are secrets kept close by the professionals who do it for a living. Detonating the bomb in a controlled environment is sometimes an option, but blowing up this particular bomb would only destroy valuable evidence. In the quiet isolation of the town dump, Corporal Meaney disabled and disassembled the bomb, preserving both the device and its contents.

Meaney turned the pieces over to a patrolman, who bagged them for evidence. Then Meaney sought out Lieutenant Kane.

"There was a significant amount of powder in it," he said.

"How bad?"

"If it went off in a car, it would have killed everyone inside," Meaney surmised. "If it blew up in that mailbox, it would have killed the homeowner."

Kane considered this for a moment. "Could it have been detonated remotely?"

"No," he said. "The fuse would have to be lit. But it easily could have gone off accidentally."

When they got back to the police station, Kane and another officer examined the bomb. The device looked like a silver dumbbell, with a hollow body made of a metal tube about four inches long. There was a round metal cap on one of the ends, the other cap having been unscrewed and removed by the bomb squad. A small hole had been drilled in the top of the pipe halfway between the two caps.

The patrolman pointed something out at the capped

end of the pipe. There was a strand of hair poking out of a piece of dirt. It wasn't possible to tell if the hair was only sticking to it because of the debris, or if the hair had been trapped within the threads of the cap. Kane hoped it was the latter—meaning it had been left there during the bomb's construction—but he didn't want to start monkeying with evidence. He wanted to get some expert help with this case. He made a mark on the pipe near the hair, then put all of the bomb's remnants in an evidence bag.

Kane went back to his desk and called the postal carrier for Vicki Bader's neighborhood. She told him she was certain she'd delivered the mail on Patricia Avenue between 2:15 and 2:30, because that was her usual time to be on that part of her route. The mail carrier also told Kane she remembered seeing the metal contraption inside the mailbox, but she'd thought nothing of it and just put the mail on top of it. Kane was shocked that the postal worker—someone supposedly trained to spot suspicious packages—had seen the explosive device in the mailbox, yet ignored it and went about her day.

The information about timing wasn't helpful. If the bomb *hadn't* been in the mailbox at 2:30, it would have meant that the culprit left it within an hour of Vicki Bader's arrival home. Someone might have noticed something in that narrow window. But since the pipe bomb was already there mid-afternoon on Monday, that meant it could have been in there for most of the weekend.

*   *   *

Kane got into work early the next morning. He put his coffee cup down on his desk, right next to the photographs of his two sons.

Richard Kane had been with the Exeter Police Department since 1981. He'd known he wanted to be a police officer since he was a boy growing up in Dedham, Massachusetts. He took criminal justice classes at Massasoit Community College and couldn't have graduated at a worse time. Massachusetts voters had enacted "Proposition 2½" in 1980, which capped local property tax rates at 2.5 percent. The results, particularly in the early years of its adoption, were layoffs and hiring freezes for municipal jobs like teachers and policemen. Kane couldn't find a job anywhere in Massachusetts. In an act of near-desperation, Kane applied to be the animal control officer for the town of Exeter, New Hampshire. He got the job, and fifteen years later, he was a lieutenant in charge of the detective bureau.

Kane pulled out a telephone book and began looking up federal listings. He dialed a number.

"This is the Bureau of Alcohol, Tobacco and Firearms," the voice on the other end said.

Kane explained who he was and why he was calling. He wanted to see if any experts on explosives could give them a hand with the case; specifically, someone who could examine the pipe bomb for clues. The ATF agent said that since the device had been found in a mailbox, the postal inspector's office would probably be interested. He gave Kane a phone number for the Boston office and offered his further services if the cop should require them.

A short time later, Kane's phone rang. The man on the other end introduced himself as Postal Inspector Willie Moores. "I'm in Kittery, Maine, this morning," he said. "I'll be there in a half hour."

True to his word, Moores arrived at the Exeter Police Department in fewer than thirty minutes. He immediately asked if he could see the device. Kane and Detective Roberts brought the postal inspector to a room where the pipe bomb, still sealed in a plastic bag, sat on a table. Without another word, Moores moved close to the device but didn't touch it.

"The bomb maker drilled a hole in this pipe in order to get the fuse in," he observed.

"There's a hair stuck to one of the caps," Kane pointed out. "There's a chance the hair is stuck inside the threads, but we haven't done a thorough analysis yet."

Moores scanned the pipe for the mark indicating where the hair was. The inspector was pleased; there was a lot to work with here.

"The Postal Inspection Service operates a crime lab in Virginia. We can use it to develop any evidence." Then the inspector said, "I can transport the evidence to the lab myself, if you'd like."

Kane knew Moores was in.

*   *   *

"What else can you tell me about the case?" Moores sat with Kane and Roberts, who glanced briefly at their notes.

"There's been a lot of trouble at this address in the past few months."

"So, it's unlikely this was a random target."

"The homeowner, Vicki Bader, reported a burglary on January 11th of this year," Kane said. Someone broke into the home and killed her pet parakeets. Otherwise, nothing else was taken.

"A month later, on February 14th, some of her windows were shot out with BBs."

"On Valentine's Day," Moores noted.

"On the same day, her tires were slashed while she was at work in Kingston. She filed a report with the Kingston Police," Kane said.

"Mrs. Bader told me yesterday that she is recently divorced and in a nasty custody battle over her three children," Roberts said. "Given the nature of these other incidents, we think that maybe the pipe bomb and these other things are tied to the custody battle."

Moores took careful notes. "What has the ex-husband said?"

"We haven't talked to him yet. Taken alone, the other incidents weren't really much of anything. Even Mrs. Bader said she hadn't accused him of the other events. But she said we should talk to her ex-husband about this one."

"Why's that?"

"Because she said she'd seen him make bombs before," Roberts replied. "She said he'd fill a pipe with gun powder, then put Vaseline on the threads of the cap."

"Did she say why he'd use Vaseline?"

"To prevent a spark when he'd screw the cap on."

Moores put his pen down. "That's an awfully specific detail for the average housewife to know about bomb making."

Kane and Roberts nodded at each other. "That's what we thought."

"Could she have made the bomb herself?" the inspector asked. "Be responsible for the other acts, too?"

Roberts wanted to say something, but Kane noticed she seemed unsure of how to phrase what she was thinking.

"Mrs. Bader kept saying she knew what would go into such a bomb, though she said she didn't know how to make one. Then she said she didn't even have a drill to build the bomb." Roberts raised an eyebrow. "At the time, no one had said anything to her about a hole being drilled into the bomb."

Three sets of eyes darted between the metal device on the table and one another. "She might have gotten tired of waiting for us to accuse her husband for the vandalism, so she kicked it up a notch," Kane offered.

"Why would she do that?"

"I've seen people do crazier things to get an edge in custody battles."

* * *

Vicki Lynn Bader walked into the lobby of the Exeter Police Department at noon on Tuesday, March 12, less than twenty-four hours after calling the police about the explosive device in her mailbox. She still appeared shaken. Vicki had a youthful and pretty face, curly strawberry blond hair, and a warm smile. She was on the short side, and she weighed around two hundred pounds, but Vicki looked like a woman carrying unfamiliar baggage, not at all like someone who had always been obese.

Vicki followed Detective Kim Roberts into the station's interview room. The detective asked her permission to tape their conversation.

"Sure," Vicki said.

Lieutenant Kane watched the interview from the department library.

"You should know that you're not under arrest and you can leave any time you wish," Detective Roberts told her.

Roberts listened to Vicki describe her movements in the hours leading up to the bomb's discovery and what she had done since. After running into her house and calling the police, Vicki said she'd called her attorney, Heidi Boyack. They agreed that the police should question her ex-husband, Seth Bader, about the possibility he built the bomb. The detective asked if Vicki would write out a statement about everything she had done between checking her mail on Saturday, the ninth, and discovering the mailbox bomb two days later.

After writing out the statement, Roberts asked Vicki if she would be willing to take a polygraph test. Vicki was taken aback.

"Can I call my lawyer and ask her what she thinks?" Roberts provided her with a telephone. After hanging up, Vicki seemed apologetic. "My lawyer says I shouldn't take the polygraph. And she says I should end the interview."

With that, Vicki Bader left the police station.

Roberts returned to the interview room and examined the chair on which Vicki had been sitting. There, she found a couple of strands of hair. Roberts carefully collected them and gave them to Postal Inspector Moores, along with the remnants of the bomb and Vicki's handwritten statement. Moores was on his way to catch a plane to Virginia and the crime lab.

TWO

The Shell Game

On the morning of Thursday, March 14, 1996, Detective Kim Roberts was anxious for her lieutenant to get into the station. It had been two days since Postal Inspector Willie Moores left New Hampshire with what remained of the pipe bomb, but preliminary results were in. Roberts was a young woman eager to impress her senior officer, and she was as meticulous as she was attractive, ambitious as she was enthusiastic. It wasn't unusual that something as tiny as a hair could get her pumped up about an investigation.

"The hair on the pipe bomb *was* caught in the thread, so it got there during the bomb's assembly," Roberts told Lieutenant Richard Kane when he got in. "But it wasn't human hair. The hair came from a cat."

"Seriously?"

"And the hair we recovered from the chair that Vicki Bader sat in? Also from a cat."

"Can they tell if it's from the same cat?"

"I don't know," Roberts said, "but Moores promises to get back to us as soon as they have more information."

Kane had been collecting his own information about the second suspect in the pipe bomb case, Vicki's ex-husband, Seth Bader. He lived in Stratham, the next town over from Exeter, in a beautiful gated home only three miles from Vicki's place. Seth was a lawyer, and this played no small part in his divorce and custody cases against Vicki, which were as vicious as she had let on. There were dozens of filings on the docket, most made by Seth's attorney. Much of the ground contested by Seth was about money; he already had custody of the three children. The two older boys, twelve-year-old Joey and seven-year-old Matthew, were distant cousins to Seth and had been adopted by the couple. The youngest child was Samuel, a two-year-old who had been born not long before the Baders' marriage ended. Many of the filings characterized Vicki Bader as unstable, pointing to several suicide attempts between 1994 and 1996 after her divorce from Seth. Vicki had been granted only structured, supervised visits with Sam, and her legal strategy focused on getting more time with her baby. Kane was not surprised to discover that everyone in the family, including the boys, was in therapy.

Police in Portsmouth—about twelve miles from Exeter—informed Kane that a local physician, Dr. David Shopick, had reported some criminal mischief a month earlier and had told police he suspected Seth Bader was responsible. Kane called Dr. Shopick at his office to see what the connection was. Shopick said he was a therapist who had once treated Seth and Vicki as a couple and still had Vicki as a patient.

"I know Seth Bader to be a sociopath," Shopick told the detective. "I feel Seth is capable of doing terrible things."

Shopick said that on the eighth of February, his car had been vandalized while it was parked outside of his office. The therapist thought little of the damage until the following week, during his session with Vicki Bader. She told him about the damage to her own car on Valentine's Day and that she believed her ex-husband was behind it. The two of them started comparing notes. Shopick said the day his car was scratched was the same day that Seth would have taken twelve-year-old son Joseph to the boy's therapist, whose office shared a parking lot with Shopick's.

Vicki and Shopick agreed to take their cars to the same auto body shop. After the repairman examined both vehicles, he agreed that the damage was probably done with the same instrument.

A Dutch national named Kees Oudekerk was watching the local news when he saw the report about the pipe bomb found in Vicki Bader's mailbox. He walked into the Exeter police station the next day and asked to speak to a detective. Oudekerk told Lieutenant Kane that he was a former client of Seth Bader's and had remained friendly with both Seth and Vicki after their divorce. Oudekerk said that Seth had once brought him into the basement of his home in Stratham and had shown him a room specially designed for storing his guns and ammunition.

"He has a radical point of view when it comes to guns," Oudekerk said, explaining that the room was protected with a vault lock and was filled with weapons, powder, bullets, and reloading tools. The man claimed Seth owned about thirty long guns and more than fifty handguns. While parading the Dutchman through his basement cache, Seth had also shown off a couple of books on graphic gunshot wounds and how to build bombs.

"I wouldn't put it past him to do this and think he can get away with it."

During her police interview, Vicki Bader mentioned having had some difficulties at her previous place of employment, so Kane and Roberts went to visit her former job site. Vicki had worked for a subcontractor who provided trucking services for Sears. The assistant manager, Jack Benjamin,* was very open about Vicki. He said she was a conscientious employee who'd worked as a part-time bookkeeper.

---

* Denotes pseudonym

"A couple of the truck drivers had been giving her some grief," Benjamin told them. The issue revolved around some payroll matters that had nothing to do with Vicki personally. "They were just 'killing the messenger,' so to speak. But she was the one they blamed."

Detectives asked for those drivers' schedules for March 11 and ruled them both out, as they had been out of the state making deliveries.

Kane and Roberts asked Benjamin if they could look around. He showed the detectives the large trucking warehouse filled with major appliances. He took them to the "deluxing room" where refrigerator doors were changed and lawn tractors were assembled before being delivered to customers. The room included a workbench with tools and a drill press. Kane remembered that the hole for the pipe bomb fuse was likely made with a similar drill.

"Would Vicki have had access to this room?"

"I suppose she would," Benjamin said.

"Would she have been able to come in here after hours and use the tools?"

Benjamin said it was possible, since Vicki had worked some night shifts. But he also said that Vicki had recently quit the job, saying she didn't feel safe at work.

Based on Vicki's statement about her schedule from Saturday to Monday, Detective Roberts reconstructed her weekend step-by-step. Vicki provided a list of things she did: she'd had a visitation with her youngest son, gone to the library, played racquetball with a friend, and made phone calls to various people. Roberts ran down everything on the list and was able to verify Vicki's whereabouts for the weekend in question.

When Kane and Roberts returned to the Exeter police station, there was another update from Inspector Moores at the crime lab. The technicians had analyzed the masking tape used to secure the fuse and had found some more animal hair affixed to the back of the tape. They identified the hairs as coming from both a short-haired dog and a cat. Officers had seen a cat in Vicki's house, but no dog. Kane contacted the animal control officer in neighboring Stratham to see if Seth Bader had any dogs licensed to him. Turned out, he had several. Seth had a Lab, a dachshund, and an Akita all licensed under his name; even the vanity plate on his Trans Am read "AKITA." Plus, his new live-in girlfriend, Mary Jean Martin, was a dog breeder who raised pit bull–type dogs. In fact, the SPCA was currently investigating the many neighbor complaints about dogs barking. Seth had already paid two tickets for violations.

The Stratham animal control officer told Kane that there were crates all over Seth and Mary Jean's stately, spacious house. He said that at any time there were more than thirty dogs in the house, and while he had told Seth Bader that he needed a license to operate a kennel, the man had insisted the dogs were all just family pets.

*　*　*

Postal Inspector Willie Moores called Kane that afternoon to tell him the crime lab had made another discovery. They had narrowed down that the two-inch metal caps on the end of the device had been manufactured by one of two companies—either Grinnell or U Brand.

"Grinnell is right here in Exeter," Kane exclaimed. The cop drove to the company headquarters and explained to a supervisor he was trying to track down where the caps had been purchased.

Kane learned that each year, more than a million two-inch caps were made in the Midwest and then shipped to a warehouse in Canton, Massachusetts. When Kane called the warehouse and asked if they could send him a list of all the places to which they had sold two-by-eight-inch galvanized pipe, the office manager said he'd need to check with his corporate supervisors first, but he mentioned in passing that there was a whole hardware division for the company located in Illinois.

Kane then called the Illinois office, where a woman explained that they supplied those items to a True Value warehouse in Manchester, New Hampshire, which, in turn, supplied True Value stores across New England.

Kane felt he was getting close now. Manchester was only twenty minutes away from Exeter, and there were only a handful of True Value stores in the area. He called the Manchester warehouse and asked to speak to someone in the inventory section. After Kane explained what he was looking for, the worker on the other end of the phone dove into his records.

"We have sold thirty two-by-eight-inch galvanized pipes between November 1, 1995, and today," he reported. "But I can't identify which stores they went to."

Kane was exhausted from his telephone chase back and forth across the country. It was nearly a week into the investigation, and he now had more questions than the day it began. He accepted that he had hit a dead end trying to piece together the bomb.

Instead, he would try to take apart his suspects.

THREE

Kitchen Nightmare

On Friday, March 15, 1996, Vicki Bader returned to the Exeter police department with her attorney, Heidi Boyack, for a second interview. Vicki had Boyack on retainer, representing her in the ongoing custody case against her ex-husband. After learning that Exeter police wanted to give Vicki a lie detector test about the pipe bomb, Boyack wanted to be present for any further questioning of her client.

The pair were greeted by Lieutenant Richard Kane and Detective Kimberly Roberts and taken to the same interview room Vicki had walked out of three days earlier. After they had taken their seats, Roberts repeated to Vicki that she was not under arrest and the purpose of the interview was to gather information about her ex-husband,

Seth Bader. Vicki's demeanor changed when she heard that; she seemed to relax and appeared eager to share information about the man she had been telling police to examine more closely.

"We moved to Stratham from Brooklyn in May of 1992. I moved out of the house two years later."

"What kinds of hobbies does Seth have?"

"Chemicals. Firearms. Dogs. Ham radio. He's adept at electronics." Vicki said Seth was a passionate Second Amendment advocate, was an officer in Gun Owners of New Hampshire, and was involved in gun clubs in several New Hampshire towns. Vicki told the investigators that Seth knew how to reload his own ammunition and would refill used cartridges with loose gunpowder to make his own ammo.

"He likes to buy things from catalogs," she said. The two companies she mentioned specifically were Brownells, a firearms and accessory provider, and Loompanics, an outfit that offered unique and unusual books—some with anarchistic themes. She said 90 percent of her ex-husband's purchases were by credit card. "UPS delivers a lot of stuff to the house."

"Have you ever seen Seth make a bomb?" Kane asked.

"I have," she said, claiming to have witnessed her husband create two or three bombs before. "He likes to blow things up."

Vicki's story piqued Kane and Roberts's interest. She told them she saw Seth first create an improvised explosive device out of PVC pipe. He tried to detonate it in the backyard, but instead of blowing up, the device had melted. She said it had rounded caps, but she couldn't recall the type of fuse he'd used.

"Where did he get the PVC pipe?"

"I think he bought a long piece of pipe and just cut it down. I believe he got it at Home Depot, maybe the one in Manchester, but I'm not positive."

"Were the other bombs he made created with PVC pipe?"

"No. The next bomb he made was made from a metal pipe he bought at ArJay's Ace Hardware. He also bought two metal caps. He bought some type of cord that would burn at so many feet per second, I don't know how fast. It might have come from Riley's gun shop in Hooksett or from Brownells magazine."

Vicki talked at length about one incident that had happened in the Stratham house. She couldn't remember exactly when it happened, but she knew their now two-and-a-half-year-old son Sam had been an infant at the time.

"I was out of the house and when I came home the kitchen was filled with smoke. The cabinets were charred and the walls were covered with soot." Vicki told the detectives that Seth had been playing with a device in the kitchen when it blew up. But Kane and Roberts were frustrated that Vicki could remember few details about the event. She didn't remember exactly where it happened, other than that it was in the kitchen. But she insisted there had been a lot of damage done to the room, enough that a handyman had had to come in to repair the ceiling.

"What happened to Seth?" Kane asked.

"Nothing happened to Seth," she replied.

Kane shifted a bit in his chair. Something didn't seem right. "Wait a minute, the explosion was so big that it charred the cabinets and caused damage to the ceiling—but Seth, who was there mixing all the chemicals, was not hurt in any way?"

"No."

"Did he have soot on him or on his clothes?"

"No."

"Did he have any medical problems whatsoever?"

The woman said that he did not.

Before the detectives escorted Vicki Bader and her attorney from the police station, Vicki told them she suspected her ex-husband's motivation for putting the bomb in her mailbox was because he was losing the custody battle. She felt that he might have been trying to make her look bad in court by making her the target of a mad bomber. Her attorney, Heidi Boyack, agreed that it seemed things had turned in the ongoing custody case, and it looked like Vicki had a reasonably good shot at getting the kids back. Kane told them that if anything developed, they would let Vicki know.

On Sunday, March 17, 1996, Lieutenant Richard Kane celebrated St. Patrick's Day by checking out Vicki's claim that Seth had set off a bomb in the kitchen of the house they'd once shared.

His first call was to a carpenter named Scott Gould, who said he had known Seth Bader for a couple of years. The lieutenant quizzed him about any damage done to the Baders' kitchen, and Gould said he'd been hired to paint the ceiling twice. Kane asked if an explosion had caused the damage either time he'd been hired. Gould scoffed and said there was no way the repairs he did could've been related to an explosion. The workman was very sure that it had been water damage he'd been hired to fix, and that a plumber had also needed to come in to fix a problem with the upstairs bathroom.

Kane then called the plumber Gould had named, Joe Pollard. Pollard said he had done work for both Baders in both of their homes, mostly fixing pipes and toilets. Kane asked when the last time was that he'd been to either home, and Pollard said he'd recently been to Seth's house to remove a toy stuck in a toilet. He'd been unable to reach it, so he'd had to break the toilet and install a new one. This had caused some water damage to the kitchen ceiling below.

"Have you ever had to leave plumbing supplies at either of the houses?"

Pollard said he never had. Kane asked more specific questions about metal piping of the type that was used to make the bomb, but the plumber said he didn't stock that size on his truck. Pollard looked through all his bills to both Baders and found one from March 4, 1994, before the couple's divorce, when he'd had to replace a toilet that was leaking when it was flushed. He remembered that this problem had caused some water damage to the kitchen ceiling below it.

Kane hung up the phone, uncertain of what to make of Vicki's accusation that Seth had once accidentally set off a bomb in their Stratham kitchen. None of the workmen recalled seeing any telltale signs of an explosion in the home. Kane hoped to clear up the confusion the next day, when he would finally question Seth Bader about his connection to this crime.

On Monday, March 18, 1996, Postal Inspector Willie Moores returned to the Exeter Police Department to brief Kane and Roberts about what physical evidence the crime lab had uncovered on the pipe bomb.

"The fuse was red. Most kinds of fuses you can buy over the counter at a gun shop or fireworks stores are green. This fuse was a pyrotechnic type typically used to light a cannon." He continued, "The masking tape removed from the bomb was not the tape that was taken from Vicki Bader's home."

Moores said the hole in the pipe was 3/32 inches around. Inside the pipe, there was a wadded-up paper towel. The powder inside the bomb was identified as Hercules 200, but it had been mixed with a type of flaked aluminum that would make the powder burn faster. He also told them the lab was still working on examining the pipe for fingerprints, as well as analyzing the hair that had been found in the threaded portion of the bomb assembly.

*   *   *

After Vicki named ArJay's Ace Hardware as one of the places Seth got pipe supplies, Kane asked her for any documentation of her own purchases at the store. She later told him that a few weeks before the bomb was discovered, she had shopped at ArJay's and bought three packages of magnets. Vicki said she had only found the receipt that morning.

Kane sent a patrolman over to Vicki's Patricia Avenue home to get the receipt. The time stamp showed that she had been in the store on the twenty-seventh of February. The officer went to ArJay's to see if any pipe or caps had also been purchased on the twenty-seventh. An inventory check turned up nothing from that day. A single two-inch cap had been sold on February 22, but it was a cash transaction and the clerk couldn't remember what the customer looked like.

Richard Kane's secret weapon for dealing with Seth Bader was Detective Kimberly Roberts. He guessed that Seth would be taken in by the young detective's good looks; if so, he wouldn't be the first. Kane decided to let Roberts lead the questioning of Vicki's ex-husband. He would watch on video from the library.

Seth Bader arrived at the Exeter police department at noon on that Monday, a week after the pipe bomb's discovery. He had been asked to prepare a statement about where he had been, and with whom, during the three days prior to the bomb's discovery on the eleventh.

Seth Bader was not an imposing figure. He was short and stocky with a full head of thick, curly hair framing a chubby, boyish face. He was dressed well, but his suit didn't quite hang on him the way the designer had probably imagined it. He talked quickly, loudly, and with a distinctive Brooklyn accent. He had trouble making eye contact, and it could be exhausting to converse with him. Seth was highly intelligent and let everyone know it, including Detective Kimberly Roberts.

"All of a sudden, this is my fifteen minutes of fame," Seth said bombastically as he entered the interview room. He seemed at ease, or at least as at ease as a man with so many peculiar mannerisms *could* seem. Although he was a practicing attorney, Seth brought his own lawyer, Barbara Taylor, who represented him in his custody case as well as other legal matters. Kim Roberts closed the door and directed them to sit down.

"I spoke with you directly," Taylor said to Detective Roberts, "and you told me that Mr. Bader was not a suspect." Roberts agreed, saying the door was only shut for privacy.

"I'm concerned about my public image and now this. People are looking at me like I'm the O.J. of New Hampshire, and I'm rather sensitive about it," Seth claimed. O. J. Simpson's televised trial had recently begun in Los Angeles.

Roberts smiled at Seth and asked if he knew anything

about the pipe bomb found in his ex-wife's mailbox. He said he didn't, but he had three theories.

"By far the most likely one is that Vicki did it herself," he said, moving his hand to the top of his head and massaging his scalp. Roberts didn't react to his theory, which was one the police had also considered. Seth then took off on a verbal sprint that the detective would soon come to recognize as his signature style.

"She's done some weird things to get attention. She's made these suicide attempts that I don't think were genuine suicide attempts. You don't try to kill yourself seven or eight times and still be living, unless it's attention getting. There's a lot of weird things that have happened. You know, the parakeet incident. I mean, basically she's losing the case against me. I have custody. It's likely to become final in a few months. She's gonna be financially ruined by the case, and I think she's just looking to do something desperate to get sympathy or get attention. It's not rational, but that's her."

As Seth told this story, he continued to unconsciously rub the top of his head.

"Number two, she's been hassled by someone at her former employer. Supposedly, she screwed up someone's paycheck and got a threatening phone call. The third theory—and this is really far-fetched and I'm kind of going to the bottom of the barrel here—it's not beyond the realm of possibility that this was aimed at me and they just got the wrong Bader. In my line of work, I upset a lot of people. I do divorce work. I do criminals—who obviously aren't the most wonderful of people in the world."

Roberts had a hard time keeping up with the fast-talking Seth. She asked whether Vicki would have the knowledge to construct a bomb.

"Vicki knows everything I know about guns," Seth claimed. "Vicki knows everything about it that I do. When we were together, she avidly followed my hobbies."

Seth freely admitted that he kept gunpowder in a locked room in his basement. He said he used the powder to reload cartridges. Seth had containers of Hercules black powder, but other brands as well. He said the police were welcome at any time to come to his home and examine his gun collection and armoring tools.

"Did you ever see Vicki build anything that could explode?" Roberts asked. Seth said his ex-wife enjoyed fireworks, including some that were a little too big to be considered "legal" in New Hampshire, but that was all. He said the job of lighting the fuses in the backyard had always fallen to him because his ex-wife had a fear of matches.

"Was there ever a time when you and Vicki were together in your house in Stratham that you blew up the kitchen with something? [With] some sort of chemical or any explosive device?"

Seth Bader seemed puzzled. "I had a fire in the kitchen due to cooking. But not from a bomb." Seth told Roberts that two years earlier, he had been cooking with a wok when the hot oil flashed, leaving a thick, greasy coating on all the cabinets. Vicki had been out at the time and hadn't returned until hours after the incident. Seth said the whole room stunk, so he had a handyman refinish the cabinets, scrub the light fixtures, and paint the walls and ceiling. There had also been some ceiling stains from a leaky pipe in the bathroom above.

"I feel I should be looked upon as a victim in this. I don't know if you're aware, but I'm a co-owner of that house on Patricia Avenue. So to some extent, I'm getting looked at by the newspapers like a criminal." Seth seemed sincerely troubled by the thought. "The bomb wasn't in my face when I opened the mailbox. But I feel to some extent victimized by the whole thing."

Kane didn't know what to make of the interview. Seth Bader had been candid and cooperative. He had offered to let investigators come to his home. He had even agreed to be fingerprinted before he left the station so that detectives could eliminate him as a suspect. Seth had made a big show of how his fingerprints were already all over his statement and in dozens of files of criminal cases he'd worked on in Exeter.

"I think it's safe to say," Seth added on his way out, "that if you had witnesses to who put it there, or you had fingerprints off the bomb, you would have already arrested somebody at this point."

Roberts just shrugged and said that obtaining those kinds of things took time.

The only thing that Seth said he was disinclined to do

was take a lie detector test. He said he'd been polygraphed twice in relation to the custody case—passing both times—but the results had failed to advance his legal position one iota. Seth said the whole process of being hooked up to the machine was uncomfortable. "They ask you things about your taxes and shit, just for comparison. That's the annoying part."

Kane gave both Vicki's and Seth Bader's handwritten statements to Postal Inspector Willie Moores. He promised to send them to an analyst in Arizona who might be able to determine their levels of deception by looking at changes in the patterns of their handwriting. Kane and Roberts agreed not to interview either of the Baders again until they got some more data from the lab.

After comparing notes with Roberts, Kane was most troubled by Vicki's tale of what happened in the Stratham kitchen. Everything they heard from the workers and from Seth contradicted her story about her ex-husband building and detonating bombs. It sounded like Vicki was exaggerating Seth's proficiency with explosives, while at the same time downplaying her own. Seth was probably right: the court would likely perceive Vicki to be a victim, which might elicit sympathy from the judge. She could benefit from the crime. The pipe bomb, as Seth had argued, might actually help Vicki win her legal case.

Kane knew Vicki Bader's world was troubled. What he couldn't tell was whether or not her troubles were of her own making.

FOUR

A Loving Daughter

Vicki Lynn Buzby was born on September 29, 1961, in Abington, Pennsylvania, the only daughter sandwiched between two boys, John and Jimmy. The family was decidedly middle-class. Her father, Jack Buzby, worked for Pitney Bowes as a service manager, fixing business-class postage machines. The only way he'd eventually get a raise was to transfer to a bigger office, so the family moved from Pennsylvania to Dayton, Ohio, and then again, when Vicki was ten years old, to Nesconset, a small town on eastern Long Island, New York. The house, a 1950s-era white cottage, was only about six hundred square feet and had just two bedrooms for the five of them. Vicki spent her teen years in Nesconset and was an honors student, much to the delight of her parents. She enjoyed music and played the clarinet. Vicki was slender, pretty, and funny, and she was often asked out on dates. This didn't always go over well with her parents or her protective brothers, but she was a good girl and never gave them much reason to worry about her.

In the mid-1970s, Jack and Lois Jean Buzby's marriage fell apart. After they divorced, he moved back to Pennsylvania, then in 1985, to Melbourne, Florida, where he remarried. Less than three years later, Buzby died of a heart attack at the age of fifty-eight and was buried at Arlington National Cemetery.

Lois reassumed her maiden name, Stewart, and remained in the white cottage in Nesconset. The boys eventually married and moved out (John, the oldest, moved to a town just outside of Boston; Jim stayed on Long Island with his wife and children). Vicki moved into an apartment in Smithtown, about five minutes away from her childhood home in Nesconset. Lois loved her boys, but her relationship with her daughter was especially close-knit.

For Lois's birthday one year, Vicki purchased her an answering machine. Lois had never had one before. When she plugged it in, she was puzzled to see the device blink at her, indicating she already had messages. When she played the tape, she found that Vicki had asked all of her mother's friends to call and leave her birthday greetings. Much in the way someone might put in the first dollar when giving a gift of a wallet or purse, Vicki felt her mother's new answering machine should already be stuffed with messages. Lois thought her daughter was the most considerate person in the world.

When Vicki was twenty years old, she became engaged to a man named David Alexander* after dating him for just a few months.

Vicki planned a big wedding for the spring of 1981 at Terrace on the Park in Flushing Meadows. The facility was originally the heliport for the 1964–65 World's Fair and had been converted into a popular catering hall for New York–area brides. The reception had all the trappings, including an extended guest list made up of numerous aunts, uncles, and cousins from Lois's large family.

In the weeks leading up to the wedding, however, Vicki confessed to her mother that she had cold feet. Lois Stewart thought David was a nice enough guy, but she never wanted to see her daughter in a marriage she'd later regret.

"Back out if you want to. We'll still support and love you," she told her daughter. Yet despite Vicki's misgivings (and likely due to the massive financial commitment already made to the wedding), she soldiered ahead with the marriage.

It wasn't until they lived under the same roof that Vicki acknowledged how vastly different she and David really were. She was commuting daily to New York City by train to her job as a real estate consultant. The money was excellent and she felt she had a knack for the business. Yet

---

* Denotes pseudonym

even though she continued to earn a sizable salary, her new husband thought she ought to live on a thirty-dollar-a-week allowance. He insisted they save every other nickel in order to purchase a house in a good neighborhood. But six dollars a day was not a reasonable per diem for a Manhattan commuter. The disagreement underscored all of Vicki's apprehensions about the marriage.

Six weeks later, the couple agreed to an annulment and went their separate ways.

At age twenty-eight, Vicki Lynn Buzby found herself intrigued by a lonely hearts ad she read in the personals section of her local newspaper. She answered the ad—which described a good-looking, considerate man—on a whim. Although Vicki knew better than to take any description in a personals ad at face value, she called the voice mail box listed to leave the bachelor a message.

He responded almost immediately. The man's name was Seth Bader, and he was thirty, two years older than she was, but still a student. They had both gone to the State University of New York at Stony Brook on Long Island, but at different times. He had studied engineering there but now was in law school at Hofstra University. Seth sounded nice on the phone, but also nervous. He talked very fast but was prone to long pauses Vicki felt begged her to fill the void. The call went well, and they agreed to talk on the phone again.

Seth called Vicki the next day, and they agreed to continue their blind courtship. Although they didn't live terribly far from each other, Seth preferred to keep it a telephone romance at the outset.

In a series of phone calls, Seth began to paint a picture of his life for her. He was the only child of older parents who were both academics of some renown. His mother was a concert violinist, a skill he said she'd been ruefully unable to pass along to her son. His father had assumed Seth would be a physicist or engineer, but Seth told Vicki that he'd continually disappointed his father with his choices of loves, both professional and personal. None of his girlfriends had been Jewish, a considerable point of contention between Seth and his father. Vicki wasn't Jewish, either, but Seth told her that wasn't something he cared about. Seth and Vicki talked on the phone for an entire month before they ever laid eyes on each other, but she already saw him for who he was: a lonely little boy looking for someone to love him.

If Vicki was disappointed by Seth's looks when they finally met, she never told him so. To her, he looked like a lovable schlub, part Woody Allen, part Lou Costello.

Seth Bader didn't make the same positive impression on Vicki's mother. Lois Stewart thought the fat little man was boorish. He seemed in love with the sound of his own voice, which always was too loud and too fast for meaningful conversation. On one occasion, Lois recalled serving the couple spaghetti when they came over for dinner. Seth enthusiastically devoured the pasta, a compliment to the chef's cooking. But then he brought the plate up to his face and began to lick the sauce off the surface of the china. Lois was nauseated by the animal-like noises Seth made as he lapped the plate, marinara sauce staining the tip of his pug nose.

Vicki was surprised to learn that her new boyfriend was a firearms enthusiast. Growing up in the Long Island suburbs, she hadn't had much exposure to guns. It seemed slightly peculiar that this brainy law student from Brooklyn would be so adept at handling weapons and so passionate about shooting. She could understand how the constitutional aspects of the freedom to bear arms could make for stimulating debate and intellectual discussion, but Seth was a true believer, not just a rhetorical warrior for the cause.

In order to get closer to him, Vicki asked her new boyfriend to teach her about guns. He showed her how he liked to target shoot small-caliber weapons indoors using a bullet trap, a metal box designed to capture the projectile after it pierces the paper target. The report of the weapon echoed madly off the walls, and the room filled with blue smoke. Soon, Vicki was also hooked on the hobby.

Vicki Lynn Buzby married Seth Bader on May 18, 1991. Seth had just graduated from Hofstra University School of Law in neighboring Nassau County. The couple relied on the help of Vicki's friends to pull off the wedding. One friend who owned a local restaurant catered the event, and another offered his riverfront home in Smithtown as a setting, transforming his home with white tablecloths and fresh flowers.

The guests who attended were largely there for the bride. Seth only invited two aunts and a few friends. His father had passed away two years earlier, and his mother, whose ring he planned to put on Vicki's finger, was living in a nursing home with Alzheimer's. When they got to the "speak now or forever hold your peace" part, no one objected, although many of Vicki's relatives privately thought she was making a mistake marrying Seth, who they thought was a lout. Instead, they tried to be as supportive as they could, especially as she repeatedly told them how happy Seth made her.

The couple honeymooned on the East End of Long Island, then moved into Seth's family home in Brooklyn.

After the wedding, Seth told his wife that she owed him $1,500 for "her part" of the wedding. Vicki thought he was joking. They were a married couple, after all. Weren't all the expenses—of a wedding, no less—their joint obligation? Seth insisted. There had been extras that only she had wanted. They added up to $1,500 and she needed to pay him back just as soon as she could. Despite the fact that her first husband's attitude toward money had driven them apart, Vicki capitulated and agreed with Seth.

No sooner had the thank-you notes from the wedding

gone out than the couple announced that Vicki was pregnant with twin girls. Everyone was ecstatic, especially Seth, who very much wanted to be a father and right the wrongs he believed his own parents had committed against him.

FIVE

Boy, Interrupted

Joseph Fitzgerald was born on May 6, 1982, in Brooklyn, New York, to Bernard and Jaye Fitzgerald. Joey didn't remember too much of his early childhood, except for his father going off to jail. No one ever bothered to explain to him why his father was in jail. He was six years old at the time, and Jaye, his mother, was pregnant with his little brother, Matt.

Jaye and her son went to live with her great-aunt Mildred. Though she married an Irish-Catholic, Jaye had grown up in a Jewish family. Aunt Mildred, like most of Jaye's older relatives, was from a generation that cherished family above all else and would never let an outsider help a loved one in need. No one ever asked the elderly aunt if it was an inconvenience to have a pregnant mother and her little boy living with her. They didn't need to. It was a matter of both pride and principle.

Jaye gave birth to her second son, Matthew, on September 20, 1987. Not long afterward, Mildred passed away and left the apartment to Jaye and her children. It was a place they could barely afford with Jaye's welfare check.

Jaye was a heroin junkie. Joey would later say that their house was always littered with crack pipes, pot paraphernalia, and old syringes. He would also say his mother never did drugs in front of him or his brother, but he was fairly young when he realized that the plastic bag of yellowish powder had something to do with the reason Mommy was usually too tired to get out of bed. Joey began coping with it the way so many children of drug users do; at just seven, he became the parent of the house, taking over the care of his younger brother. Joey changed Matt's diapers. He fed them both breakfast. He bathed Matt and got himself off to school. He did all these things with competence far beyond his scant years.

When Joey was nine, his father, Bernard Fitzgerald, was released from jail and came to live with his wife and kids in Brooklyn. But Fitzgerald had terminal cancer, and the only reason he'd been let out was because he was dying. He lived in the apartment with them for about a week before he got so sick he had to be admitted to the hospital. He died shortly thereafter.

It didn't take long after Bernard's death for the family to get evicted. Another aunt in the Bronx took them in for about a month before Jaye's drug use got to be more than the woman could take. The family then moved in with an uncle on Staten Island, but soon he kicked them out because of the drugs, too.

Despite the instability in his life, Joey had initially done well in elementary school. But after his father died and the family began migrating all over the five boroughs, Joey's grades started to slip. With each move came a new school, a new teacher, and a new set of classmates. By the time he was in fourth grade he started really falling behind.

When Joey was a toddler, Jaye would bring her children around to visit some of her relatives, including Yvette and Abram Bader, Seth Bader's parents. Abram Bader was Jaye's mother's cousin. Joey liked Abram very much, and the feeling was mutual. Abram showered Joey with positive attention, something the child didn't get much of at home. Despite the distant family connection, Abram viewed the boy as a blood relative and thought it was scandalous that Jaye was living off welfare instead of seeking financial help from her family.

By the time the Fitzgeralds found themselves homeless, Abram Bader had passed away and Yvette Bader had been moved into a nursing home. Jaye had long since run out of friends and relatives willing to put them up for any length of time. She was still shooting heroin, and she decided the only option available to her was to move to a homeless shelter in the city.

* * *

Seth and Vicki Bader had moved into Seth's parents' old home on a postage-stamp lot in Brooklyn. One day in 1991, a social worker knocked on their door explaining that Joey Fitzgerald would be taken from his mother and placed "in the system" if a relative didn't claim him. The last time Seth had seen Jaye's boys was at a family wedding. He knew his late father would be appalled at the idea of Joey living in foster homes. The authorities had determined that Joey's brother, Matthew, could stay with his mother at the shelter, but Seth insisted Joey move in with him and his new wife, Vicki.

Life in the Bader house was not like anything Joey had experienced before. For once in his life, there were two adults around who actively took care of him. They made his bed and cleaned his clothes. He didn't have to cook his own food or clean the kitchen. He didn't have to take care of his little brother; he only had to take care of himself.

Joey described his early relationship with Vicki as affectionate and encouraging. She would read him stories before going to bed and then tuck him in under the covers. For his birthday, she threw him a proper party. He got to invite all his friends from school, and they had cake and presents. Unlike the other adults he was used to, Vicki didn't seem to have any motive for her kindness other than just caring about him.

To hear Joey tell it, he never got along with Seth. The

man was not as demonstrative with his feelings as Vicki was. There were days when they would just pass each other in the kitchen and say nothing at all.

"I stayed out of his way and he stayed out of mine," Joey would later say. But Seth did spend some time with Joey doing the things Seth enjoyed, and brought the boy to firing ranges with him to teach him about guns. At this point, Seth's firearm collection was modest, but growing rapidly.

In November of 1991, Vicki and Seth planned a weekend getaway to Maine. Vicki was six months pregnant with the twins. They had reservations at the Wagon Wheel Motel in Saco and had made arrangements for Joey to be cared for by a relative.

Although she had been looking forward to the trip, Vicki didn't feel quite herself as they left Brooklyn. Soon, she began to feel some pelvic discomfort while driving across southern New England. As they were traveling through New Hampshire, still a good hour or more from their destination, Vicki began to miscarry.

"I'm going to lose the babies," she cried. Seth stopped the car and tried futilely to calm his wife down and halt her contractions. He called for an ambulance. The couple held hands and looked into each other's panicked eyes. They didn't know what else they could do.

The loss of the twin girls was devastating to Vicki. For Seth, it was a crushing blow. The miscarriage was a turning point in their relationship they'd both later admit they never got over.

*   *   *

In May of 1992, Seth Bader purchased a large, beautiful house in Stratham, New Hampshire, at the end of a long cul-de-sac called Doe Run Lane. On paper, Seth was the sole owner of the property, which was easily worth a half million dollars, though he paid just $380,000 for it since the builder had run out of money before completing construction. There was plenty of land, close to eight acres—something the New Yorkers were not accustomed to—and a small creek that ran through the back end of the property and fed into the Squamscott River.

Joey had just turned ten and was amazed at the size of the new house. His eyes grew wide looking at the backyard of green grass and trees, not to mention a swimming pool. The home's interior needed to be finished and painted, but Vicki told Joey that meant they could design the rooms any way they wanted to.

On moving day, some kids on bicycles came over to see who had moved in. Joey was a little older than them, and the fact that he grew up in New York City made him a sort of exotic traveler to the grade school kids who lived on his new street.

Seth Bader was also a fish out of water in his new neighborhood. He told Joey he was getting the best Medeco locks for the doors—just like they'd had on his parents' home—but couldn't understand why the neighbors thought it was overkill to do so. Like most New Englanders, the residents of Doe Run Lane were die-hard

Red Sox fans who believed in the mythological rivalry between the Sox and the Yankees. They couldn't conceive of someone from New York who didn't follow baseball.

The Steinway piano that Seth inherited from his parents was placed in the sunken living room of the new house. But that instrument paled next to Seth's most impressive possession, his mother's G. B. Guadagnini violin. It had been crafted in the 1800s and was appraised at $400,000. As a child, Seth had reluctantly played the violin, but he had refused to pick up the bow since he was old enough to protest. Unlike his ostentatious display of the Steinway, Seth sensibly kept the Guadagnini in climate-controlled storage to protect it.

To Joey, it seemed like the move to New Hampshire really suited Seth and Vicki. They had both been melancholy since losing the twin girls. Now, in their new home, they seemed affectionate once again. He'd see them holding hands, hugging, and kissing. Much of what Seth and Vicki's marriage was really like was kept hidden from his view; either that, or as a ten-year-old boy, he simply didn't notice it.

The person Joey Fitzgerald loved the most in the whole world was his little brother, Matt. Everyone else had let him down, abandoned him, or, he assumed, would eventually. It was Joey's idea to send for Matt to live with them in New Hampshire. He hadn't seen his brother in months, so he decided to ask Vicki, thinking she would be more open to the idea than her husband.

"You're right," she said to Joey. "That would be a very good thing to do. Let me talk to Seth." Joey was very happy at the thought of his brother moving in. He never heard the conversation between the Baders but figured it must have gone well because Vicki told him shortly thereafter that Seth had said yes.

Within a few weeks, Matt moved to New Hampshire and into the bedroom across the hall from Joey. But his arrival had an odd effect on Seth Bader. It was clear to everyone—including Vicki and her mother Lois Stewart—that Joey was Seth's favorite. He made no bones about expressing it, even in front of Matt. Seth often said he could see Joey growing up strong and handsome, calling him a "Big Wheel." The young man would have the athletic ability Seth never had. He would be a crackerjack shot. In Seth Bader's eyes, Joseph Fitzgerald was the Golden Child, and Matt was a nuisance.

Despite Seth's overt displays of favoritism toward him, however, Joey wanted less and less to do with him. Seth's voice was so loud it always seemed like he was yelling. The more Joey was exposed to other kids in his new neighborhood and saw how they interacted with their parents, the more he thought Seth was mean, even strange.

Seth Bader was admitted to the New Hampshire Bar in November 1992 and began running a law practice out of his home office in Stratham. Seth took on all kinds of cases, from family law to criminal defense, but was not heralded by peers as a rising star. He was seen instead as running a workaday practice. He quickly got the reputation for being single-minded; not necessarily a bad trait in a lawyer, but Seth was also abrasive and stubborn, and his loud, fast New York staccato and ill-fitting double breasted suits seemed out of place in country courtrooms.

Vicki returned to her professional roots and began scouting choice real estate investments along the state's Seacoast region. The couple purchased rental properties in Exeter, Portsmouth, and Newmarket. The venture quickly became a profitable revenue stream for them. She also helped Seth do legal research, digging through law books or the state Revised Statutes Annotated (RSAs) to assist with cases.

To both boys, Vicki never seemed so happy as when she told them she was again pregnant in early 1993. There were only three bedrooms in the house, but the boys were assured that nothing would change right away. The baby would sleep in a bassinet next to Seth and Vicki's bed. The child was due in August. Joey would be eleven years old by then.

When Samuel Robert Bader was born at 11:36 on August 7, 1993, Joey was braced for considerable changes in his family life. Sam cried at night and smelled up his diapers like any other baby, but Joey wasn't burdened with the task of caring for him, not like he had been when Matt was born. Sam was an easygoing baby, and Joey liked him.

If anyone seemed to be put out by his arrival, it was Matt. He would constantly complain that the baby made too much noise.

Sam's arrival officially made the Baders parents, but they already felt like the older boys in the house were more than merely third cousins. Seth and Vicki formally petitioned the Rockingham County Probate Court to adopt Joseph and Matthew. Their mother, Jaye, didn't object, and the adoptions became official after a hearing on February 28, 1994. The boys changed their names from Fitzgerald to Bader, and the five of them finally made up a true family, at least on paper.

At the same time she was adopting Joey and Matt, Vicki was coming undone. The week before the adoption hearing she began therapy with a counselor in Exeter. Vicki felt she needed help sorting through her feelings about an increasingly hostile home life. Vicki had hoped the arrival of baby Sam would be the tonic her relationship with Seth needed. His anger, his pettiness, surely these were a result of his pain and disappointment at losing the twins, she'd thought. She'd hoped that becoming a father to Sam would heal those wounds. Instead, living with him became intolerable.

Seth belittled Vicki. Marginalized her.

"You're a fat pig," he would say, referring to the baby weight she had yet to lose. "I don't know what I was thinking of when I married you."

Her pregnancy with Sam had been difficult and, to hear Seth speak of it, unwanted. If the couple thought that the birth of a healthy child would solve all the problems in their marriage, they were wrong.

Seth had also been particularly petty about Vicki's inability to work during her pregnancy with Sam, during which she'd been advised to take it easy in light of her earlier miscarriage.

"I'm keeping track," Seth had told her.

"Of what?" Vicki asked him.

"All the money you're costing me by not working," he replied bitterly. Vicki had hoped that Seth would come to his senses once Sam was born, but when he presented her with a detailed invoice for her half of their living expenses during the pregnancy, she realized the man she married wasn't the lovable schlub she'd once believed he was.

In April of 1994, things took a turn for the worse when Vicki announced she was once again pregnant. Joey noticed there was no jubilation over the news from Seth, who seemed just as surly and distant as ever. On the night of the twenty-eighth, he got into his blue Jeep and drove off, only to return before dawn looking drawn and haggard.

SIX

Broken Home

Lawrence, Massachusetts, lies just south of New Hampshire's border. It's the kind of city where no one brags about living; when people say they're "from" Lawrence, what they're really saying is that they *escaped* Lawrence. For those who do live there, it's generally a matter of necessity or convenience, but rarely one of choice.

On April 28, 1994, Lawrence police detective Jeffery Shannon* set out on an undercover sting operation. Following him in a second unmarked car were two other detectives. Driving down Green Street in one of the city's most notorious neighborhoods, Shannon spied a young woman standing on the sidewalk. If it hadn't been the

---

* Denotes pseudonym

middle of the night, and if she had been wearing a coat in the chilly weather, he might have thought she was waiting for a taxi. But there was no doubt why she was really there. He pulled up to her, pushing the button to open the window on the passenger's side.

"I'm looking for Wanda." This was Detective Shannon's standard opening. It wasn't always Wanda, though. Sometimes it was Denise, sometimes Maria. The name didn't matter. The response was nearly always the same.

"Wanda's not around, baby. But *I* can take care of you."

"How much?" The detective pulled a wad of bills out of his jeans pocket.

"Twenty, baby."

"What do I get?"

"A blow job."

Shannon leaned over and opened the sedan's door, letting the woman in. He asked if she wanted the money first, and she replied that she did. He handed the woman a twenty, which she promptly slid into the top of her left sock.

"You're under arrest," he said, "for prostitution."

It only took fifteen minutes for Shannon to bring his first collar back to the station and return to the operation. Nabbing hookers in Lawrence had become a high-efficiency assembly line. At the end of his shift, Shannon would write up just one report, detailing all the evening's arrests in two single-spaced pages.

By 1:25 A.M., the detective had brought two more hookers to the station and had seen to their booking. One had directed him to drive to an isolated dirt road off Green Street before she'd initiated the transaction. Shannon had let her, because going to these places gave him new locations to stake out on future patrols. After dropping her at the station, he cruised back to Green Street, where he saw a navy blue Jeep pulling up to yet another prostitute standing on the sidewalk. The Jeep had a New Hampshire vanity plate: SB-ESQ.

Two for one, Shannon thought. If arresting hookers had become a rote part of his job, nabbing johns was like earning bonus points. Radioing the detectives in the tail car, he followed the Jeep, which now carried a passenger, to a desolate parking lot on Methuen Street. The cops drove another block, parked their unmarked units, and returned to the Jeep on foot.

Approaching from an alley at the rear of the lot, Shannon saw the woman in the Jeep pull up her shirt, exposing her breasts. Then he saw the driver's hand push the woman's head down, out of view.

Walking up to the driver's side of the Jeep, the detective got an eyeful of exactly what was happening inside the vehicle. The driver had his pants down by his ankles, and the hooker's head was bobbing rhythmically in his lap. Shannon used the butt end of his flashlight to rap on the vehicle's driver's-side window. The man inside started, reflexively pulling up his pants. Shannon ordered both of them out of the car and read them their rights.

"What's happening here?" He addressed the girl first, and she pointed at her companion.

"This guy, he paid me twenty dollars for a blow job."

Shannon looked at the man standing in front of him.

He was short and oily, with a smarmy expression on his sweaty, round face.

"I don't know this girl," the man said.

"I know you don't," the detective replied. "You're both coming with me."

Back at the station, the john didn't have much to say as he was booked, watching passively as the detective counted the money he'd confiscated from his wallet. But when Shannon started to process the prostitute, she had plenty to say.

"Hey, can I have the twenty bucks he owed me? I mean, I did go down on the guy."

At 3:00 A.M., Jeffery Shannon found himself back in his unit, watching the corner of Broadway and Whitman streets. It was a slightly different part of the map, but that didn't prevent the detective from experiencing a distinct sense of déjà vu.

"What the hell . . . you guys see this?" Jeffery got the affirmative response from his tail car. Straight ahead of the cops was a blue Jeep Cherokee with a New Hampshire vanity plate that read "SB-ESQ." The driver of that Jeep must have barely posted his bail before heading back downtown to pick up another hooker. A woman got in the car, and as soon as she closed the door, the Cherokee sped down Broadway, toward the neighboring city of Methuen.

When Shannon crossed city lines chasing the Jeep, a Methuen patrolman pulled him over for speeding. Shannon explained what he was doing, and the patrolman lit his light bar and joined the chase. When they finally caught up to the Jeep, Shannon strode over to the driver's window.

"Hi, there," the cop said to the little man, who looked far less embarrassed than a man in his situation ought to look. "Remember me?"

Shannon asked the man to exit the vehicle and then arrested Seth Bader for soliciting his second prostitute in under three hours.

To Vicki, who had for months felt unloved and unwanted by her husband, his arrest was the final straw. She decided her only choice was to get away from Seth Bader. In early May 1994, a pregnant Vicki Lynn Bader gathered her three children and a bagful of clothes and left Doe Run Lane. Joey had just turned twelve years old, Matt was six and a half, and Samuel was nine months. Vicki also took with her a 9mm Sigarms pistol, which had been a gift to her from her husband in happier times.

She left no forwarding address.

Seth Bader responded to what he perceived as Vicki's insolence the best way he knew how: he went to court. He enlisted an attorney he knew, Barbara Taylor, to be his lawyer.

Barbara Taylor grew up in Dedham, Massachusetts. A bright student, she attended the prestigious Winsor

School in Boston before starting college at Northwestern. In what she'd later call an "idiotic" decision, she transferred to the University of Pennsylvania, where she graduated in 1966 with a degree in archaeology, and enrolled in the graduate school there, before dropping out as a result of then-legal academic discrimination. After working three jobs in New York, she saved enough money to take an extended trip to the United Kingdom, where she met her husband. The couple moved back to Massachusetts and settled down.

After working in a variety of fields for many years, Taylor decided in 1988 to finish the academic journey she'd given up as a young woman. She enrolled at Suffolk University Law School in Boston, graduated in the top half of her class, and was admitted to both the Massachusetts and New Hampshire bars by 1992. She looked forward to a nice, quiet practice in New Hampshire. But then she met Seth Bader, who lived in a neighboring town, at a training they attended together after their concurrent bar admittance. After she agreed to take him on as a client, nothing about Taylor's practice was nice or quiet.

Seth hired Taylor to represent him in court proceedings but acted as his own counsel when it came to strategy and direction. Together, they drew up his motion, *Libel For Divorce*. It was the first filing in what he vowed would become an epic divorce case. He accused his wife of taking virtually none of Joey or Matt's clothing and no diapers, bottles, formula, or pediatric prescriptions for

Samuel when she took the boys from their house on Doe Run Lane.

Seth then filed for ex parte custody of the children, asking the court to grant him custody without hearing from Vicki. He stated that his wife was suffering from "severe depression" and that "her whereabouts [were] presently unknown."

Vicki had enlisted an attorney herself, who competently refuted Seth's allegations. Vicki warned her lawyer that Seth would be relentless and would not give any quarter in the upcoming fight. But then one day, with no other warning, she suddenly informed her attorney that she had settled the case with Seth.

Seth Bader had crafted a postnuptial agreement on his office computer. In a moment of mutual weakness, he and Vicki realized that a tooth-and-nail fight between them would be more than either could stomach. The agreement stipulated that Vicki would live in a rental property the couple owned on Patricia Avenue in Exeter, and Seth would pay the taxes and utilities on the home. She and the boys would all stay on his Blue Cross and Blue Shield health plan, and instead of child support or alimony, Seth would pay Vicki a flat $20,000 a year labeled as "income from rental properties."

The boys would split their time between the two homes. It seemed a fair and expedient solution, and both parties willingly signed off on it on June 3, 1994. It appeared that only six weeks after running away, Vicki would be free from Seth Bader.

*   *   *

While waiting for the court to approve their postnuptial agreement, Vicki scheduled a prenatal appointment with her physician. She sat on an exam table, staring at the ceiling. She was due in January, and mentally she was preparing to go through the pregnancy on her own. Unlike when she was carrying Samuel, though, this ultrasound technician was not cheerful and chatty. Vicki kept waiting for video images, but instead, the technician just turned off the scope, told her to wait for the doctor, and left the exam room.

A sober-faced ob-gyn entered the exam room to tell her the child she was carrying had died. Vicki was stunned. She hardly comprehended what the doctor was telling her. He told her a nurse would come in shortly to prep Vicki. She was going to have a D & C. There was no baby, and she was all alone.

When the boys returned to their father's home for the first time after the separation, there was an immediate change of atmosphere, and not one for the better. The house was in disarray. Seth gave both Joey and Matt a long list of chores. Joey had to do the laundry, change and dress Sam, and clean up after Seth's three dogs: an Akita, a Labrador, and a dachshund. The routine reminded him of living in Brooklyn, taking care of his baby brother so his mother could get her fix, just like he was now working around the house so that Seth could get his fix. Except Seth's addiction wasn't drugs. It was women.

On June 20, 1994, the court accepted the Baders' post-nuptial agreement. It was finally official. The Baders were divorced.

On June 21, 1994, Vicki asked a babysitter to watch the kids at her home in Exeter. After kissing them good-bye, she drove her blue Cadillac Coupe DeVille to the Wagon Wheel Motel in Saco, Maine. Vicki got the same room that she and Seth had reserved on their ill-fated weekend nearly three years earlier. There, she ingested a bottle of Tylenol with Codeine, closed her eyes, and waited to die.

SEVEN

Trash Talk

Postal Inspector Willie Moores called Exeter Police lieutenant Richard Kane on Tuesday, March 19, 1996, to tell him that preliminary attempts to recover fingerprints from the bomb and masking tape hadn't been successful, but they were going to run some more tests. The inspector promised to keep Kane updated.

Kane would have been sure he had a really good suspect for the bomb in Vicki Bader's mailbox were it not for the way the victim kept behaving. Her inconsistent stories about her ex-husband and his kitchen explosives experiments were a problem, as was her potential motive for portraying Seth as a threat to her safety.

The police chief told a reporter that Seth Bader was not a suspect in the bomb scare at his ex-wife's house.

Detective Kim Roberts told Seth's lawyer the same thing. But, of course, Seth Bader *was* a suspect. Spouses are virtually automatic suspects in crimes involving their partners or ex-partners. At least one of the local newspapers knew it was a possibility. They had sent a reporter to Seth's home after the pipe bomb incident to interview him.

"My jaw hit the floor and hasn't come back up . . . my head is spinning. I don't know what to make of it," he was quoted in the paper. "If this was New York, this would be normal. But this is New Hampshire. Stuff like this doesn't happen here."

Seth Bader played the "innocent as a lamb" role very well, but Kane knew that the attorney was a wolf in sheep's clothing. Seth had the know-how with explosives and by his own admission had plenty of the supplies on hand needed to fabricate a pipe bomb. He had plenty of motive, too. A child custody battle can be the worst kind of dispute. There was also a financial motive as far as alimony and child support might be concerned. Not to mention that something about the little man just seemed greasy.

But Seth Bader had been nothing but cooperative with the police. He'd made a big show about giving them his fingerprints and issued a standing invitation to look around his gun room. He wasn't acting like a man with something to hide.

It would have been much easier to focus solely on Seth Bader if it weren't for Vicki Lynn Bader. She tripped and stumbled at every step with the police. Whenever they thought they could rule her out as a suspect, Vicki said or did something that only made her look worse.

Exeter patrolman Dan D'Amato's unmarked car crept down the sleeping cul-de-sac on Doe Run Lane on March 21. It was 4:00 A.M. on the first day of spring, but in the dark it still felt like winter. D'Amato hoped that Seth Bader had the same habits as his neighbors; otherwise he'd have to sit in an idling car until someone woke up to do their morning chores. A quick inspection of the curb was all the officer needed. Apparently Seth was one of those who liked to put his garbage out the night before and sleep in the following day.

D'Amato collected all the trash bags in front of the Bader residence—thirteen bags in all—and brought them back to the Exeter Police Department. Lieutenant Kane met D'Amato in the sally port and closed the doors once the car was inside. Kane laid a tarp on the floor and emptied the bags one by one to examine their contents.

The process was painstaking and at times nauseating. Seth's trash was full of soiled diapers and the plate scrapings from unfinished meals. But there were also other items that might be of evidentiary value. Seth had thrown away two bottles of PVC glue and two tubes of sealant. There was a Dixie cup that was charred on the inside, as if someone had lit black powder in it. There was also a box of plumber's tape and a couple of receipts. Kane recovered paper towels of the same brand that had been mixed in with the powder in the pipe bomb device. Large amounts of animal hair were also among the bags' contents.

Kane also came across some crumpled-up sheets of yellow lined paper. He flattened them out to get a better look and was stunned by what he read scrawled in blue ball-point ink.

Poison mother, whole story, shot mugger, not charged, shot and killed hold-up man, not found, stalked, shot, killed man, stalking Vicki

Tires, windows, packages, letters, calls, bomb

$

On Monday morning, March 25, Detective Kim Roberts got a phone call from Heidi Boyack, Vicki Lynn Bader's attorney. Over the weekend, Vicki had had an encounter with a suspicious man at the Exeter Public Library that she wanted to report.

Roberts informed Kane, who immediately called Vicki at home. He asked if they could come over to talk about what had happened at the library. Vicki agreed, and they set the time for 12:30 that afternoon. A few minutes later Vicki called back and said that after speaking to her attorney, she felt the best place to talk would be the police station.

When she arrived, Vicki told them about the incident. She said she arrived at the public library on Friday between noon and 2:00 P.M. She asked the reference librarian for access to the historical room, a locked section that included rare books, genealogies, and historical documents as well as a complete set of books containing New Hampshire state laws, called RSAs.

"I was researching RSAs when a man came into the room and asked whether he could read the supplemental portion of the RSA I was reading," Vicki said. "He looked at it for a minute, then returned it to me and said, 'I don't look like a dangerous man, do I?' Then he left. At the time I didn't think it was important, but I thought you two should know."

Vicki described the man as white, with bushy gray hair, a mustache, and a small beard. He was of medium height and medium build. She said she had never seen him before and didn't know where he went after he left the historical room.

"I'm just curious, Vicki," Roberts asked. "What were you reading when this man approached you?"

"I was reading the RSAs on arson and explosives." Then she added quickly, "And custody and taxation RSAs, too."

Kane was dumbfounded. "Why would you be looking up laws on arson and explosives?"

"I was curious about them."

"But of all the RSAs, why were you reading these?"

Vicki didn't have a good answer. "I just wanted to know."

Boyack had earlier told the detectives that her client felt Seth Bader was under a lot of pressure.

"Why did you tell your attorney that you felt Seth was under a lot of stress?" Roberts quizzed Vicki now. "She said you felt like something was going to happen."

"Seth is going to be deposed by my insurance company on Wednesday about some things he stole from my house last January. And on Thursday, we're going back to Superior Court for another custody hearing."

Vicki said that in the past, it had been during times like this that strange things would happen to her. "I'm just afraid of coming home and finding my house set on fire."

When Vicki left, Kane and Roberts were again struggling to deal with what the woman had told them. They found it odd that Vicki would be looking up the laws regarding arson before telling the police that she felt her house would be set on fire. This only added to the list of reasons why Vicki Bader was still a suspect in the pipe bomb case, even as she was still, technically, the victim.

Kane and Roberts went to the Exeter Public Library and tracked down the reference librarian. She said she remembered Vicki coming in and looking for the RSAs around noon on Friday. The detectives asked if the librarian had also seen a man approach Vicki Bader while she was in the historical room, but the librarian said she had not.

"I left for lunch around 1:00," she said. "The library director covered for me while I was gone." The cops quizzed the director, but she hadn't seen anyone talking to Vicki, either.

Later in the day, Kane received a call from Vicki. She said she had returned to the library to double-check which books she had been looking at on Friday.

"I was *not* reading about arson and explosives. I'm sure I was looking at laws relating to custody issues," Vicki said unconvincingly. "I was mistaken about the arson. I must have been thinking about something else."

Kane and Roberts were again bewildered by Vicki's actions. All the talk about arson was unsettling to the investigators. With a busy week of stressful legal hearings ahead for the Baders, the lieutenant was very worried that something was indeed about to happen. The Patricia Avenue home might be again targeted for criminal mischief, but it was also looking just as likely that Vicki could damage the house herself in order to implicate her ex-husband.

Kane ordered that both Seth's and Vicki's homes be placed under surveillance for three days.

On Tuesday morning, March 26, detectives waited for Vicki Lynn Bader to put the trash out for that day's pickup. After the terry cloth–robed woman placed the rubber bins at the end of her driveway, the police took the bags back to the station.

Kim Roberts helped Kane sift through the rubbish strewn across the tarp. Unlike Seth Bader's trash, Vicki's was slim pickings for the investigators. They found some handwritten notes that Vicki made about the case, but the content seemed to merely parrot the information they'd given her at previous interviews. There were a couple of receipts, none of which corresponded to anything remotely criminal. Nothing of value was found.

For the next three days, the Exeter detectives took turns staking out both Vicki's and Seth's houses. Both Baders' patterns were mundane and predictable. Vicki went to the store and the library. Seth went to the post office and the country store and brought his sons to school. In the evening, his girlfriend, Mary Jean Martin, would visit.

On the third day—Thursday, March 28—the Baders both made it to the courthouse in time for their hearing. While they were inside, Kane peeked into their car windows, but he didn't see anything suspicious in either vehicle.

Lieutenant Richard Kane met with Postal Inspector Willie Moores on Tuesday, April 2. Moores told him that the national lab had failed to turn up any physical evidence from the pipe bomb. No fingerprints, no DNA.

Inspector Moores told Kane they had had some luck analyzing the handwriting samples given by Vicki and Seth Bader. Moores had given copies of the statements to Avinoam Sapir, a former Israeli police officer and Mossad operative considered to be the father of a technique known as Scientific Content Analysis. Sapir studied the statements given by both Baders and analyzed the words and phrasings they used. He concluded that Vicki's statement had several lines in it that indicated deception. Sapir's professional opinion was that this deception was most prominent in the section where she wrote about finding the pipe bomb in the mailbox.

Kane couldn't shake the feeling that Vicki wasn't telling the truth about the bomb. But he also worried that she might simply have a gift for putting her foot in her mouth, and if so, that she might be in actual danger. Unfortunately, the case was now a month old, and it didn't seem likely they were going to turn up any new evidence at this point.

But just as Kane was about to back-burner the investigation, Postal Inspector Moores called his office. The paper cup that they had recovered from Seth Bader's trash *had* been used to ignite a small amount of gunpowder. The lab said the powder found in the cup was a mixture of black powder and aluminum flake, just like the powder discovered inside the pipe bomb.

EIGHT

Femme Fatale

At five feet six inches, with curly blond hair and striking green eyes, Mary Jean Martin was easily the prettiest woman Seth Bader had ever dated. She was alluring and graceful. She was also ambitious. She knew exactly what she wanted, and either people gave it to her or she cut them loose and moved on. The advantage to being Mary Jean was that it usually wasn't until she was out of someone's life that they finally understood what she'd been all about. It wasn't until she was long gone that they started to call her a gold digger.

Mary Jean Martin was born in Waltham, Massachusetts, in March 1964. She had two younger brothers, Steven and James Paul. When she was a teenager, her parents divorced and most of her family moved to Florida, but she decided to stay behind in New England. She was an unremarkable graduate from Waltham High School and then bounced around from college to college attempting to scratch out a business degree—she started at Brandeis, then transferred to Bentley for night school, then spent some semesters at Bridgewater State and Stonehill—without ever graduating.

When she was eighteen, Mary Jean got into a serious relationship with an older man named Alan Achorn. He worked for his family business, the Achorn Steel Company, but held a second job at Mary Jean's father's company, National Folding Box. They bought a house and got married within a year. The union dissolved when Mary Jean was twenty-two, with "irreconcilable differences" written on the divorce decree. Many years later, long after Achorn had remarried and had children, Mary Jean would discover that he had passed away due to complications from diabetes. She only found out about his death because of a glitch on her credit report.

In the mid-1980s, Mary Jean married Nathan Byrne.* It was a rocky relationship from the start, and when the couple tried to get a divorce, they learned their marriage had never been valid because the wedding ceremony hadn't been performed by a legal minister in the first place. Instead of trying to sort through the legal confu-

---

* Denotes pseudonym

sion, the pair agreed to just let things go and walked away from each other. Mary Jean later heard that her second husband had died in prison.

By November 1989, Mary Jean was ready to try marriage again, this time to a Boston man named Brian Messenheimer. The celebration was held at a restaurant in New Bedford. Messenheimer worked as a toll collector on the Massachusetts Turnpike; a good career, until he got hurt on the job and went on workers' comp. In 1988, the couple had a daughter, Courtney, though Messenheimer was troubled that even after the birth of their child, Mary Jean's priority seemed to be spending her weekends at dog shows. Their rift grew, and soon she was walking away from yet another husband, but this time, with a shared custody agreement in hand.

Seth Bader continued to pursue new women after his prostitution arrest and Vicki's exodus from the house. Within a week of his estranged wife leaving with the boys, Seth fell into a relationship with a twentysomething call girl from Boston named Jill Provenza.* Their first meeting was a dinner at a fancy restaurant in the North End. Provenza thought Seth's table manners were embarrassing, and she didn't foresee spending any more time with him, but Seth won her over by demonstrating just how fat his wallet was. When he described his empty New Hampshire

---

* Denotes pseudonym

mansion, Provenza made an indecent proposal. "I will come live with you and attend to all your sexual needs," she said, "for twenty thousand dollars a month."

Seth pondered her offer. He seemed embarrassed by the moral implications of the deal. The price was steep, but that wasn't the reason he turned her down.

"I can't," he told Jill Provenza. "I would fall in love with you and I'd want an emotional relationship with you, too."

Without Mary Jean's knowledge, her friends put together some photographs and signed Mary Jean Martin up for a personals ad account in *Boston* magazine. Her ad generated dozens of responses, and Mary Jean eventually went on a number of hit-or-miss dates. After that, she decided to pick from the bachelors who posted and not the other way around. Mary Jean selected three ads from the May 1994 issue of *Boston*. One was from a "handsome, New Hampshire Seacoast attorney" who was looking for a beautiful girl to "sit by the pool with him and his [dogs.]" By day, Mary Jean worked as a paralegal in a small law firm, but on the side, she also bred dogs for sale and to show. This ad seemed like a promising fit.

Mary Jean's first date with Seth Bader was on Saturday, June 18, 1994, two days before his divorce from Vicki was made official. It was a memorable day for Mary Jean— not because of the date, but because a dog she had bred and sold had placed at the Middlesex County Kennel Club's show. The American Staffordshire terrier, named

Once Upon a Blue Moon, had won Best in Class and several other prizes.

After the excitement of the show, Mary Jean was running late for her dinner with Seth. They'd arranged to meet at the Legal Sea Foods restaurant in Burlington, Massachusetts. By the time she arrived, the place was packed and the wait promised to be more than an hour, so they went somewhere else. Over dinner, they talked about their mutual love of animals. Mary Jean told Seth about her hobby breeding American Staffordshire terriers, dogs almost indistinguishable from pit bulls. Before the night was over, they made love at Mary Jean's house, and made a date for the following Tuesday for Mary Jean to come to Seth's home for a barbecue and to meet his dogs.

By the end of the summer, Mary Jean had moved into the house on Doe Run Lane and was freely spending Seth Bader's money.

Mary Jean worked for a personal injury lawyer outside of Boston, earning $27,500 a year as a paralegal. She told people that she didn't make any money as a dog breeder and that she spent more money on food and care and traveling to dog shows than she ever made selling her animals.

Mary Jean was an asset to the attorney because she had a good head for figures and knew the ins and outs of insurance adjustment. Mary Jean had been an adjuster for Aetna while she was married to Brian Messenheimer. Her ex-husband later claimed that Mary Jean left the company because of irregularities with her paperwork, and that her cozy relationships with some personal injury attorneys connected to her claims didn't smell right.

With her cascading blond hair and tight skirts, Mary Jean was very popular with the law firm's clients—some of whom were not the most upstanding citizens in the Commonwealth. But her job did give her an advantage; she now had an eclectic group of friends that she could call upon should she need them.

Seth Bader was deeply infatuated with Mary Jean, or "MJ" as he called her. She was willing to be his sexual plaything and he couldn't get enough. There was immediate talk of her moving from Massachusetts to live with him in Stratham. Seth did all he could to lavish her with dinners and gifts, giving her full access to his checkbook and credit cards and letting her go on frequent shopping sprees with them. He even paid for her to get liposuction. This was behavior far removed from his life with Vicki, in which he'd made her document every dollar she took from the family coffers and had set to memory every nickel he felt she owed him as a result of her bed rest while pregnant with Sam.

Mary Jean loved concerts and live theater. She would pay for the best seats to plays in Boston's theater district with Seth's credit card and buy front-row concert tickets in venues all over New England. Seth would often accompany her, but she was just as likely to go alone.

Another of Mary Jean's obsessions was Disney collectibles. She spent thousands of dollars on studio artwork and expensive figurines. When she sold her home to move in with Seth, she invested much of the proceeds into Disney items she felt certain would increase in value.

Three days after Seth's date with Mary Jean and the day following the court granting the Baders' divorce, Vicki Lynn Bader was rushed to the hospital from the Wagon Wheel Motel in Saco, Maine. It was the evening of June 21, 1994. She was barely conscious. Earlier that day, she'd had a difficult therapy session with Dr. David Shopick; one so intense that he'd tried to contact her afterward. Vicki had also skipped a meeting she was supposed to attend after her therapy appointment. Her absence resulted in a series of phone calls from Vicki's worried friends to the police, who then called Vicki's home and spoke to her babysitter. The sitter said Vicki had just called her, and the police were able to trace that call back to Maine. When the Saco police forced the motel room door open, they found Vicki lying on the bed next to an empty bottle of Tylenol with Codeine pills. Vicki was taken by ambulance to Southern Maine Medical Center in Biddeford. She was admitted and voluntarily agreed to stay for a week.

Seth Bader heard the news about his ex-wife from the Exeter police while Mary Jean was at his house for their second date. With Mary Jean in tow, he collected the boys from the babysitter Vicki had hired and brought them back to Doe Run Lane to stay with him.

After the separation, Joey preferred staying at Vicki's house. When he had first moved in with the Baders in Brooklyn, Vicki had seemed very much like a caring aunt. But as the years passed, Joey began to appreciate her more and more, as he would a mother. Despite his adolescent feelings of confusion about his past and Vicki's role in his life, she didn't make him cook his own dinner or change Sam when she was in the middle of something else, the way Seth did. But Joey could also tell that Vicki was sad. She told the boys that she had lost the baby she'd been carrying, and it reminded Joey of when she'd lost the twins, and how hard that had been on her.

Vicki had kissed all the children good-bye when she left them with the sitter on the night of June 21. Joey went to bed and was awakened in the middle of the night by Seth Bader, who had shown up at Vicki's house with a blond woman Joey had never met. A groggy Joey rubbed his eyes as Seth shook him awake.

"This is MJ," he told the boy, pointing to the woman with the curly golden hair.

Seth and Mary Jean had planned to go to the movies later that night, but Vicki's crisis had put a crimp in their evening. Now they would all instead go along to Saco, Maine, to retrieve Vicki's blue Cadillac Coupe DeVille from the parking lot of the motel where she'd attempted to take her own life. It was to be Mary Jean's responsibility to drive Vicki's car back to New Hampshire.

Even after she was discharged from the hospital, Vicki didn't feel right. Emotionally, everything was still a tidal wave, and she had far to go in order to crest the surface and breathe in the air.

Why am I so sad? she asked herself.

She clearly didn't love Seth, so she couldn't be depressed about the end of her marriage. If anything, it should have felt like a relief to no longer be in that house. She had been through a horrible miscarriage once before, but this time her whole body felt different. She didn't feel like she was in complete control of her own emotions. Dr. Shopick told her it was the pregnancy hormones still rushing through her body that had her feeling out of sorts.

When she was released from the hospital, she and Seth agreed to continue to share time with the boys, but they were to spend more time at Seth's house until Vicki felt better. Before he dropped the boys off at her house on Friday, July 22, 1994, a month after her suicide attempt, Seth took Vicki to an appliance store to purchase a washer and dryer for her Exeter home. Joey, Matt, and Sam all came along. Vicki seemed in good spirits that afternoon. She thanked her ex-husband for buying the washing machine and watched him drive away, leaving her alone with the three boys.

That night, while the boys watched television, Vicki

again swallowed a handful of pills. She called Dr. Shopick, and he notified the Exeter police. At their urging, Vicki waited for the patrolmen outside, away from the eyes of her children. The cops talked to her calmly. They strongly encouraged her to check herself into the Portsmouth Pavilion, a psychiatric facility about ten minutes away.

This time, while Vicki lay in a hospital bed recovering from her second suicide attempt in as many months, Seth Bader was preparing a legal blitzkrieg against her. When her attorney showed her the motions her ex-husband had drafted, she was furious. He was suing for sole custody of the boys.

In his filing, Seth claimed that on the day he'd purchased the washer and dryer, he'd observed several small cuts on his ex-wife's wrist, evidence of another undocumented suicide attempt.

"That's not true!" Vicki had protested aloud when the filing was read to her. "They're scratches from the cat!"

In the brief, Seth said that Vicki had appeared calm and collected earlier in the day when they went shopping for appliances, only to attempt suicide hours later. He pointed to this as proof of Vicki's instability. Seth also wrote that he had spoken with Dr. Shopick about Vicki's state of mind. He told the court that Vicki had relayed to Shopick that she was having "dreams, visions, and/or hallucinations" that the children she had miscarried were "calling to her from Heaven," and the doctor was concerned that she might attempt "to take her living children with her to Heaven to join the miscarried children."

Shopick blanched at Seth's characterization of their conversation. He insisted his words about mothers taking their children to Heaven had been prompted by direct questions from Seth, and that his answers were meant only in the most general of terms, and had been given with Vicki's permission. He had started Vicki on a combination of lithium, to stabilize her mood, and Zoloft, an antidepressant. At the request of Vicki's attorney, Shopick wrote to the court saying she was responding well to treatment and remained a nurturing, supportive mother.

"I do not think her past psychiatric problems are interfering with her ability to be a highly effective parent at this time," his letter to the court read.

After Mary Jean moved into the house in Stratham, she often brought her six-year-old daughter Courtney over to stay with them. Courtney was a precocious blonde who lived most of the time with her father in Charlestown, Massachusetts. She was just a year younger than Matt, and Joey came to see Courtney like a little sister, something he'd never had. But just as with his little brothers, twelve-year-old Joey was left to take care of Courtney whenever Seth and Mary Jean decided to hit the town or sleep in late.

Mary Jean's relationship with Seth's boys was initially friendly and supportive, though it was clear to her from the beginning that Seth was incapable of taking care of his kids. He didn't change diapers and was always happy to let someone else cook dinner or put the children to bed. But Mary Jean thought very highly of Joey. When she was around, she would help him with his chores and with changing Sam's diapers. She even entrusted him with the care of her precious dogs; she never fooled herself into thinking that Seth was the one feeding and cleaning up after them.

Mary Jean's closest relationship in the house, however, was with Matthew. She knew the seven-year-old had been born to a drug-addled parent who had passed him around to relatives, and then was left behind when his brother was taken to New Hampshire by Seth and Vicki. Following Vicki's suicide attempts, Matt hadn't seen his adoptive mother at all, so when Mary Jean arrived, he clung to her for affection. Mary Jean often invited Joey and Matt to come along with her to work and to weekend dog shows, driving them all over the Northeast and staying in modest hotels. They had fun, but it also meant leaving Seth alone in the house with Sam. Inevitably, the toddler would have a fully loaded diaper when they returned Sunday night.

Mary Jean had moved into Seth Bader's house but continued to maintain her independent lifestyle, seeing no need to account for her time when she left Doe Run Lane, sometimes for unexplained overnights. Her indifference to Seth's concerns about her whereabouts flummoxed him. He wanted to be with her every day and did all he could to win her over, yet she still held him at arm's length.

"Where I go when I'm not with you is none of your goddamn business!" she would tell him.

Seth would try to lay into her, just as he had with Vicki. But Mary Jean was a completely different animal. She gave it right back. Seth, for all his egotistical tendencies, was sharp enough to know when he wasn't going to win an argument. Where Mary Jean went and what she spent money on were topics Seth quickly learned to avoid.

Over time, Mary Jean's view of the situation between Vicki and Seth transformed from sympathy for Seth and the boys to no small amount of irritation. Vicki's suicide attempts were an annoyance. The never-ending legal maneuvering was a constant conversation that Seth couldn't stop having, even when he and Mary Jean were alone. Worst of all, the money that was siphoned to Vicki—the whole gestalt of Vicki—in alimony and medical bills and legal fees and a thousand paper cuts of indignities, was money that wasn't going to Mary Jean.

Mary Jean claimed the whole situation gave her headaches. She said she was prone to migraines and had been taking painkillers for years to cope with them. Bader, however, noticed that Mary Jean rarely went to the doctor, yet was able to somehow obtain and fill painkiller prescriptions at will.

*   *   *

Mary Jean did a little bit of dog training—but her true specialty was making *men* do her bidding. Mary Jean knew exactly how to lead Seth and get him to roll over.

Both of them were hotheads, and arguments were part of the landscape almost from the start. Mary Jean had no problem storming off and leaving her fidgety lover to ruminate. Invariably, a bouquet of roses would turn up at work the following day, or Seth would come crawling with a piece of jewelry in hand to entice her back. A fancy dinner was a common gesture of apology. And if Mary Jean was sufficiently placated, she would reward Seth with what he wanted: attention in the form of sex.

Seth followed MJ like a puppy, doing whatever she wanted him to do. To outsiders, it was hard to determine just what kind of feelings Mary Jean had for Seth. One weekend, the couple was invited to go hunting with Kees Oudekerk, a client of Seth's who shared his interest in guns. Oudekerk brought his girlfriend, and the four of them found a secluded area in the woods of Maine. At heart, Seth was a target shooter and didn't enjoy hunting, but he liked Oudekerk and wanted to cultivate the friend-ship. The men walked off into the trees. Mary Jean wasn't pleased with any part of this activity and stayed behind with Oudekerk's girlfriend to make lunch.

While they waited for the hunters to return, Mary Jean went on about how Seth's law practice wasn't what it was cracked up to be, that he only had a few clients and too much of his time was focused on the damned custody case. Mary Jean had been surprised to learn that much of Seth's wealth was not a result of his legal acumen. He had inherited most of his money from his parents, and he'd made a nice profit selling their home in New York, as well as that of a pair of elderly aunts who'd been placed in a nursing home.

The nest egg was considerable, but the burn rate was high and the lifestyle unsustainable. Mary Jean lamented to Oudekerk's girlfriend that she should have gotten involved with an older doctor instead of Seth Bader.

"I told Seth if he wants to marry me, it's going to take at least a seven carat diamond ring," she said.

NINE

Driven to the Brink

While Vicki was hospitalized—and while Seth was actively petitioning the court to have her child custody rights marginalized—Seth still insisted that his ex-mother-in-law care for the boys during Vicki's three scheduled days of visitation. He called Lois Stewart on Long Island and demanded she come up to New England to take the children off his hands. Lois didn't mind watching her grandchildren; it just struck her as both ironic and mean-spirited that Seth was on the one hand fighting so hard to keep his kids from their mother, while simultaneously insisting that someone else assume the caretaker role so he could have a vacation from parenting.

To Lois, it didn't seem Seth was doing much in the way of parenting at all. When she was alone with Joey, she'd press the boy for details of his home life in Stratham. Joey said that Seth would spend his days holed up, either in his office or in his special gun room. The only person Seth seemed to give attention to was his new girlfriend, Mary Jean. Joey said it fell upon him to change Sam's diapers and make lunch for Matt, but he was used to it after all those years in New York when his mother was high and he took care of his younger brother.

On one Saturday morning while Lois watched the boys at Vicki's house, Seth called and asked if he and Mary Jean could pick up the children and take them to the Stratham Fair, which was taking place that weekend. Lois asked what time he wanted the boys ready, and he told her 11:00 A.M. She dressed them, prepared a diaper bag for Sam, and then waited for Seth to show up. He didn't arrive until 5:00 P.M.

Lois waited through the evening for them to return, peeking out the window every time the beam of head-lights would gleam down the street. When they hadn't returned by 10:00 P.M., Lois called his home in Stratham.

"When are you bringing the boys home?" she asked Seth.

"I'm not," he said. "They were tired so I put them to sleep here."

"Well, weren't you going to call me and tell me?"

"It was late. I thought you were asleep."

The following morning, Lois drove to Doe Run Lane to pick up the boys. She had swallowed her anger and decided to be pragmatic. She needed to have a stern but respectful discussion with the father of her grandchildren.

She entered the hallway and said, "Seth, I need to talk to you like a Dutch uncle."

Seth looked at her quizzically. He wasn't familiar with that expression.

"The way you don't keep to your time commitments, it's not fair to the children. It's not fair to me. They were confused; they waited hours for you to pick them up . . ."

Seth's eyes blazed. "You don't get to talk to me like that!" he shouted. He then reached out and placed both hands on Lois's shoulders—in plain view of the children—and shoved her. The woman tried to find her footing but tumbled backward down the two steps into the sunken living room. Lois landed hard on her backside and momentarily felt stuck to the floor. Collecting her feet beneath her, she got up, walked back up the stairs, and slapped Seth hard across the cheek. Seth's head snapped back around, the side of his face reddened like a fire engine. Again, he placed both hands on Lois's shoulders and prepared to shove her again.

"Are you really going to push a fifty-nine-year-old woman down the stairs *twice?*" an incredulous Lois Stewart blurted out.

Seth hesitated, then turned on his heel and stomped off to the kitchen telephone. "I'm calling the cops," he declared victoriously. "*They'll* make you leave."

With hands fluttering, she waved the shell-shocked children through the hallway and out the door to her car. "I'm leaving on my own."

* * *

Sometime after the shoving incident, and after getting the blessing from an increasingly stronger Vicki, Lois decided to file a domestic violence petition against Seth Bader. The immediate result of the filing was the confiscation of Seth's vast and precious firearms collection. Now the man was really furious. He countered, seeking his own domestic violence petition against his ex-mother-in-law.

At a district court hearing on both petitions, Seth told the judge that he'd never laid hands on Lois, but that *she* had struck him with her shoe.

"I knew lawyers lied, but I didn't think they lied under oath," Lois told the court. "I guess I was wrong."

Lois could tell that the judge seemed unconvinced of Seth's claims but uncertain what to do about the conflicting petitions.

"If I just sign both of these orders, do you think you can stay away from one another?" the judge asked Lois, as if the infractions were offsetting penalties in a football game.

"That's fine by me," she said. "I have no intention of being around that man."

In New Hampshire courts, judges don't often sit to hear divorce or custody cases. They're presided over by marital masters, mid-level judicial officials who review evidence and make rulings in the cases, which are then rubber-stamped by a sitting justice. Though they wear robes and sit at the bench, the marital masters' function is to move the backlog of divorce cases along, primarily recommending mediation in order to resolve conflicts amicably and in the best interest of children. If a particular case—like the Baders'—required multiple hearings, it wasn't uncommon for a different master to preside over each of the hearings.

On August 1, 1994, the court ruled in favor of Seth's custody motion and gave primary custody of Joey, Matt, and Sam to him. For Seth, the case was about making a point, and he privately agreed to work out a near fifty-fifty time split with Vicki, but he remained devil-may-care about dates and times for drop-offs and pickups.

The court said it would reevaluate the custody situation in January 1995, but Vicki was sure the two older boys did not like Seth and would say that they preferred to stay with her if they were asked.

Near the end of 1994, Seth Bader gave Mary Jean a four-carat diamond engagement ring worth $10,578 and she accepted his proposal. When Seth told Vicki about the engagement, he said the ring cost $20,000. Vicki felt it was a one-two punch designed to flaunt his deep pockets and to remind her that he'd never once bought her jewelry while they had been married.

On January 11, 1995, Seth and Vicki Lynn Bader returned to Rockingham Superior Court to review their case with a different marital master. He refused to alter the custody agreement. Vicki walked out of court a broken woman.

* * *

Seth Bader received a call from Vicki on the evening of the court ruling. She asked for an overnight visit with Sam, but Seth refused. It was his night with the children and that was that, he said.

After Seth refused her request to see the baby, Vicki again swallowed a handful of pills and called Dr. Shopick. Vicki said that the baby she'd miscarried would have been born that month and that now, thanks to the court, she had suffered yet another loss.

Shopick called the police and asked them to check on Vicki. Outside it was a near blizzard and the patrol car drove as fast as it could in the snow. The front door was locked. The officers kicked in the door and searched the house for Vicki, calling her name over and over again. She was not in the kitchen, nor in the living room, nor the bathroom. All the lights were on, and there were no footprints or tire tracks in the snow, so they knew she must still be somewhere in the house.

The cops went through the home's bedrooms and found them empty. When they paused to regroup, a sound came from behind a bedroom wall. It sounded like someone snoring. Opening a closet, they discovered a crawl space behind it, where they found Vicki's near-lifeless body. She was completely unresponsive. The responding EMTs had to inject her with Narcan, a narcotics antidote, to stabilize her for transport to the hospital. Vicki was put on a respirator. There was a legitimate concern that she would not live through the night.

Seth Bader got a call from the Exeter police telling him his ex-wife was comatose and on her way to the hospital. They asked him to secure the front door, which they had damaged while kicking it in. Seth and Mary Jean drove over, and once the authorities left, the couple scoured the house, rifling through drawers and cabinets. In one drawer they found some pornographic cartoons drawn and signed by Vicki. They were mostly coarse sketches of naked men and their faceless lovers. In one, a buxom blonde was on her knees before her lover.

"When you told me your ex-wife left you because you lost your marbles," the cartoon woman said while pointing to the man's crudely drawn shaft, "I thought you meant your *mind!*"

Seth also discovered that Vicki had been reading several books on the topic of suicide. There was also a will and a series of suicide notes written to Vicki's family and friends.

Dear Dr. Shopick,

I'm sorry I was beyond even your help. I tried and so did you but the pain was too great . . . I can't think at any more losses [sic]. Let Sammy grow up with Seth + Mary Jean. If they stay together it will be a nice nuclear family.

I'm truly sorry I couldn't make it.

Vicki Bader

Some notes were written to friends, mostly apologies to them for her suicide. There were no letters addressed to the children, but there was one brief note written to Lois Stewart.

Dear Mom,

Get this witnessed + present to Seth so you'll get paid. Sorry I couldn't take anymore.

This letter likely referred to the will found nearby. In it, Vicki bequeathed all her furniture, a cat named Q-Tip, and $5,000 to her mother. She left her stereo to Joey and her birds and fish to Matt. She also requested "to be buried by my miscarried daughters, non-embalmed with a small ceremony."

The final letter discovered—the only one written with any kind of passion—was addressed to Seth.

Dear Seth,

I hate you. Thank you for destroying me [. . .]. You put so many demands on me I couldn't work, now you are destroying me economically. You stole away 2 of my kids and won't quit till you get the third. Well—here he is. You can expect all types of problems due to the loss of his mother but you have what you wish.

I hope you rot in hell.

Vicki

While Seth went to grab a few things from the boys' rooms, Mary Jean went through Vicki's bedroom dresser. Although Seth was not its supplier, Vicki did have a modest collection of jewelry. There were some gold bracelets, necklaces, and a few diamonds. Mary Jean took them all. She knew just what to do with them.

When Vicki got out of the hospital, she and her mother were furious about the items taken from the Exeter house. Lois Stewart mistook the kicked-in door as the work of burglars, not the police, and initially reported the jewelry stolen as part of a break-in. Seth was noncommittal about what he might have taken. He offered to return the children's things personally, but Vicki didn't want him back in her home. Instead, Mary Jean drove the boys to Exeter where they went into the house and dropped off the things Seth had taken for them.

There were many arguments about the jewelry. Seth claimed to have no knowledge of what became of her rings and bracelets, and in a way, he was probably telling the truth. Most of the good stuff had already changed hands.

Later, when people asked Seth what had happened to Vicki, he spun her latest suicide attempt into an allegation of attempted murder as well, telling people—including his adopted son Joey—that Vicki had crushed up her pills and mixed them in a bowl of vanilla pudding, which he said had been meant for Sam. He claimed that Vicki wanted to be with all of her children in heaven. Seth said her actions only further proved his contention that his ex was unstable and dangerous.

The claim that the pills were meant for Sam shook Joey. In fact, Vicki's suicide attempts had fundamentally changed the way Joey viewed her. They scared him. He didn't understand why she would try to do that to herself, even with all the problems she'd faced. For years, Joey had emotionally aligned himself with Vicki. She had taken the place of the mother he no longer had in his life, but her attempts to kill herself felt like just another person looking to abandon him. And even worse, according to Seth, she was even willing to kill Sam, a baby who had done nothing to anyone.

Why would she do that? Joey asked himself. *She should be there for us, like a mother should. Why can't she stick it out for us?*

But when talking about the situation with the boys in the neighborhood, Joey was far less sentimental. "Whatever," he'd shrug.

Joey Bader found himself in an unenviable position. He did not want to live with Vicki because he was now angry and afraid of her. He also didn't want to live as an indentured servant in Seth Bader's house. The thought of leaving both homes, of going into foster care or some other arrangement, scared Joey into believing he'd be split up from Matt and never see him again. He needed to figure out which was the lesser of these evils.

*   *   *

Despite the pleas from Dr. Shopick to do nothing to upset Vicki, Seth wasted no time seeking an emergency order from the marital master granting him permanent, sole custody of the children.

On February 7, 1995, Joey was interviewed by a social worker from the New Hampshire Division of Child and Youth Services at an office in Portsmouth. The counselor had one task: to figure out what kind of residential setting Joseph and Matthew Bader should be in. Before going in, Joey had already made up his mind.

"Vicki's made it clear she doesn't want me around," he told the counselor with Matt sitting at his side. "She hates me."

"You get the feeling she hates you?" the worker replied.

"Yeah. It's just like an aura."

Joey said Vicki was fat and lazy and did nothing but eat. He said Vicki was "a lousy mother" who never even bothered to change Sam's diapers herself. He said it was up to him to take care of his younger brothers and clean up the house. The social worker made notes of all of this.

The court ruled that Joey and Matt could make their own decisions about how much time to spend between the two homes. The ruling also stated that Vicki could only have visits with baby Sam if they were supervised by a third party.

She would be limited to seven hours of visitation a week under the close watch of a nurse or social worker. The structured visits with Sam were intrusive and humiliating, but Vicki hoped visits with the older boys were still a possibility.

"Joey and Matt don't want to see you," Seth told her.

Vicki was stunned. "What do you mean? I love them."

"The boys want nothing to do with you. They're afraid of you. They don't ever want to talk to you again." There was no sympathy in his voice. Seth was quite clear that he felt this was the outcome Vicki deserved.

Vicki sobbed, heartbroken at the thought that the two boys she'd adopted were turning their backs on her. Both legally and emotionally, Vicki Lynn Bader had effectively lost her children.

TEN

Not Yet Begun to Fight

Once she was released from the hospital, Vicki Bader was in need of new legal representation. Her psychiatrist referred her to an attorney named John Lewis of The Legal Clinics in Portsmouth, New Hampshire. Lewis agreed to take on Vicki as a client, but he was already overwhelmed by his present caseload. He asked his associate, Heidi Boyack, if she would be the lead lawyer on Vicki Bader's case.

Boyack was a pretty, single attorney about the same age as Vicki who grew up on the Massachusetts shoreline north of Boston. Her uncle was a successful attorney, and many of her relatives were in the legal profession. By the time she was in the seventh or eighth grade, Heidi Boyack knew she was going to law school. She graduated from Suffolk

Law in 1990 and worked for three years in the Massachusetts Department of Revenue, securing child support payments from deadbeat parents. By the time Vicki Bader came to her Portsmouth office on February 16, 1995, Boyack had handled dozens of similar cases in private practice.

Boyack found Vicki very bright and easy to talk to. It was clear that she was extremely concerned for the children but also had a level of compassion for her ex-spouse. In Boyack's experience, not every party involved in a custody case was so magnanimous. In fact, she found the whole postnuptial agreement drawn up by Seth to be extremely peculiar. It seemed to tie Vicki closer to Seth, not give her the liberty afforded most divorcées. Boyack wasn't sure if this was some legal stratagem Seth was slipping by his ex-wife or whether the man was—on some subconscious level—trying to keep Vicki close to him.

Vicki was open about her past suicidal episodes, but the woman did not seem to Boyack like a fragile flower about to wilt. She came off as a strong-willed, determined mother. But Boyack did note that Vicki spoke a mile a minute and tended to unconsciously repeat herself. The lawyer wondered if it might have something to do with the medication she was taking.

After the meeting, Lewis asked Boyack, "Do you think she's got a chance at getting her kids back?"

"With those suicide attempts? Probably not." But Boyack thought Vicki did have a reasonable chance at expanding her time with Sam.

Boyack soon found that crossing swords with Seth

Bader was a formidable task. Between January 17 and March 10, 1995, there were twenty-seven filings in the *Bader v. Bader* case file, nearly all of them instigated by Seth himself. To Boyack, everything Seth did seemed deliberately complicated or obstructionist. She began to wonder if his plan was to rack up as many hours toward Vicki's legal fees as he could. When Boyack needed to communicate with the plaintiff and his attorneys, it took numerous phone calls to get a response. Vicki had paid her lawyers a $5,000 retainer, but it was quickly being depleted.

Up until this time, Vicki had been living off of the rental income Seth had provided her in lieu of child support or alimony. It worked out to be about $1,700 a month. After she got out of the hospital in January, the checks from Seth stopped, despite the promise of payment in the couple's postnuptial agreement. He didn't return Boyack's calls and sidestepped any inquiry or confrontation about where the money was.

According to Boyack, withholding cash wasn't the only tactic Seth used to taunt his ex-wife. It was clear the children were being used as pawns in this vicious chess match. Boyack requested that a guardian ad litem (GAL) be appointed in this case. A GAL would be an attorney who represented the legal interests of the boys, not the parents. Boyack filed the motion, which Seth immediately objected to.

Mary Jean Martin liked to hang out after work at a Massachusetts pool hall named Brighton Billiards, more than an hour from Seth Bader's Stratham home. It had an authentic *Color of Money* kind of feel to it. Customers brought in their own expensive cue sticks carried in black leather cases lined with red felt, and pool sharks passed cash back and forth after games of nine ball.

Mary Jean could play well enough, but she wasn't there to make money. In addition to his box business, her father had also once owned a pool hall, and she liked the atmosphere. She had made friends—some through work, some through other connections—who also liked to hang around this particular pool hall. They would have drinks, then go to someone's house and play cards. It was a scene that belonged exclusively to Mary Jean, one that Seth knew about but was not invited to partake in.

"Here she comes. My fiancée." Though they weren't actually engaged, that's how Sebastian Caradonna typically greeted Mary Jean. The two had met several years earlier at the law firm when he was a client in a civil case. They weren't lovers, but they struck up a friendship and eventually started moving around in the same social circles at the billiard room.

Caradonna was in his late forties and had a persnickety manner about him. He liked to dress neatly and was stick thin, with sunken cheeks and a trimmed mustache. He was Boston Italian, not Old Country. He liked nine ball but wasn't nearly as sharp as his friends who guiltlessly took his money during his frequent losing streaks at the tables. Caradonna liked to pretend to be a big shot, though no one in the pool hall actually made him for one. He enjoyed dropping faux-subtle references to connections he had, people he knew, and "jobs" he'd had a hand in.

Sibby, as Sebastian Caradonna liked to be called for short, was not a "made" man as much as he was a trust fund baby. But although his family was wealthy, Caradonna was on the outs with his kin. The details he gave were all intentionally opaque, but the pool hall crew knew that Caradonna had physically attacked his brother in a dispute over how to handle their mother's declining health. He was on probation, and the rumor was that he'd tried to run his brother over with a car. Now the family was essentially paying Caradonna a stipend to stay away from them.

One afternoon at Brighton Billiards, Mary Jean was showing off some gold jewelry she wanted to sell. The prices she was asking were way too low, and she made no secret of why she was getting rid of it.

"They're Seth's crazy ex-wife's," she told her friends. Mary Jean's attitude toward Vicki Bader was one of indifferent hostility. Vicki was a financial obstacle, not a rival for her lover. The suicide attempts didn't move her heart. They only reinforced what Seth said about her: that Vicki was fucking crazy.

The girlfriends of the pool players fingered the bracelets and convinced themselves they were must-have items.

"What do you have there, my fiancée?" Caradonna peeked into the crowd of ladies passing over twenty-dollar bills. Mary Jean showed him what was left: a diamond ring that was likely some family heirloom. Caradonna bought it and had the diamond reset in a gold tiepin.

*   *   *

Vicki continued to work on herself. Although she was heavily medicated, she still felt antsy, ill at ease. Something wasn't working, but she couldn't put her finger on it.

Just before Valentine's Day, Vicki decided to write a letter to Joey and Matt. She figured it would be a low-risk way of rekindling their relationship. If they responded with a letter of their own, it could be a good indicator of whether or not the boys truly were done with her, or whether Seth was deceiving her about their feelings.

She pulled out a piece of stationery and began in a hopeful tone.

2/13/95

Dear Joe + Matt,

I'm writing to say Hi and keep in touch. I'm seeing Sam and would love to see both of you but Seth says you refuse to either see or speak to me. I hope you change your mind. Please feel free to call or write to me anytime.

Things are going well here. I've left your rooms exactly as you left them (Aack!!!) and am looking for a job.

How's it going with you? [. . .]

Well boys, keep in touch and if you want to see me let me know.

I love you.

Vicki then surprised herself when she signed the bottom of the letter, because it was not a term she had used before with the older boys.

Love,
Mom a/k/a Vicki

Very neatly, she placed the letter in an envelope, attached a Garfield return address label in the corner, and addressed it to "Joe & Matt Bader c/o Seth Bader." Then she took her letter to the post office and sent it certified mail for $2.52.

On February 28, 1995, Vicki Lynn Bader strode down her driveway to her mailbox, reached in, and pulled out the day's mail, only to find something unexpected. She turned around and headed right back inside.

Vicki put aside the bills and coupon flyers in favor of a single letter addressed to her. She could tell by the handwriting and the postmark that it had come from Joey. She hadn't spoken with him in many weeks, and now, she would finally be able to hear what he had to say.

She ran a finger under the flap of the envelope and tore it open on the seam. She pulled out the paper and stared at it for a moment. It was the letter that she had lovingly written to the boys two weeks earlier. *Why did they send it back? Did they even read it?*

She noticed there was writing on the other side of the paper. She turned it over to find another letter written on the back.

"Dear Fat Ass . . ."

What is this? she thought. Vicki didn't know what to make of it. It was definitely Joey's handwriting. Unbelieving, she blinked her eyes and started to read the letter over again.

Dear Fat Ass,

I'm sorry I didn't send you a gift for Valentine's Day. I was going to send you some rat poison and pudding but Seth wouldn't let me. It would be purchased by me (secretly) and sent to you on Mother's Day (even though I have never thought of you as a mother except as a mother fucker). Although I do think of you as a fat asshole who tried to trick us into loving you.

    If you cared for us even a little, you'd let us be where we want to be. Get a job so you won't have to make Seth pay you money, and leave us alone (this goes for Matt too for he encouraged me to in the note). I feel also that Sam should not see you because you are a very dangerous person. I don't want to waste too much effort on something like you, so I'm going to end this letter.

        Hatefully,
        Joe and Matt

All of the air left Vicki's lungs. There were tears in her eyes, but she didn't feel like crying. The room started to spin, and her hands shook so violently she had to put down the letter. The letter was so vile, so deeply hurtful; she felt the world closing in all around her. She picked up the phone.

"Dr. Shopick," she said through heaving breaths. "I want to voluntarily commit myself to the hospital before I do something I regret."

Vicki's voluntary admission to the Portsmouth Pavilion on March 1, 1996, was both a step back and a step forward for her recovery. Although it was her second breakdown in three months, this time Vicki had done the responsible thing by seeking help. She stayed in the hospital for four days and was released on March 5.

Upon her discharge, Vicki learned that Seth had dropped her from his health insurance policy the month before. She was confused. *He's not supposed to do that. That's in our agreement.*

Vicki phoned Boyack and asked if she'd call Seth's attorney about the health insurance mix-up. But to Boyack, it wasn't a "mix-up" at all. She was sure that Seth Bader had dropped Vicki's insurance on purpose, just as he had purposefully stopped sending her money from the rental income. He was trying to choke off Vicki's access to the two things she desperately needed: legal representation and psychiatric care.

Boyack drew up a motion to ask the court for visitation time with Joey and Matt. The lawyer suspected that the boys' reluctance to see Vicki was engineered by Seth and that some time alone with them could repair the once-vibrant relationship Vicki had shared with them.

When she returned home from the hospital, the light on Vicki's answering machine was blinking red. She pressed the button and listened to the pinch rollers click into place against the cassette inside.

"Vicki, it's me." The recorded voice was calm. It was Joey's. "I have heard that I am being forced to go and visit you by the judge. And I basically don't want to. And if you're gonna try and make me, um, you're gonna have to get the cop to drag me, kicking and screaming, near your house. Because I will not go ever of my own will."

The tape clicked off. There was no anger in Joey's voice, but clearly he remained afraid of her.

The following day, another letter arrived in Vicki's mailbox addressed in Joey's hand. Vicki was torn as to whether to open it. It could be another poison-pen letter or it could be a remorseful note from the young man she treated like a son.

It didn't start off sounding remorseful.

"Dear Psychotic Bitch . . ."

Vicki folded the letter closed and pushed it aside. She tried to ignore it, tried to put it out of her mind. But it proved too hard to disregard, and Vicki had already tasted the poison.

Dear Psychotic Bitch,

You are not our mother, you never were and you never will be. The only way you have anything to do being a mother is as a mother fucking fat asshole.

By the way, we don't need to get together to pick out my birthday present. It's already at your house. You just need to swallow all of it this time.

Back in January when we heard you might die I called up some friends and made plans for a party, but Seth said to call them back and cancel it . . .

Die slowly and suffer,
Joe
a.k.a. not your son

Vicki reeled again under the weight of words. Why were the boys so angry with her? It didn't make sense.

In order to sleep that night, Vicki took some pills. The next morning when a friend called to check in on her, Vicki confessed that she might have taken too many pills the night before. Although the error seemed innocent enough, and no damage was done, there was plenty of concern all around for Vicki's safety. Dr. Shopick sent an ambulance to her house to assess her. She readily agreed to another voluntary admission to Portsmouth Pavilion, but had she refused, the responders would have involuntarily admitted her anyway.

* * *

It wasn't long before Joey Bader's resentment at the way Seth treated him around the house began to deepen. He was becoming a teenager. He wanted to hang out with friends; he wanted to meet girls. There was so much that he wanted to do, so much that he felt Seth was keeping him from.

Living in the Stratham house after Vicki's first suicide attempt was almost like living with no parents at all. At first, Seth was out most nights on dates, leaving Joey in charge of Matt and Sam. That meant cooking and cleaning up after dinner, changing Sam's diaper, and getting his little brothers into bed. The next morning there would be no breakfast waiting, either—it was up to Joey to drag himself out of bed and feed himself and the other hungry children. Within weeks, Mary Jean had moved in. But instead of more help and supervision, it meant even more nights out for Seth and his girlfriend, and sometimes meant an extra child, Courtney, for Joey to take care of.

And then there were the dogs. Joey was used to taking care of Seth's dogs in the house, but Mary Jean brought her whole breeding operation with her to Stratham. The number of dogs was always fluctuating based on the size of litters and the demand of customers. Plastic dog crates were piled in the kitchen or the dining room, with overflow in the basement. Whenever the doorbell rang, the sound of twenty to thirty baying canines would explode from the home. A fenced-in kennel was put in the back-yard to give the animals some time to run off leash, but the panic of noise from the dogs jumping, growling, and fighting with one another shattered the quiet of the cul-de-sac.

The dogs all had names—something that made them more desirable as future show champions—but they didn't get full-time affection. Mary Jean would dote over them when she stayed in Stratham, but when she wasn't there, Seth didn't step in as their caretaker. The respon-sibility for feeding, watering, and cleaning the cages—of as many as sixty dogs at a time—fell to Joey.

Attorney Heidi Boyack was stunned each time she learned about Vicki's commitments to the psychiatric facilities.

"You gotta be kidding me," she'd say to John Lewis.

It wasn't that the attorneys were ignorant about Vicki's state of mind. It was just that the incidents of self-harm were so out of character with the surprisingly resilient woman they'd come to know. There had been, however, some obvious signs that Vicki was in medical turmoil. They'd noticed her face was changing; her lips looked swollen. And she no longer spoke in a frantic, repetitive manner. Again, Boyack had assumed these were all the results of a constant rejiggering of her medications.

Despite watching her client—and her case—slowly crumble, there was a bit of good news for Boyack. On March 14, 1995, the marital master scheduled a new two-day custody hearing for May, giving Vicki a chance to make her case. Also, the marital master appointed a guardian ad litem to advocate on behalf of Joey, Matt, and Sam Bader. At last, there was a neutral third party who could better assess what was really going on in the heads and hearts of the children.

But the victory was not merely that a new ally was to join the fight. The GAL, Yvonne Vissing, was an academic with decades of study in child abuse and family relationships. She was a PhD with a curriculum vitae that ran more than a dozen pages, filled with published papers, academic appointments, and memberships in professional organizations. It could be said that she was Seth Bader's intellectual equal, if not his superior.

Boyack thought Vissing was going to see right through him.

Vicki continued her quest to get better. She wanted to be strong and ready for the two-day hearing in May. There was a lot riding on this for her. In April, a third letter from Joey had arrived in the mail. She wasn't going to read it, knowing what happened to her the last two times. But Vicki wanted to believe that Joey and Matt would eventually come back to her. The more she thought about it, the more she didn't want to live a life in which she'd never believe in anything again.

She ripped open the envelope and pulled out the letter. She braced her emotions and dove in.

Dear Psycho,

Everything has been going well, very well, since we have not been seeing you. Can we introduce your dog to our 90-pound hungry Akita? I'm sure he would like some lunch. Chardonnay [Vicki's dog] makes me want to throw up, and you don't deserve a dog like Bandit [Seth's Akita]. I was seriously wondering when the ASPCA is going to take him back, since I think he'd rather be put to sleep than live with you . . .

By the way, when are you going to stop writing to us? We're trying our best to forget you were born. I hope you're glad to hear that Matt is happy. He and Mary Jean have built a very strong mother-son bond. We're really one big happy family.

I was wondering where did you get the idea that we loved or even liked you?

Hatefully,
Joe

Then, signed below his older brother's signature, as if an endorsement of the letter's contents, was:

Matt

It hurt, but Vicki stood strong. She folded the letter and sent it—along with the previous two—to her attorney. Vicki had finally accepted that she had lost Joey and

Matt. But she remained hopeful she'd be able to salvage her relationship with Samuel.

The inspiration for the hate letters to Vicki was not Joey's. The idea had come from Seth. The man had not merely suggested that Joey write them; he stood over him at their round kitchen table dictating what they should say.

"Sign it like this," Seth instructed. "Die slowly and suffer. Joe, a.k.a. not your son."

"What does 'a.k.a.' mean?" the twelve-year-old asked.

"Also known as." Seth then photocopied all the hate mail and placed it in a folder.

Seth would talk to Joey about Vicki, saying how the "fat leech" needed to get a job and stop squeezing so much money out of him. Seth would complain to Mary Jean about the situation, and she would pile on, too. All this was done in front of the children with no concern for their feelings.

When Joey left the message on Vicki's answering machine saying he refused to go back to her home, Seth was standing in front of him mouthing words and pantomiming things for him to say.

"And if you're gonna try and make me, um . . ." Joey looked up from the blue Trimline phone and paused to see what Seth was doing. He was waving his fists and kicking his feet. Joey shrugged, giving him a look that said, *I don't know what the hell you're doing.* Seth then started mouthing the words "kicking and screaming."

". . . You're gonna have to get the cop to drag me,

kicking and screaming, near your house." After he hung up, Seth slapped him on the back, pleased with what the boy had done.

Despite what he said, Joey didn't really spend a lot of time wondering how the messages or the letters might hurt Vicki. Seth might've been the puppet master, but Joey never objected. He just did what Seth told him to, part of the deal he'd made with himself in order to not be separated from his brothers.

He would later say he was too afraid of what might happen if he didn't.

The two-day hearing in May was going to be brutal. Seth Bader had hired additional attorneys from another law firm to supplement Barbara Taylor's work. The deposition of Vicki by Seth's legal team was among the most vicious interrogatories Boyack had ever witnessed.

"Why do Seth's lawyers hate me so much?" Vicki asked.

Boyack honestly didn't know what to say. She had no idea why, no idea what Seth must have said to his lawyers to motivate such antipathy.

When they got to court, Seth and his team took every quarter they could. His attorneys presented the suicide notes Seth had collected from Vicki's house in January 1995 as evidence that she remained unstable. They presented Vicki's pornographic cartoons, taken that same night, as evidence that she was unfit. They accused Vicki of putting her crushed-up pills in a bowl of pudding with the intention of killing Sam, an allegation that Vicki and Boyack vigorously denied.

The hate mail from Joey and Matt was presented by Seth as evidence his ex-wife was unwelcome as a mother. Boyack wondered how Seth had copies of the letters that had been sent through the mail to Vicki. The answer was telling: he had photocopied the letters in his home office before the boys mailed them. At that point, Boyack realized nothing Seth Bader would ever do could surprise her.

But Vicki's attorney wasn't going down without swinging. She was just as aggressive, offering evidence that Seth Bader was an absentee parent. She said all of the care of young Sammy was done either by Joey or by Mary Jean Martin. Seth didn't feed, dress, or bathe his son, let alone change his diapers or play with him. The photocopies of the hate mail proved Seth condoned—if not outright instigated—the rift between mother and children. She argued that Seth Bader wasn't there fighting for his children; he was only there for the fight.

Heidi Boyack asked for a change in the custody arrangement: more time for Vicki with Sam. She also asked the court to void the 1994 postnuptial agreement and order Seth to give Vicki a proper alimony payment.

In mid-June, when attorney Boyack learned what the court's ruling was, she asked Vicki to come to her law office to hear it. Boyack and her colleague John Lewis thought it best to discuss it face-to-face with Vicki, not over the phone.

Vicki sat in a comfortable chair, nervously playing with her hands. "There is some good news," Boyack told her. The marital master had agreed to order Seth to temporarily pay Vicki $1,700 a month in alimony, at least until a final hearing on their case could occur. The figure was roughly equal to the $20,000 annual payment for rental income promised in their postnuptial. Seth was also ordered to put her back on his health insurance policy and carry her indefinitely.

"What about visitation with Sam?" Vicki begged. "Did we get any additional time?"

"No," Boyack said softly. "The master has decided not to make any change to the visitation arrangement. You'll continue to have limited, supervised visits with Sam."

Vicki grabbed the court order from Boyack's hands and began flipping through the decision, looking for a reason why the marital master would keep her baby at arm's length from her.

. . . While the court can sympathize greatly with the defendant's request, given the extensive documentation of the defendant's severe psychiatric problems, including her numerous attempts to take her own life, . . . the Court has great concern relative to the placement of any of the children with the defendant in an unsupervised manner.

The issue before the Court is not one of reward or punishment. The Court's order is not rewarding the plaintiff nor is it punishing the defendant . . . At this point, the Court does not find that allowing any of the children to be unsupervised with the defendant would properly and adequately provide for said child's safety.

Vicki hung her head in despair. Her disappointment was palpable. Boyack and Lewis tried their best to console her, but Vicki stumbled out of the law office a weeping wreck. She was broke, having borrowed from friends and family to pay a portion of her legal bills, and she was also emotionally spent.

On June 17, Vicki drove herself to the Portsmouth Pavilion, the same facility at which she had been treated before, and sat in her blue Cadillac Coupe DeVille in the parking lot. She swallowed a fistful of pills and waited for someone to find her.

Vicki's physical health had been yo-yoing just as her mental health had been. Her primary care physician, Dr. Richard Stebbins,* had charted the changes in Vicki's well-being over two or more years.

She complained often about headaches and stomachaches. Her blood pressure was always a little too high. She'd gained more than fifty pounds. She had insomnia. Stebbins had diagnosed Vicki with irritable bowel syndrome about a year earlier. He felt like a broken record, telling

---

* Denotes pseudonym

her as he did all of his patients that better diet and exercise would go a long way toward curing her ills.

Vicki struck Stebbins as morose. She told her doctor that she felt like she was going to die. Stebbins, who had braved that blizzard the previous January to get Vicki an emergency admission to the hospital, was aware of her suicidal past. But this time he clearly heard her saying something different.

Vicki was telling her doctor that she thought her ex-husband was going to try to kill her.

Stebbins prodded Vicki about controlling her weight and her hypertension. Vicki's response was unforgettable. "It was probably one of the most bizarre things I've ever heard in my life as a physician," he would later tell people.

"I don't want to lose weight," Vicki said, "because I want to make it difficult for Seth when he tries to move my body."

PART TWO

By Evil Example

How sharper than a serpent's tooth it is
To have a thankless child!

—WILLIAM SHAKESPEARE, *KING LEAR*

ELEVEN

Hot Seat

While Vicki Bader was again languishing in a mental health facility, Seth Bader was slowly losing his cold war with the guardian ad litem. Dr. Yvonne Vissing was particularly concerned about the dynamic in Bader's home. She suspected that the animosity shown toward Vicki in the boys' letters was actively encouraged by Seth. She was also concerned about the signs of neglect Sam showed.

Seth felt attacked by her honest inquiries into his parenting abilities. Dr. Vissing was going to be a problem, and he needed to eliminate her from the equation.

Aside from the GAL, the only other outsiders who frequently saw Seth's parental interaction with the kids were the women assigned to supervise Vicki's visits with Sam. Most often, one of them would pick Sam up at Seth's home and transport the child to a clinical setting or to Vicki's house.

Caseworker Sue Benoit tried to speak with Seth about Sam's care. When she came to pick up the boy one morning, he wasn't dressed, fed, changed, or washed. It was 11:00 in the morning, and she suspected Seth had kept the child confined to his room since he'd woken up.

On another occasion, Benoit arrived to discover Sam covered in diarrhea. She urged Seth to bathe and change his son before they left. Seth wanted *her* to clean the baby, but she said that wasn't one of her duties. Seth placed Sam in the kitchen sink and sprayed the toddler down with the faucet hose.

"This will be the fastest Bader shit, shine, and shower ever," he said.

Another day, while running late for court, Seth dropped Sam off at a babysitter's home by placing the child on the floor of the living room and yelling to the caretaker that he had to rush out. The sitter, however, wasn't at home, and Sam wandered around the empty house for several hours.

It's unclear who got the babysitting date wrong, but Seth was loath to enroll Sam in a different child care setting. He knew that kind of screwup was exactly the sort of thing that Vicki's lawyer and the guardian ad litem would jump on.

*   *   *

On Friday, July 7, 1995, Seth brought Sam to his pediatrician, Dr. Donna Moussette,* for a skin problem on the boy's backside. "It doesn't seem like diaper rash," Seth said. "I've been putting Neosporin on it. I want it cleared up before his next visit with his mother."

It was not the first time that Seth had brought Sam to the doctor under irregular circumstances. One month earlier, he'd insisted Moussette see his son after Sam tripped and fell into the outside corner of a wall. Sam had a bump on the middle of his forehead about six centimeters long. It was a little purple, but not a very serious injury.

"Has there been any change in his verbalization?" she asked while examining the reflexes in Sam's meaty legs.

Seth said that even at twenty-two months old, Sam didn't talk much.

The doctor asked what kind of social interaction the boy was getting. Seth said at the time that Sam didn't go to day care or preschool; he spent much of his day in Seth's home office when he wasn't with a sitter.

"He hears me talking on the phone all day long. Is that enough exposure to teach Sammy the language?"

Moussette remarked that simply hearing his father talk on the phone was not sufficient for a developing child. She said Seth needed to engage him in verbal interaction.

---

* Denotes pseudonym

If no progress was gained in the coming months, she told him they could explore speech and hearing evaluations.

Now, back in her office a month later, Moussette asked to look at the inflammation beneath the toddler's diaper. The doctor was immediately alarmed by what she saw on the twenty-three-month-old's backside. It wasn't a rash. It was a burn.

The red marks were below the waistline on the upper part of Sam's buttocks, near the tailbone. The wounds were nearly symmetrical. The one on the right was almost five and a half centimeters in diameter, or the size of a shower drain; the mark on the left was the size of a quarter: two and a half centimeters. There were also two other spots on the bottom of Sam's buttocks where dried skin was flaking off.

"I want to send him over to the hospital," she said. "Can you take him there directly or would you like me to call an ambulance?"

Seth did as he was told and brought Sam to the hospital for an emergency evaluation. The doctors were already expecting the child. Moussette had contacted the police, the state Division of Child and Youth Services, and the Baders' guardian ad litem, Dr. Vissing. She made sure Sam's chart reflected all she had seen.

Superficial skin injury—appears consistent with burn, second degree. Difficult to imagine how this could have occurred unintentionally or silently. One possible mode of injury would be pressure with a hot flat object being applied to the skin. Of concern is length of time it took father to seek medical attention—wounds are rather shocking in appearance to this examiner.

Dr. Vissing called Dr. Moussette to find out more about the injuries and told the pediatrician that she suspected Sam was frequently left unsupervised at home or alone in the house. She also believed that Sam was left in his diaper for hours on end, perhaps from the afternoon until the next morning. Vissing explained that her investigation into the Bader boys' well-being was being hampered by Seth Bader; he was filing a lawsuit against her and trying to have her removed as guardian ad litem in his case.

"Do you feel that Samuel is in danger and should be removed from the home?" Vissing asked. The pediatrician said she did.

Stratham police officer David "Butch" Pierce called Seth and asked if he'd come to the station to discuss the burns on Sam's rear end. Twenty minutes later, Seth arrived with his son and his lawyer.

Seth was advised of his Miranda rights, and both he and Barbara Taylor signed papers indicating he understood them. He then told the cop that he first noticed the red marks on Tuesday, July 4. He claimed that Vicki had called him and said she, too, had noticed the red marks on Monday before she returned the child to him.

Seth told the officer that Dr. Moussette told him that the burns were serious and had sent him directly to the hospital. The emergency physicians prescribed an ointment and scheduled a follow-up.

Pierce asked if the burns had blistered. Seth looked blank, then responded that no, they had not blistered.

"May I see the wounds?"

Seth gently pulled Sam's pants and diaper down. Pierce thought that the wounds must have blistered and popped at some point, as the skin along the edges had peeled. Pierce asked permission to take a couple of photos, and Seth said it would be fine.

"Why didn't you take your son to the doctor before today?"

"I thought I could treat it with Neosporin. Sam didn't appear to be in any pain."

Seth walked through the timeline again. He said Vicki had returned Sam very late and the boy was already asleep. He said he'd put Sam to bed without ever checking his diaper.

Pierce asked how the burns might have occurred, and Seth said it was possible that when Vicki wasn't watching him, Sam could have brushed up against a low grill. He didn't mention that all of Vicki's visits with Sam were supervised. The officer asked if Sam's diaper or clothes had been charred or burnt, but Seth said they hadn't been.

"When was the last time Sam had a bath?"

Seth squinted his eyes and thought very hard. "I don't know. My son, Joe, might have given him a bath a couple of days ago." The cop wrote this in his pad, noting that Sam's face and hair were visibly dirty.

Seth told Officer Pierce that on Wednesday he had left Sam with a babysitter while he went to court. After Seth and his lawyer left the station, Pierce placed a call to the sitter, Jean Walker,* and asked if she'd file a report. The woman was very distressed, saying the incident had been on her mind the whole week.

"Seth dropped Sammy off at 9:30 at my house on Wednesday morning and he never said anything about any burns," she told Pierce.

She said she had changed him at 10:00 before she brought him outside to play, and that's when she'd noticed the burns. Walker's fourteen-year-old niece had been helping babysit and was also shocked by the red marks. They took out a camera and snapped two pictures of the burns and for the rest of the day kept the wounds as clean as possible.

When Seth picked Sam up, Walker told Pierce, she asked him about the burns. Seth said something about a bruise and Vicki, but Walker would have none of it. "Those aren't bruises. Those are burn marks."

Seth admitted he hadn't changed Sam recently, so he wouldn't know.

"Sam likes to slide down the stairs," he then said to Walker. "He might have gotten a rug burn or something."

The babysitter said Seth called on Friday and told her he wouldn't be dropping Sam off that day because he had

---

* Denotes pseudonym

a pediatrician's appointment that afternoon. She told the cop she hadn't known what to do and had been worried about the child ever since.

Pierce decided to talk with all of the people in Sam's life individually. The officer met with Vicki Bader, who said she'd had a supervised visit with Sam on Monday, July 3. Both she and the woman who'd supervised the visit, Sue Benoit, had noticed the marks on Sam's bottom that day. However, Vicki said, the marks had not looked terribly serious at the time and Sam wasn't fussing. The pair took Sam to see the town fireworks display before returning the sleeping child to his father.

Vicki told Pierce that she'd talked to Seth by phone the following day and asked him how the marks had happened. Seth said he hadn't changed Sam's diaper and didn't know anything about the marks. He promised to apply some ointment and see a doctor if it didn't clear up.

When Pierce interviewed Mary Jean Martin, she told the cop that she'd first noticed the burns on Tuesday morning, after Sam's mother had taken him to see the fireworks. She said Joe got up to change Sam in the morning, and when he saw the pink splotches he came to find her. They both examined the marks but thought a rug burn might have caused them. Mary Jean said while Joe put a clean diaper on Sam, she went to tell Seth about the injury. She didn't know if he ever checked on it himself.

*   *   *

With Seth's attorney, Barbara Taylor, sitting next to him, seven-year-old Matt Bader said he was ready to answer Officer Pierce's questions.

"Do you know how Sam got burned?" Pierce began.

"Mary Jean and Joe think he got burned on the clothes dryer," Matt replied. "But Seth says it's impossible because it doesn't get that hot."

"Is there anything else in the house that Sam might have gotten burned on?"

Matt said the desk lamp that was in his bedroom could have burned him. It had been on the floor and Sam could have rolled over onto it.

"Is there an iron in your house?"

"I don't think so," Matt said frankly. "No one irons."

"Do you like your brother?" Pierce asked.

Matt just shrugged. "He's annoying."

"How is he annoying?"

"He's always screaming unless he has something to eat."

"When was the last time you heard Sam scream?"

Matt said, "A couple of days ago."

"Why was he screaming?"

"Because I was playing with him."

Pierce asked if Sam's screams were because he was happy or because he was hurt. Matt said that Sam was screaming because he was happy.

"What were you doing to make him scream?"

"Just playing," Matt said.

The officer asked again what they had been doing. Matt shrugged and said they were just playing with toys. Attorney Taylor asked Matt if he wanted to answer any more questions, and the child said no. Later, Joey Bader told Pierce he had no idea how Sam got the burns or why anyone might want to hurt the toddler. When Pierce told Joe about Matt's theory that Sam could have rolled over onto a lamp in his bedroom, Joe responded that it was impossible. Matt's bedroom only had a ceiling light.

The state Division of Child and Youth Services opened up an investigation into the circumstances around the burns and into the condition of the children in Seth Bader's household. The caseworker for the state was frustrated by what she felt were efforts by Seth and his lawyer to interfere with the investigation. They grumbled about Barbara Taylor's presence at Officer Pierce's interviews and her eagerness to cut off questioning of the children whenever it seemed they were getting somewhere.

Seth's solution was to insist his sons prove their innocence with lie detector tests. The caseworker objected, saying such a method was unreliable for children and likely to cause a lot of confusion for them. Seth decided he would get a polygraph himself to prove to the naysayers he wasn't responsible for Sam's injuries. The polygraph indicated Seth wasn't being deceitful when he proclaimed his innocence.

As a result of the investigation into the burns on Sam

Bader's backside, DCYS asked the district court for an emergency hearing in mid-July to hear evidence and decide whether the boys should be removed from Seth's home. Their recommendation was that Sam and the other boys should be placed in the care of Vicki Bader.

Yvonne Vissing agreed with DCYS's recommendation. But the guardian ad litem was having her own troubles with the case. Seth Bader was foiling her every attempt to get information about the children. Vissing alleged Seth's legal team was pressuring the boys' court-ordered therapists against sharing their findings with her. Now Seth was suing Vissing personally. He claimed the guardian ad litem was biased and wanted her removed from the case.

The emergency hearing was brief. The witnesses were the pediatrician, Dr. Donna Moussette; the guardian ad litem, Dr. Yvonne Vissing; the DCYS caseworker; and Seth Bader. Heidi Boyack argued on behalf of Vicki Bader and in favor of custody.

The marital master denied the motion to give Vicki custody, saying her emotional state was still too volatile, but the master was in agreement that Seth didn't appear to be in any condition to take care of Samuel, either. DCYS suggested foster placement for all three boys, but the master noted he did not have the authority to take that action.

A full administrative hearing would have to be held in order to determine the long-term placement of Joey, Matt, and Sam.

*   *   *

Details about juvenile cases remain among the last bastions of confidential information in American society. The court hearings that resulted from the burns on Sam Bader's backside generated hundreds of documents regarding whether the state should take the children away from Seth Bader, but all of these documents remained sealed or redacted.

The only indication about the outcome of these hearings was that Joe, Matt, and Sam were back in the Stratham home by September 1995—and that Vicki continued to fight for them.

TWELVE

Runaway

Joey Bader started junior high school in September of 1995. The thirteen-year-old no longer had the build of a child; he was growing into a young man. He was nearly as tall as Seth and would soon be taller. He didn't want to be called "Joey" anymore. He wanted people to call him "Joe."

Classes were getting harder, and Joe had little time to study. There were dozens of dogs barking and pissing all over the house, and his list of chores continued to mount. There were not enough hours in the day to keep up with his schoolwork.

The lackluster grades on Joe's November report card enraged Seth. Joe wanted to tell Seth it was all his fault for treating him like a slave and not letting him be a kid. Certainly his adoptive father had made no effort to help him with his studies or work with him, something Vicki had always done. But Joe didn't get a chance to fight back, because Seth did most of the yelling. Joe turned away and walked into another room, but Seth followed him in a rage. Joe tried to block it out, as he did every time Seth yelled at him.

"If you don't bring these grades up, I'm going to send you to private school!"

That got Joe's attention. The implication wasn't that Seth was going to spring for some fancy prep school like Phillips Exeter Academy down the road. This was a threat that he would send Joe away to some military or reform school.

Joe turned away again and walked up the stairs to his bedroom on the third floor. He closed the door and waited for Seth to burst in, but he never did. Joe stared at the ceiling, looking at his posters of *Pulp Fiction*, Pearl Jam, and John Lennon. He absently strummed chords on his electric guitar, turning Seth's words over and over in his mind.

Seth was going to send him away, leaving Matt behind in the house. He knew his little brother wouldn't be able to care for Sam and all the dogs. Seth already was cruel in his dealings with Matt, and the whole reason Joe had put up with a year of servitude was because it seemed to be the only option that would keep the brothers together. This threat was a game changer.

On the morning of November 22, 1995, the day before Thanksgiving, Joe woke up and stuffed some clothes into a large olive green army knapsack. He then went down into his brother's room and told him they weren't going to school.

"We're leaving," he said. Joe went to Matt's dresser and put some clothes in a red duffel bag. It was close to 8:00, and the school buses had already rolled through the neighborhood. They sat quietly in Matt's room waiting for their opportunity to slip out of the house. When they heard Seth turn on the second-floor shower, they made their move.

As Joe opened the front door and felt the morning chill bite his face, the stacks of dog crates in the dining room came alive with guttural baying. Matt closed the door behind them, and the brothers jogged toward the wooded line at the end of the property.

A noise cut through the silent neighborhood. A scraping slide and a click, like the pump of a shotgun. Joe spun around and saw what the sound was. Seth had thrown open the sash on his bathroom window.

"You two get back in this house this goddamn minute!"

The boys turned around and kept running. It was the first time either of them had disobeyed an order from Seth.

All the naked man in the window could do was yell, "Get the fuck back in here!"

Joe had some experience driving Seth's Jeep. He got to putter down the driveway in it once a week to bring out the garbage. But Joe's runaway plan was not that deeply thought-out, and he passed on borrowing the vehicle.

Instead, Joe and Matt ran through the woods that surrounded Doe Run Lane and kept going until they got to the main road, Portsmouth Avenue.

"Where are we going, Joe?"

The older brother stopped to think while watching cars zip by the secondary highway. He looked up and down the road for a pay phone, but he knew there wasn't one for miles.

"Follow me."

Joe led Matt across the busy street and went to the nearest business he could find, a travel agency. He asked if he could use their phone and borrow a telephone book. Joe looked up the name of a cab company and asked the dispatcher to send a car to pick them up.

"Where are we going to go?"

"Vicki's house," he said. "She's probably going to her mother's house on Long Island for Thanksgiving. The place will be empty. We can go there."

The cab dropped them off in Vicki's driveway, and Joe paid for the ride with some of the money he'd squirreled away. The house was still and the door was locked, but Joe remembered where Vicki used to leave the spare key. He went into the garage and looked underneath the bicycle pump. The key was still there.

The boys let themselves in through the front door and dropped their bags in the living room. Matt complained about being hungry, so Joe rummaged through Vicki's kitchen for something to eat. There wasn't much in the pantry except some oatmeal. He found a package of Steak-umms in the freezer, so he heated up a pan and tossed them in.

After eating, they sat on the couch and watched daytime television. They had been chilled to the bone while walking in the woods, and the warmth from the furnace was making them drowsy. The couch pulled open into a bed, so they moved some furniture around so they could both sprawl out and watch the TV. Joe walked around the house a bit, a home he had not visited in many months. Q-Tip the cat pounced back and forth. Joe peeked into his old room. In the letter she wrote in February, Vicki had promised to keep the boys' rooms just as they had left them. She was true to her word. They were a little cluttered, but all of his things were still there.

Propped in the corner was his old Louisville Slugger. *So* that's *where that went*, he thought. He closed the door, then joined his brother on the sofa bed and dozed off. Outside, the November temperatures continued to drop, and the purplish twilight sky left long shadows on the quiet neighborhood as afternoon turned to evening.

A slumbering Joe was stirred by another presence in the room. He opened his eyes to see Vicki sitting on the pullout bed next to him.

"Hi," he said. She had been rubbing his sleeping back.

"Hi," she replied.

Vicki did not seem scared, nor angry at them for being there. She did look surprised.

"What are you guys doing here?"

"We thought you were going to New York for the holiday."

Vicki explained that, no, she had just been at work and was having Thanksgiving dinner at her brother's home in Massachusetts.

"I'm going to give Seth a call," she said softly.

"No," Joe blurted out. "Don't."

"Why not?"

"We don't want him to know where we are."

Joe didn't know what to expect from Vicki. Here was the woman who had rescued him from the mean streets of New York City and brought him to bucolic New Hampshire, opened her home and heart to him, and adopted him as her own son. She had shown him nothing but love. And how had he repaid her? With letters and phone messages so vicious and mean-spirited they drove her to attempt suicide. Now, with no other place to go, Joe had turned to her. Would Vicki kick them out?

Vicki smiled and nodded at Joe. She agreed not to call right away and instead offered to make them dinner. There was nothing left to eat but the oatmeal, so the three of them ate that. They played a board game and laughed together.

Afterward, Vicki called Seth to let him know the boys were with her and didn't want to come home just yet. He was angry but relieved. She asked if they could spend the night with her, and Seth said they could.

The next morning, Vicki dressed up, even putting on

some department store jewelry she'd purchased, just in case Seth was the one who picked the boys up. She didn't want to appear broke and run-down to her ex-husband anymore.

But instead it was Seth's lawyer, Barbara Taylor, who arrived at Vicki's home to retrieve the boys. Joe grabbed a couple of things from his room, including his baseball bat, and left with the lawyer.

When they returned to Stratham, Seth and Mary Jean asked to see Joe in Seth's office.

"Why did you run away?" Seth asked calmly.

"I don't want to go away to private school." The excuse seemed to satisfy Seth, but Mary Jean seemed troubled by something else. She nudged Seth into speaking up.

"If anyone asks you why you went to Vicki's house," he said, "you should tell them you went there to hurt Vicki."

Joe was confused. He knew another hearing over custody of Sam was coming up in December. Was Seth afraid of how it would look if his sons ran away to Vicki's house?

"The baseball bat," Mary Jean prompted. "He could say he was going to hit her with the baseball bat."

Joe left the office agreeing that if anyone were to ask him about his intentions, he would repeat what Seth said to him. And Seth had no fear that Joe would not comply. Because Joe always did what Seth told him to do.

* * *

Within a matter of months, Vicki Bader would be dead. Joe had no way of knowing that his fear of being separated from his brother would make him an accomplice in her murder and that this one agreement would lead to an elevated terror campaign against her. Just hours after being fed and cared for by a woman who loved him, this impressionable teenage boy had unwittingly set foot on a one-way path he'd be unable to escape.

A path that led to a shallow grave in a secluded forest in Maine.

THIRTEEN

Gaslight

Heidi Boyack refused to give up the fight for her client. The custody hearing that had taken place the previous May was hardly enough to settle all of the outstanding issues in *Bader v. Bader*. An additional hearing to focus on financial matters was slated for December 1995.

Vicki was in debt because of this case, a case made intentionally expensive by her ex. While Vicki didn't have two nickels to rub together, Seth's assets were listed at well over a million dollars.

In July 1995, Boyack filed a motion to have Seth Bader pay $10,000 of the $18,000 balance on Vicki's legal fees. In her motion, Boyack was able to list the numerous ways that Seth had acted in bad faith.

Seth Bader was ready for a counteroffensive. In

October, he filed a motion to have Vicki's alimony payment reduced from $1,700 to $700 a month. He reasoned that Vicki was paying her attorneys at least $1,000 a month and he should not be compelled to pay for legal counsel. Later that month, Seth moved to have Vicki pay *him* child support.

On December 15, 1995, the marital master awarded Vicki's attorneys $5,000 to cover their legal fees. All of Seth's motions were denied. The master then referred the case to a bench judge for a full and final hearing sometime in the spring or summer of 1996.

If Seth could claim one legal victory, it would be the replacement of Dr. Yvonne Vissing as guardian ad litem. The master found no bias or fault in her work, but giving the Baders a new GAL was a path of least resistance. The new guardian was Tim Cunningham, and although Seth may have believed a man would be more sympathetic to his cause, he was mistaken. If anything, Cunningham would see the situation even more clearly than Vissing had.

After losing his motions to have Vicki pay him child support and being ordered to pay a portion of her legal bills, Seth was angry. He renewed his fixation on his custody case. Soon, he'd be inspired to try a more creative approach to solving his problems with Vicki.

One night, Seth took Mary Jean to the movies to see *Never Talk to Strangers*. It starred Rebecca De Mornay as a criminal psychologist and Antonio Banderas as her boyfriend. In the film, as De Mornay's character becomes more attracted to Banderas, she also becomes the victim of a terror campaign. She receives strange gifts in the mail, like wilted flowers. Her beloved cat is murdered. De Mornay hires a private eye to learn if her new boyfriend is the culprit. In the end, the detective discovers that De Mornay's character had killed her own cat and mailed the gifts, all in a psychotic episode resulting from some past trauma.

While the movie was itself unremarkable, Mary Jean would later claim it had a profound effect on Seth Bader. She claimed Bader told her watching the film had inspired him with a plan to get rid of Vicki. In *Never Talk to Strangers*, Seth Bader saw a playbook for destroying his ex. The string of disturbing gifts resonated with him as something that would push Vicki's buttons. The twist at the end of the movie—the victim was really the perpetrator—provided the solution for escaping detection.

With her history of mental instability, Seth could make it seem like Vicki was doing these things to herself.

"That's what I want to do," Seth said excitedly to Mary Jean. "I want to terrorize Vicki. I want to do everything they did in that movie. I want to gaslight her!"

Seth reasoned that if he could scare Vicki into moving away, to even leave the state, it would be harder for her to win custody of the children. If he scared her sufficiently, she might drop the custody case altogether.

Soon after, Seth asked Mary Jean if, as a dog breeder, she had access to different kinds of animal medicines.

"Why do you want to know?"

"Joe's going to break into Vicki's house and get her cat," Seth explained. Mary Jean took it as fact that Joe had already agreed to do this. "If we bring the cat back to the house, can you give it a shot of something to knock it out?"

"Why?"

"So we can cut it up. Like in the movie."

Mary Jean's face turned green. "That's fucking sick!" she yelled. "I raise animals for a living. I'm not going to do that!"

"MJ, I thought you'd want it unconscious first."

"Then hit it over the head with a fucking hammer or something," she said. "That's just totally gross."

Later, Mary Jean went to Joe and told him she was disgusted by the idea of killing the cat. Joe told her he didn't want to do it, either.

In January 1996, Seth came to Joe with a new idea involving Vicki's parakeets.

On January 11, a year to the day after Vicki overdosed and fell into a coma, Joe got up and showered before waking up Matt for school. As usual, Joe went to Seth's bedroom door and knocked to wake him. The boy did this because his school bus came earlier than Matt's and he wanted to make sure his brother got out the door on time.

When Seth emerged from his room he handed Joe a note to give to the school office.

"This will get you out early today. I want you to do it today, then meet me at the gas station down the street from her house."

Around 1:00 P.M., Joe went to the school office and presented his note. It said he had to leave school to get to a therapy appointment with his court-appointed counselor. Joe did have a session scheduled that day, but it wasn't for several hours.

Vicki's home was only about a mile from Joe's regional junior high school. Dressed in a winter jacket and sneakers, Joe made his way back to the house he had considered a safe haven just two months earlier. Joe slipped into the garage by the side door and went for the key hidden under the pump.

It wasn't there.

Joe was suddenly stumped. Either Vicki never returned the key they used when they had gone to her house on the day before Thanksgiving, or she'd purposely stashed it someplace else. He desperately looked around the garage, under doormats and on the tops of door frames, but the key was nowhere to be found.

I don't even really want to do this, he thought. It would be a plausible explanation to Seth that the key was gone and he couldn't get in. The idea of not going through with the plan had crossed his mind during school and on the walk over. But then Joe worried about what Seth might say or do next if Joe failed at this assignment.

He tried the front door, but it was locked. The back door was locked, too. He examined the windows on the side of the house and saw that the latch was turned on the sash of the one leading to Vicki's bedroom. Joe jumped a couple of times trying to reach the first-floor window, but it was too high for him to get any leverage and open it.

Joe grabbed one of the wooden benches from the picnic table on the backyard patio and dragged it over to the window. Though it was broad daylight, the boy figured most of the neighbors were at work. Besides, if anyone were to see him, they would know he was Vicki's son and just assume he had forgotten his key. He propped the bench against the facade and climbed up into the window.

After closing the sash behind him, Joe began his search for Vicki's parakeets. He hadn't noticed them in November and wasn't sure where Vicki kept them. It was only through Seth he was even aware she had the birds at all.

When he couldn't find them downstairs, Joe climbed to the second floor, where he discovered a square birdcage in the hallway. There were two parakeets in the cage, one yellow and the other blue. Joe removed the top of the cage and reached in to grab the birds, but they flew around the cage and evaded his grasp. If he wasn't careful, the birds would flee from the cage altogether, and he'd have to chase them around the house. This wasn't working.

Joe went into Matt's old room looking for something to use. He found a red and green tin the size of a tomtom drum. It was decorated with a winter scene and had once been filled with popcorn. He placed the tin next to the opening of the birdcage, then flipped them both upside down. The parakeets tumbled into the canister, and Joe covered the opening with his body so the birds could not escape while he fumbled to put the canister's lid in place.

He took the tin to the kitchen and opened the oven door. At the metal groan of the oven's hinges, the birds responded with fluttery taps and scratches from the inside of their container. The canister was too tall to fit on the rack, so Joe turned it sideways and rolled it in, the birds flapping in panic inside the metal walls. He switched on the broiler and walked out the front door.

It took Joe about twenty minutes to walk from Vicki's home to the rendezvous point at the gas station. He waited another five or ten minutes before Seth pulled up in his Jeep.

"Did you put her birds in the oven?"

"Yes."

That was the extent of their conversation about it.

When Vicki came home to her darkened house from her part-time job doing payroll at a local warehouse, she noticed a peculiar smell, as if something was burning. She flicked on all the lights and glanced around quickly before heading to the kitchen.

There was a haze in the room, and the orange light was lit on the oven indicating the broiler was on. *Did I leave it on when I left today?* Vicki thought. She gripped the door handle and a cloud of gray smoke wafted out. Vicki fanned her hands and waited for her vision to clear.

In the oven was a round tin canister, turned on its side. Vicki used potholders to remove the canister and looked inside. She didn't know what she was looking at right away. There were blackened embers everywhere. Some burned meat and tiny bones. When Vicki realized the embers were actually the crisp remainders of feathers, she let out a horrified scream.

Her pet birds had not only been killed, they'd been roasted alive as they flapped their wings madly, trying to escape.

That night, Mary Jean came to the Stratham house to get some of her dogs and found Seth joking with Joe about what he'd done.

"You did *what*?" she shouted.

"I couldn't do it to the cat, MJ," Joe said. "But birds are different. They're like bugs or something."

Seth chuckled along. "And stepping on a bug is nothing."

Mary Jean took a long, cold look at him. "Seth, come with me and help me bring the dogs into my van."

Seth followed her into the basement and stood next to crates, waiting for Mary Jean to select which dogs she would be bringing to the next show.

"You son of a bitch!" she roared at him. "How could you use Joe for such a thing!"

Seth shrugged and offered up his hands. "He used to live there. None of the neighbors would suspect him if they saw him."

"That's bullshit," she countered. "You're just too big of a pussy to do it yourself."

Mary Jean grabbed a couple of dog crates and stormed out of the house. She drove to her friend Sebastian Caradonna's home in Medford, Massachusetts, and asked if she and the dogs could stay with him for a while. He was thrilled to play host and protector. When Mary Jean settled in, she ranted to him about what Seth had done. Caradonna seemed unmoved.

"It's not such a big deal," Caradonna told her. "I don't think you should be so mad."

Mary Jean continued her rhetorical argument with Caradonna playing devil's advocate.

"You know, if you really want to do that, fine. But be a man and do it yourself. Or pay someone. Don't involve a little kid. That's disgusting, that's what. And I don't believe in torturing birds, Sibby. I had a pet bird as a kid. But really, why not grow your own set of plums and do it yourself?"

The next day at the law office, a bouquet of flowers from Seth arrived for Mary Jean. He promised not to involve Joe in any more intimidation tactics against Vicki, and Mary Jean promised to return to the house after that weekend's dog show in Saratoga.

When she finally returned to the Bader household, Mary Jean discovered that five of the twenty-five American Staffordshire terriers she'd left at the home were sick. She brought them to an emergency veterinary clinic where it was determined they had been poisoned. All five dogs died at the clinic.

"They ingested antifreeze," the vet said. "It could have been poured into their water dishes or they could have been given some meat soaked in it."

Mary Jean was enraged. She knew exactly who to blame for the crime.

"It was Vicki Bader who killed my dogs!" she told her friends at Brighton Billiards.

"Why would Seth's ex-wife try to kill your dogs?"

"Because Seth had her birds cooked in the oven and she thinks I did it!" For all except Caradonna, the bird story was news. Mary Jean's retelling of Joe's mission brought more laughs from the pool hall crowd than the dead dog story generated sympathy.

"That was twenty thousand dollars worth of dogs that I lost!" Mary Jean complained to Seth.

"I'll put in a claim with my homeowner's insurance. Maybe they'll cover it."

"When is the next time your lawyers are going to depose Vicki?" she demanded. "I want them to grill her about killing my dogs."

Seth nervously ran his fingers on the top of his head. "I can see about that."

The poisoning of the dogs made a convert out of Mary Jean. She was now on board for any harassment Seth cooked up for Vicki. The problem was that Vicki was not responsible for the deaths of Mary Jean's terriers at all.

Several weeks later, after the insurance company denied his claim, Seth told Mary Jean the truth. "Vicki didn't do it," he said, trying to defuse another explosive harangue about the incident. "It was icy and Joe poured some antifreeze on the front steps. He wanted to melt it. When he let out some of the dogs, they must have licked it up and got sick."

Mary Jean wasn't convinced. "Why only five dogs? Why not all of them?" She began marching through the house, looking for the teenager so she could confront him.

"You know he doesn't let them all out at once. Look, Joe was scared to tell you the truth because he didn't want you to be mad and yell at him. Just let it go."

Despite the confession, Mary Jean didn't believe Seth. She was convinced that Vicki had somehow killed the dogs in retaliation, and that her ex-husband was now covering for her. Without ever knowing it, Vicki Bader had made a deadly enemy.

"How would you feel about killing someone?"

Sebastian Caradonna was taken aback by Mary Jean's question. But knowing what happened to her dogs, it was clear to him whom she was talking about and what she was getting at.

"You got the wrong person." Caradonna got aggravated that she would bring such a topic up in his home. He got up and walked out of his own house. After circling the block a couple of times, he returned to finish the conversation. "I'm not . . . eh, no . . . that's not my cup of tea."

Caradonna told her he couldn't believe she could be so serious about something like that, and she dropped it.

The following day, Mary Jean came to him with another trial balloon. "Someone should slash Vicki's tires."

"Yeah, yeah, yeah, yeah. Whatever."

Mary Jean let another couple of days pass. "It's not that big a deal. You know, there could be a couple of bucks in it for you."

"I told you, I don't want to do anything like that."

"I know some of the people in your family," she then said ominously. "They'd be interested in some of the things I know about you . . . I know your probation officer's number. A few calls could be made there, too."

For Sibby Caradonna, the big talker, the time had come to step up and take some action.

Seth Bader was getting impatient with the delay in his plans to psychologically torture his ex. It had been nearly three weeks since the bird incident, and he knew from the letter-writing campaign how susceptible his ex-wife was to mounting pressure.

"I want you to mail this to Vicki." Seth handed Mary Jean a small box.

"What is this?" Mary Jean pulled the top off. Inside was a raw, bloody steak with a knife stuck in it. "Ugh, this is so gross."

"Just mail it to her."

Mary Jean, motivated not by compassion but by a

desire not to handle the dripping package, tossed the whole thing in a Dumpster.

"Did you mail that item I gave you?" Seth asked her a short time later.

"Yeah, just like you asked."

"Good," he said. "Mail this one, too." It was another box with another slab of raw meat pierced by a steak knife. Mary Jean again took it to a commercial Dumpster and threw it out.

For a third time, a twitchy Seth gave Mary Jean a package for Vicki that contained a knife stabbing a piece of raw meat. Like the others, Mary Jean had no intention of putting it in the mail.

"How come your friends haven't hit Vicki's car yet?"

"They've gone twice to her office and missed her."

Seth didn't want to hear excuses. From the beginning he had ponied up a lot of money to have this petty vandalism done, money that Mary Jean had neglected to mention to Caradonna. If she was going to subcontract this job, she was going to have to do a much better job at it.

FOURTEEN

Short Fuse

Sandro Stuto, a.k.a. Sandros Studo, was born in Milan, Italy, in 1975, but he grew up with his parents and brother and sister in a small Sicilian town, outside the seaport city of Catania and near the Mount Etna volcano, called Ramacca known for its artichoke farms.

Stuto's mother thought the opportunities for her children in the United States were much greater than becoming an artichoke farmer, so she took Stuto and his sister to Malden, Massachusetts, to live with extended family, leaving her other son behind with her husband.

Stuto arrived in the United States on July 24, 1988, at the age of thirteen. He enrolled at Beebe Junior High School but had a very difficult time with the English language. After his first year, he was held back so he could have more time to brush up on his remedial skills. But his second year in school was no better and was only exacerbated by a prolonged absence when he took several months off to return to Italy. By the time he came back to the United States he was sixteen and considered himself too old to be hanging out with freshmen at Malden High School, so he dropped out.

A few years earlier, Stuto's uncles had purchased a little pizzeria called DiPietro's. It had been run by Italians since the 1950s, and now it was the Stuto family business. Stuto worked full-time at DiPietro's, bossed around by his hot-blooded uncles. His English didn't improve much by working all day with his Italian family, so he was left with an accent so pronounced he sounded like a Sicilian Inspector Clouseau.

When he wasn't at the pizzeria, Stuto liked to shoot pool. Over the next few years he became a regular at several pool halls around Boston, including Brighton Billiards. Among the friends he made, winning and losing money to, was Sibby Caradonna. At one point, the two of them were playing pool almost every night.

One night in October of 1995, Sandro Stuto and a buddy were cruising the streets of Boston. They had been playing pool and looking for women, but Stuto was under twenty-one and behind the wheel, so he hadn't been drinking. While driving past Kenmore Square, his car got rear-ended, folding up the backseat and totaling the sedan. Stuto's inebriated passenger scrambled out the door and onto the crowded sidewalk. He had an outstanding warrant and didn't want to be around when the police arrived. Stuto was dazed when the EMTs got there. They stuck him in an ambulance and left the wreck in the middle of the street.

Days later, the crack of a cue ball brought back the sound of the crash in Stuto's mind. He told Caradonna all about the Kenmore Square accident, and Sibby agreed that without his passenger as a witness, he was in a tough position with his insurance claim.

"Whaddya think I should do?" he asked Caradonna.

"I know just the lawyer you should talk to." After their game, Caradonna went to the pay phone and called Mary Jean to get Stuto an appointment with her boss.

Stuto and Mary Jean didn't recognize each other, despite both being regulars at Brighton Billiards. The sexy blond paralegal sat in on the meeting with the attorney, who, after agreeing to take Stuto's case, turned things over to Mary Jean. She asked him questions about the accident and took notes. The young man could not help noticing how attractive she was, and Mary Jean Martin and Stuto soon became friends.

Stuto was always eager for cash and made it known he would do odd jobs for money. When there was a small flood at the law firm caused by a broken pipe, Stuto helped move boxes of paperwork from the basement. Caradonna later hired him to resod the lawn at his Medford home.

As the pressure began to mount from Seth about needing more action in his plan to harass his ex-wife Vicki, Stuto seemed like the kind of guy Caradonna and Mary Jean could trust to get things done.

"Do you want to make some money?"

"Doing what?"

"Well, let's just say there's this person . . ." Caradonna liked to speak in conspiratorial riddles. It was his style to add layers of mystery to the most innocuous things, to imply sole knowledge of events of great import.

"So, this person doesn't like this lady, and would be appreciative if this lady got her tires slashed or whatnot. Would you be interested?"

"Sure." There was no hesitation on Stuto's part.

Stuto was later invited to Caradonna's house and found Mary Jean Martin there waiting for him.

"So you want to make some money, huh?" she said.

Mary Jean explained what needed to be done. Stuto and Caradonna would drive an hour north to New Hampshire and cut this woman's tires and vandalize her car. At first, Stuto didn't know who this victim was, only that she was "a lady." Mary Jean offered him $600 to do the deed, but Stuto inferred that the money was coming from someone else. He would be paid after his service was rendered.

Stuto drove Caradonna to Kingston, to the warehouse where Vicki was working as a bookkeeper. Her car wasn't there. It was Caradonna's second trip to New Hampshire and the second time he'd missed his chance to do this job.

When they reported their failure to Mary Jean, she was angry with Caradonna.

"You're missing her on purpose. What are you, too big of a pussy to do it?"

Stuto thought she'd yell at him, too, but instead she purred up next to him.

"Do you want to do another 'job' for me?" She then asked if he would shoot the lady's windows with a BB gun.

"I don't-a know," Stuto hesitated. "I never use a BB gun before. Maybe no."

The next time the three of them were together at Caradonna's, Mary Jean handed Stuto a brand-new BB gun. She told him to take it into the backyard and practice shooting it. Stuto tried, but the air rifle jammed and wouldn't fire. Mary Jean was aggravated that the gun wouldn't work, but she promised to get a replacement.

"The next time you two go to New Hampshire, I'm going with you," she said.

On February 14, 1996, Mary Jean Martin picked up the men at Sibby Caradonna's home. Vicki was supposed to be at work from 12:30 to 8:00 P.M., so they left just after lunch. Before they took off in Mary Jean's Astro minivan, Caradonna grabbed an ice pick from the toolbox on his porch.

Mary Jean drove, and Caradonna sat in the passenger seat; Stuto watched the streets slip by from his perch in the backseat.

The van cruised along a tree-lined road and turned left into the warehouse parking lot. The paved space was left wide for tractor-trailers coming and going from the business. The company employees parked in a smaller lot on the opposite side of the building.

"There it is."

Vicki's blue Cadillac Coupe DeVille was sitting in the lot, just as her work schedule indicated it would be. Mary Jean backed her van up to Vicki's car, then handed Stuto the ice pick.

"Here," she said. "You know what to do. Keep the damage under five hundred dollars so the insurance won't cover it and she'll have to pay for it out of her pocket."

Stuto pulled the sliding side door open and hopped outside. He plunged the ice pick through the sidewall of the Cadillac's front tire, then dragged it across the driver's-side door. He stuck the rear tire, too, then went to the other car door and scratched it some more with the hand tool's nail-like tip. Neither Caradonna nor Mary Jean got out of the Astro.

As they pulled out of the warehouse parking lot, Mary Jean had a sudden thought. "Why don't we go over to her house while we're up here and shoot out her windows now? We know she won't be home."

Stuto had no problem with it. He could imagine the target he only knew as "the lady" finding two flat tires, calling a tow truck, then coming home to find her windows broken.

The Astro drove down Patricia Avenue once, so Mary Jean could point out Vicki's red-sided house. Before they turned back onto the main road, Mary Jean handed Stuto a different BB gun than the one he had tried to practice with. This rifle had a large scope and a shoulder strap. She said it was an exhibit in a case her boss was trying. Stuto then loaded it with brass BBs himself.

"I'll let you out here. You go into those woods over there to walk up to the back of the house. No one will see you from the woods," Mary Jean told Stuto, who shouldered the weapon and slipped into the barren winter woods. It had just started snowing, and he knew his tracks would be covered by the time "the lady" got home. His footfalls made tiny squeaks and crunches compacting the snow. He came up to a bush less than one hundred feet away from the house and stopped behind it.

Stuto pumped the handle a couple of times, then fired. He anticipated a shattering noise, but instead he heard a crisp tap on the pane. He could see he had put a clean hole right through the glass. Stuto fired again and again, almost twenty times. By the time he was done, he had broken the screens and panes in four windows.

Stuto turned around and stumbled back through the woods, trying to run with icy snowflakes pelting his eyes. His feet tripped over snow-covered stumps and roots. He came to a small stream and tried to leap over it in a single bound, but he overextended his legs and banged the BB gun hard enough for the scope to come loose and land in the running water.

"*Merda!*" he cursed, leaving the scope behind.

Stuto finally made it to the main road and hid behind a tree. Mary Jean's van was nowhere to be seen. He could hear the rumbling of a car approaching from the opposite direction he expected, so Stuto remained motionless behind the tree, hoping the car wouldn't spot him.

"Get in." It was Mary Jean. She had taken the Astro the other way down the road, then spun around to come back for him. Stuto got in and slammed the sliding door closed, and the trio drove back to Massachusetts.

Mary Jean cashed the check Seth had given her and put some of the bills into a white envelope. Before she left, she gave the money to Caradonna, who was supposed to give Stuto his cut.

"Here you go," Caradonna said, using as much discretion in passing Stuto the money in his living room as if he were doing it in church.

Stuto thumbed through the bills. "Six hundred? It was supposed to be-a six hundred for the tires and six hundred for the windows. Where's-a the rest?"

"She said the deal was for two days worth of work. You did it all in one, so that's what you get paid."

Stuto was disappointed but griped no further about it. He didn't know that Caradonna had already pocketed $1,000 for himself, and certainly didn't suspect that Mary Jean had kept a chunk of the money, too.

Seth Bader, who had never met Sandro Stuto, assumed MJ's friend had received the entire amount of the check he had written out to "cash." The lawyer was under the impression that the young Italian guy was some sort of mob figure she'd dealt with at work, not a pizza-making pool shark, a high school dropout who would do anything for a buck.

Seth figured that if he ever needed more muscle, he now had someone he could call on.

Joseph Bader almost turned around on the basement stairs when he realized that his adoptive father was already down there. Joe had chores to do, which included taking care of dogs and emptying garbage. He'd assumed Seth was in his home office but instead found the stocky man at his workbench, wearing gloves on his hands.

"Joe, come here," he called. "I want to show you something."

Seth showed the teen an odd collection of materials. He was standing at the drill press with a short length of metal pipe, two caps, a jar of gunpowder, a rope fuse, and a container of Vaseline.

"Is this what it looks like?"

"You'll see," his father said.

Seth took one of the two round caps and screwed it onto the end of the metal pipe. He then put on a pair of clear goggles, took something from a box, and placed it in the press. Joe read the box and saw it was a 3/32-inch cobalt drill bit. Joe sat on one of the two stools at the workbench while the drill buzzed its way into the pipe. Through this new hole, Seth threaded a length of red cord. He tied one end off in a knot so the fuse would not pull out of the cylindrical pipe.

"Know what I'm going to do with this?"

"Yes."

If Seth had heard his son, he didn't acknowledge it. He continued, "I'm going to put it near Vicki's house. Maybe by the garage or that retaining wall. Maybe her back door. I want to scare her so bad she'll leave the state."

Joe's face and voice were devoid of expression. "Why's that?"

"If she's living in another state, it'll be harder for her to get custody of Sam. I want her to give up the custody fight altogether." Seth secured the fuse with some wadded paper towel inside the pipe and some masking tape on the outside. "Maybe I'll put it under her doorstep."

None of the assembly operation was a surprise to Joe. He had been with Seth a week earlier when he shopped for the materials. Joe stayed in the car while Seth explored an Exeter hardware store for the metal caps he needed. He came back to the car and couldn't help chatting up Joe about his plan to scare Vicki with a bomb. But Joe was used to his father's habit of repeating the same conversations, and expecting a rapt audience when he did so. He'd learned long before that it was easier just to stay quiet instead of pointing that out.

Seth placed a white funnel into the open end of the pipe. He reached for a glass container filled with black powder and began to pour it in. Joe saw the peppery flakes go right to the top of the opening. Seth carefully reached into the Vaseline container and began to rub petroleum jelly on the screw threads.

"You don't want a spark to go off while you're screwing the other side on, otherwise . . ." Seth gave a long whistle.

"You're not going to detonate it?" Joe asked.

"Right now? I certainly hope not."

"No, at Vicki's. You said before you were just going to leave it to scare her."

Seth slowly turned the final cap onto the pipe and then set the device down on the workbench. "That's the plan," he said. The whole bomb-making process had taken about ten minutes.

Seth put all of the supplies, including the drill bit he'd used, into a large Rubbermaid container, which he asked Joe to bury in the backyard. He told the teen he'd dispose of the container more permanently later.

By March 1996, Mary Jean Martin was dividing her time between Seth Bader's home in New Hampshire and Sebastian Caradonna's home in Massachusetts. She mostly stayed with Caradonna when her daughter Courtney was with her father; and when Mary Jean had the girl she would bring her to Seth's, where Joe could help look after her. Caradonna wasn't sure exactly how Seth perceived him: as a rival for his lover or a go-to guy for his dirty deeds, or both. Mary Jean didn't share the details of her Bay State lifestyle with Seth.

"I have another job offer for you," she told Caradonna during the first week of March.

"No, no. Absolutely not," Caradonna said after hearing the pipe bomb plan.

The discussion was tabled for several days. Caradonna didn't waste much time thinking about it. He was more concerned by the daily trials of dealing with Mary Jean, like her ever-increasing horde of Disney collectibles encroaching on his kitchen and living room.

One day, Caradonna brought home several cases of Pastene tomatoes from the market. He liked to fill up his pantry with plenty of Italian staples for cooking. Piled in the corner where the canned tomatoes were supposed to go were a couple of plastic shopping bags from the Disney store. *More shit*, Caradonna thought. The man grabbed two of the shopping bags and a third bag: a white plastic trash bag. Right away he felt the plastic stretch from the weight of the third bag's contents. It felt like five or ten pounds of metal was in there. The bag fell from his hands and landed on the kitchen tile with a *clunk*.

"Mary Jean," he called to her in the other room. "What's in this bag?"

"The bomb."

"The bomb?!"

"Yeah, the bomb. Seth wants someone to place it at Vicki's front door then light it. He's willing to pay seven thousand dollars." Caradonna knew that the price was probably actually closer to $8,000, since Mary Jean liked to skim a little from the top.

Later on, Caradonna would recall that he told Mary Jean he was "not interested, adamant, adamantly not interested," in anything to do with a bomb. He said he was concerned that the bomb had already been in his house for days without him knowing about it. Had his probation officer come over, or had a spiteful Mary Jean called the police, Caradonna would have been the one who went down for the bomb, not her.

Caradonna put the device in a Lord & Taylor shopping bag, put it in his car, and drove to DiPietro's pizzeria to talk to Sandro Stuto.

Stuto would later remember things differently. He recalled being at Caradonna's house one evening, talking with his friend while Mary Jean was upstairs. Caradonna nodded toward the corner of the room at a white shopping bag with plastic handles from Lord & Taylor.

"See that bag?" he said. "Remember that bag."

Stuto nodded. He had come to expect this kind of intrigue from Caradonna. At the pool hall, Caradonna was always saying stuff like, "Look at the guy over there. Remember that guy." And then he would introduce him to "that guy" weeks later, with no further explanation about the subterfuge.

They didn't pick up the bag or look into it. They had no further discussion that night about it. The men went out to play pool, leaving Mary Jean home to watch television and go to bed. They got in the car and cruised up the interstate on their way to Brighton Billiards.

"In that bag is the bomb that Mary Jean told us about. She's gonna pay seven or eight thousand dollars for someone to drop it off and light the fuse."

Caradonna didn't know that Stuto had already had his own conversation with Mary Jean about the job. Caradonna again told Stuto to commit the bag to memory.

The next time Stuto saw that Lord & Taylor bag was when Caradonna carried it into DiPietro's pizzeria while Stuto was working. Caradonna had called the restaurant looking for him.

"I'm coming down with that bag. I need to give it to you now."

Stuto was in the middle of the dinner rush and was so distracted at first that he didn't know what Caradonna was talking about. "Yeah, all right. Whatever." It wasn't until after he hung up the phone that it clicked. *He's bringing the fucking bomb* here*! I'm at work! My uncle is here. What the fuck am I going to do with a bomb?*

When Caradonna appeared in the doorway, Stuto waved a finger to signal him to follow. They went up a stairway to the offices above the pizzeria. Stuto stuck his nose in the bag. The device was covered with some crumpled tissue paper, but he could see the coil of red fuse wrapped neatly on top of it.

"Mary Jean says the fuse will burn something like a foot a minute, so you'll have plenty of time to light it and get away." He gave the kid further instructions on where to place the device. "You put this next to the garage and it's going to blow the house right off the foundation and kill anyone inside. This ain't no firecracker."

They briefly talked money. Caradonna said the payment was likely to be in the thousands. He didn't tell Stuto that Mary Jean had already paid him $6,800 in hundred-dollar bills and that the money was inside his coat pocket. Then Caradonna hinted that he and Mary Jean had had some kind of argument about the bomb. "Make sure, whatever you do, you don't give this back to her."

Caradonna slipped down the stairs, leaving Stuto literally holding the bag. His head jerked back and forth, searching for a place in the office to stash the bomb. He cleared some room on a high shelf and stuck the bag there. But before he could go back to work, Stuto's curiosity got the better of him. He kept thinking about the long fuse he saw curled up in the bag and the amount of time it would take to detonate the bomb. He had been told there were about fifteen feet of fuse and therefore fifteen minutes of getaway time. He'd be on the interstate by the time the bomb went off. Stuto reached back into the bag and cut off a six-inch length of the fuse. He brought it over to the sink and lit it with a cigarette lighter. The supposedly long-burning fuse was consumed in seconds.

"Holy fucking shit!" Stuto went into a panic. *This guy is trying to fucking kill me.*

* * *

Sibby Caradonna was with some friends at his house when he got the call from Stuto about the fuse. He took the call in the kitchen, but everyone could hear him yelling from the living room.

"What?!" he shouted. "I'm calling her right now." He slammed the phone on the receiver and dialed Mary Jean's cellular phone.

"Whaddya doing?!" he continued barking into the phone. His yelling was so over-the-top that his guests were trying to stifle their laughter. The finer details of the spat were lost on them, but they noticed Caradonna had a bullet in his hand and was twirling it between his fingers, like some movie mafioso.

Caradonna screamed into the receiver, "I could've lost my lead man!" At this, the crowd in the other room roared with laughter. They all joked about how Caradonna pretended to be a gangster—now he had a "lead man"?

One of Sibby's buddies, a nineteen-year-old guy he knew from the pool hall, tried to calm things down. When Caradonna stepped back into the living room, steam blowing from his ears, the kid told him to "let it go." Still enraged, Caradonna lunged at the teen, while the other guests jumped in immediately to break up the fight.

Days later, Caradonna, his "lead man" Stuto, and Mary Jean Martin gathered at Caradonna's home to hash things out.

"Your guy is-a playing games wid' us," Stuto shouted

in his broken English. He was still in the dark about the identity of Mary Jean's malicious patron and the bomb's intended target. "He wants to get-a me killed along with whoever's inside-a da house."

Mary Jean wore a steely poker face. "That's not true. The bomb's got a long fuse. He's assured me it'll work just fine."

"It's not. The wick, it burns up like three times as fast."

Mary Jean grabbed the handle of the Lord & Taylor bag and carried it into Caradonna's backyard. The men followed. She dug into the bag and pulled out the pipe bomb. It was the first time Stuto had actually seen what that length of cord led to beneath the tissue paper. Mary Jean measured out another six inches and sliced it from the fuse.

"Let's see." Mary Jean lit the fuse and watched it spark up and fizzle to its end within a matter of seconds. She was just as stunned as the others.

"See, I told you!" proclaimed Caradonna. "It could have taken out my lead man."

Mary Jean seemed flustered, which was unlike her. "I'm going to go talk to him now." She picked up the pipe bomb and began putting it into the shopping bag.

"Uh-uh," Caradonna said, grabbing the handles of the shopping bag. "I'm going to hang on to this for a little while longer."

A contrite Mary Jean returned to the men the next day with an apology and a new offer.

"He says you don't have to light it. You could just place it near the house. There's a cement retaining wall in the front yard. That would be enough to scare her."

"No fucking way, man," said Stuto. "I'm not-a doing anything with that bomb. Count-a me out." Stuto walked away and never saw the bomb again.

Caradonna was a harder sell. He knew Seth Bader needed the pipe bomb back, and he thought he could squeeze some more money out of the little man. Mary Jean had paid him in advance. All the cash was inside his pocket. Despite Mary Jean's insistence, Caradonna was not about to give back both the bomb and the cash. If he wasn't getting the money for doing the job, he would get it for keeping his mouth shut.

Joe Bader was feeding the dogs on the evening of March 11 when his father yelled to him from the living room.

"Joe, look at this!"

He had been watching the early local TV news. A reporter was broadcasting live from Patricia Avenue in Exeter where a bomb had been discovered in a mailbox.

"Can you believe it?" he said, never averting his eyes from the TV. To Joe, Seth seemed both genuinely happy and genuinely surprised. He had scrambled to find a videotape to throw into the VCR so he could watch the news story over and over again. He offered no illusion that it wasn't the pipe bomb he manufactured in the basement several weeks earlier. But like a kid who got an unexpected gift on his birthday, Seth was savoring the surprise.

That weekend, when Mary Jean came back to the house, Joe overheard her and Seth talking in the hallway.

"Who did you get to place the bomb?"

"I did it."

"What?" Seth was not happy. "What the hell do you mean *you* did it?"

Mary Jean told Seth she drove her Astro van to the Exeter neighborhood, the pipe bomb stashed in the backseat. She drove from mailbox to mailbox, placing flyers in each one, hoping to avoid looking suspicious by approaching a single mailbox. When she got to Vicki's, she placed the bomb inside and drove off.

Joe slipped away after that, so as not to get caught knowing more about the incident than he was supposed to.

FIFTEEN

Nest of Snakes

Mary Jean was thrilled to hear that the pipe bomb was having the desired effect of rattling Vicki Bader. She had no idea that placing it in the mailbox had triggered an investigation that included the full backing of the United States Postal Service, a tactical error on her part. All she knew was that Vicki was scared, and now Mary Jean was ready to orchestrate more terror against her financial rival.

Mary Jean went looking for Sandro Stuto. She found him at the pool hall and asked to speak with him privately. "Would you be willing to walk up to Vicki and threaten her face-to-face?" she asked him.

Stuto considered it for a bit. He hadn't been happy about getting an excited phone call from Mary Jean a few days earlier, on the night of March 11. Stuto wasn't so sure the cops weren't listening in.

"There was a bomb found in Vicki Bader's mailbox!" she'd squealed.

"Why are you-a telling me this?" he'd said, raising his voice. "I don't know-a nothing about it. Why are you-a telling me this?" He wondered just how careless Mary Jean could be. But he had some gambling debts and a new girlfriend, so the money he knew she could provide would be nice.

"I don't know if I want her to see-a my face," he cautioned.

"What about Danny?"

Stuto smiled. Danny Payne was a kid Stuto had gone to school with. Stuto had stayed in touch with him even after he dropped out. Danny was a big, scary-looking guy. He had rings in his ears, in his nose, and in his mouth. He had thick arms covered with tattoos from wrist to shoulder. His entire scalp was illustrated with tattoos, hidden when he let his hair grow. Not everyone in the pool hall knew his name was Danny Payne. A lot of them knew him simply as "Danny with Tattoos."

Stuto asked for $2,000 to go to Vicki's house and threaten her. Mary Jean countered with $1,500, and he took the deal. Tired of getting cheated by Mary Jean and Caradonna, Stuto thought this time *he'd* be the one to keep $1,000 and offer the muscle the smaller cut. Danny with Tattoos was happy to get $500 to do the job.

*   *   *

On April 30, 1996, Mary Jean called Stuto and told him her plan would go down that day. Stuto called Danny with Tattoos and asked him to meet him at his house. Mary Jean arrived first, driving her van, and Stuto jumped in.

"Here's a map, your money, and some photos of Vicki," she said, passing him the information.

Just then, a black Mustang slid up behind the van. It was Danny with Tattoos, driving his girlfriend's car. Stuto quickly counted out the cash and stuck $1,000 in one pocket and $500 in the other. He took the map and photos, and Mary Jean drove away the instant he stepped out of the van.

The men drove directly to Exeter and made a loop down Patricia Avenue. Danny with Tattoos parked the Mustang near Vicki's house, partially hidden behind a neighbor's hedges, with the car's nose pointed toward the main road.

Stuto waited in the passenger seat as his partner walked up to Vicki's front door. From his vantage point, he couldn't see if Danny with Tattoos rang the bell or knocked on the door, but after a moment's pause the front door opened inward. A figure appeared in the outline of the screen door.

Vicki Bader opened the door without reservation. A man with tattoos and piercings on his face outlined the screen door.

"Are you Vicki?"

"Yes."

"You need to get out of the state."

"Leave me alone . . ." she said, closing the door before the stranger could say anything further. Her knees were buckling, and tears sprang up in the corners of her eyes. From the safety of behind a window drape, Vicki watched the tattooed thug walk back toward a Mustang at a fast clip. He looked like he was trying to stay casual, trying not to run.

Unknown to Vicki at the time, several other pairs of eyeballs were also on the tattooed man as he left Vicki's property. Neighbors shaken by the bomb incident had become extra vigilant about suspicious activity at Vicki's house. After she reported the incident, they were able to confirm for Detective Roberts that a man in a dark car had indeed approached the home and that Vicki Bader was definitely not making it up.

Mary Jean Martin saddled up next to Sandro Stuto at the bar in Brighton Billiards. They were celebrating the successful job in Exeter. They were both drinking heavily and watching some big wagers going on at the pool tables. Mary Jean leaned in to Stuto so she could speak in his ear and he could smell her perfume.

"Have you thought of any new ways to make money?"

Stuto knew what Mary Jean meant—did he have any more ideas on how to harass "the lady." "Danny's got this-a fifteen-foot pi-foon," he said.

"A what? A patoon?" Mary Jean quizzed.

"A pi-foon. It's a big snake."

"You mean a *python*?"

"Yeah, that's-a it. A pi-thoon. It's-a pretty scary look-ing snake," Stuto said. "He could-a slip it into her house, maybe while she's having a sleep. It's not gonna to kill her or nothing, but it will make her piss her pants."

Mary Jean laughed out loud. The motion of her body placed her right in Stuto's lap. She put her lips on his and pulled at them. They kissed for a long moment before Stuto broke the seal.

"I got a girlfriend," he said.

Even as he continued his quest to gaslight Vicki, Seth Bader was slowly driving himself mad with jealousy. He needed to know more about where Mary Jean was spending her nights when she wasn't with him. There was a place in Mas-sachusetts she went the night she stormed off because of the bird killings. There was an older man who took care of her dogs, but he knew little else. Mary Jean told him she'd got-ten a job working nights as a dispatcher for a plumber out-side of Boston. Suspicious of the additional time away this job would provide, Seth called the plumbing company. They said they didn't have a Mary Jean Martin working for them.

"Tell me where you're going at night. Are you two-timing me?" he asked.

Mary Jean wouldn't answer him. But Seth had to know.

He hired a private investigator to find out everything he could about her. The first order of business was learning who she was staying with when she wasn't with him. It wasn't a difficult task for the PI to follow her to Medford.

Sibby Caradonna was unaware of Seth's suspicions until he received a letter from him. Inside the envelope was a piece of paper with a deer drawn on it and a target superimposed over the animal. It had a single bullet hole in it, right through the deer's head. Caradonna was rattled. He complained to Mary Jean, then called the FBI.

Mary Jean and Seth, who'd been pushed over the edge when the FBI called him about the letter he'd sent, finally had it out when she returned to Stratham.

"Are you sleeping with Sebastian Caradonna?!" he demanded.

"Why? You jealous?"

"Jesus Christ, MJ, you know I'd kill for you. Are you sleeping with him or not?"

"That old man?" she said dismissively. "He's good to me and he's connected to the kind of people you're looking for to do certain jobs for you."

Seth remained suspicious of Caradonna's intentions, but now he was equally suspicious of Mary Jean's.

Mary Jean told Stuto that "the man" was willing to pay $2,500 for the snake attack. Stuto said he'd talk to Danny with Tattoos and see what he thought about the idea.

"By the way," Mary Jean said, "I'm sorry Sibby screwed you out of the money."

Stuto looked puzzled. "Whaddya mean? How did he-a screw me?"

Mary Jean said Caradonna had gotten paid $17,000 in total for all the "jobs" he'd been doing in New Hampshire, including the pipe bomb. She knew Caradonna hadn't given Stuto his fair share. Stuto's face turned red thinking about it. Then Mary Jean pulled a box from her pocket.

"Here." It was a tennis bracelet. She had stolen it from Vicki more than a year earlier. "For your girlfriend."

Stuto spotted Sibby Caradonna and his beat-up 1986 Trans Am parked at a little garage. His plate was 888 MKM, a play on the pool term "making the eight ball." That was another thing Caradonna's cohorts made fun of. Eight ball was so eighties; nine ball was what everyone was playing these days.

Stuto marched up to Caradonna, who was fiddling with his engine. "What the fuck is-a going on here?" he yelled. "She's-a telling me you're screwing me out of money."

Caradonna just put his hands up in confusion. He didn't know what Stuto was talking about, but the Italian was already on a roll.

"If you screw me outta the money, then you give me the money! I never fucked over anybody! Nobody's ever-a fucked-a me over and I'm not about to just-a let anybody fuck-a me over!"

"She's trying to manipulate you. She wants to keep us fighting so we don't trust one another." Caradonna calmed Stuto down, and eventually the Italian let the issue of what money he might be entitled to drop.

Despite the threatening incidents of the previous few months, Vicki Bader was feeling very good about her chance of winning back custody of Samuel. She still remained frustrated by the criminal investigation into the pipe bomb. The police had told her that an FBI profiler had predicted some further action from the assailant, but nothing significant had happened.

Vicki was meeting in her kitchen with her lawyer, Heidi Boyack, who was bringing her client up to date on all the court motions swirling around them. Boyack, too, was frustrated with the police. She felt they'd failed to demonstrate an understanding of Vicki's mental health issues. It was like her client's past suicide attempts were all the excuse the police needed to turn every good deed of Vicki's against her.

Vicki had told the cops everything she knew about bomb making in an effort to be helpful. Instead, they'd treated her knowledge as suspicious. She had worked as a paralegal for Seth when they were married, so it was not uncommon for Vicki to go to the library and research statutes for cases. She had done the same thing to reduce the workload and subsequent bill for Boyack. But her presence at the library had only created more circumstantial evidence against her. In Boyack's mind, it was crystal clear who was behind the pipe bomb and all the other shenanigans: Seth Bader.

Sitting at the counter and pouring coffee, Vicki told Boyack that her doctor thought she'd been misdiagnosed. She said it was possible that she had ADD. "People with ADD don't respond to anti-anxiety medicines," Vicki said. "In fact, it makes the symptoms worse."

Boyack was dumbstruck. Could it be true? Could Vicki's strange behaviors be the result of an interaction with her medication, the medication that was supposed to make her better? Her rapid speech patterns, the changes in her face? Were they all side effects—and not failures—of her treatment?

"Vicki, this is wonderful news. If there is a medical explanation to some of this behavior, we need to make that part of the custody case," Boyack said enthusiastically.

Vicki and Boyack sat talking at the kitchen table, thrilled with themselves and the prospect of seeing this journey to completion. While their coffee grew cold, the doorbell rang.

Boyack followed Vicki to the door. A figure of a tall man cast a shadow into the hallway.

"Are you Vicki Bader?" the man said.

"I am," she replied defiantly.

"My name is Brian Messenheimer," he said. "I'm Mary Jean Martin's ex-husband."

Vicki turned to Boyack, who simply shrugged her shoulders. He didn't seem angry or threatening, nor did he seem to be there at the behest of Mary Jean.

"What can I do for you, Mr. Messenheimer?"

"Your ex-husband is dating my ex-wife. I thought there were some things in her background that you would want to know about."

Stuto let himself into Sibby Caradonna's house, as he often did. Sibby Caradonna and Mary Jean Martin were lounging on the fastidious man's couch, and Stuto asked to speak with Mary Jean alone.

"I talked to Danny about the snake and he says-a no way. It's-a not enough money."

"What do you mean? Twenty-five hundred dollars is a lot of damn money."

"Yeah, but the pi-foon costs like-a eight hundred dollars or something. And he says he's not gonna get it back, so."

Mary Jean said she'd go back to her man and see if he was willing to pay more for the python, but she couldn't promise anything. There was already going to be even more money needed for a bigger job down the road.

On Tuesday, May 21, Lieutenant Richard Kane, Detective Kimberly Roberts, and Postal Inspector Willie Moores went to Seth Bader's home on Doe Run Lane. They had finally decided to take Seth up on his offer to examine his gun safe and workbench—more than two months after the pipe bomb was found. The gate at the end of the driveway was open. There was a small wooden sign by the mailbox that declared this the home of "The Baders." The sign was in the shape of a doghouse; there were cut-outs of a pair of dogs on either side, and another pair of dogs was peeking out through the opening in the dog-house door.

Seth had said he would be home because he worked out of an office on the first floor. As soon as the investigators rang the doorbell, a chorus of barks and growls emanated from inside the house. Seth opened the door to his home, revealing a virtual puppy mill. There were dozens of dog cages stacked in the dining room; more dogs were baying from the cellar. The dogs were a mix of both long-haired and short-haired breeds, but Seth told them that most of the animals were American Staffordshire terriers. In their notes, however, the detectives referred to them as pit bulls.

Seth escorted the group to the basement and showed off his gun collection and reloading operation. There were two separate rooms. One of them contained ammunition and numerous containers of black powder. Its door was secured with a padlock. Kane noted that many of the containers were the same popular Hercules brand used in the pipe bomb, but he didn't see any aluminum mixes.

In the other room, Seth showed off the work area where he did the reloading. It contained all the tools necessary to make a bomb: a vise drill press, paper towels, and cutting tools. Kane noticed all the tools were covered in a thin layer of dust, as if they hadn't been used in some time. When Seth wasn't looking, Kane shook his head at Roberts as if to say *there's nothing here we can use.*

The three investigators scanned the basement and the rest of the house but turned up nothing of evidentiary value. Kane asked if they could search the rest of the property. Seth obliged them by walking them to the dock at the far end of his yard, which provided easy access to the creek. Finding nothing there, the law enforcement officers left.

In the days immediately following the March 11 bomb incident and his initial interview with Exeter police, Seth had dug up the plastic container he'd asked Joe to bury in the backyard and disposed of it permanently. The box contained the remaining mix of black and aluminum powder, the funnel, the fuse, the Vaseline, the cobalt drill bit, and the books he owned with bomb-making instructions in them.

Though he told Joe he'd taken care of the evidence, Joe didn't know exactly when Seth had dug the box up, or where he'd gotten rid of it.

On June 26, 1996, Detective Roberts got a telephone call from the secretary at Heidi Boyack's law office in Portsmouth. She reported that their office had received two anonymous calls from a man who claimed to have information about the Bader case.

The first call had come in a week earlier, on Tuesday, June 18. The secretary said the man called from a pay phone. He said he knew the name of the man who had approached Vicki in the Exeter Public Library. He claimed the man was Sebastian Caradonna of Medford, Massachusetts. Caradonna was—according to the caller—a friend of Mary Jean Martin.

The second call came in on Tuesday the twenty-fifth and was answered by a different office worker. The man on the phone said he was very concerned that the call was being recorded, although it was not. This time, the caller claimed he knew who'd put the pipe bomb in Vicki's mailbox, threatened her at the library, and come to her door. The caller also said that police were looking in the wrong state for the men who did it.

"Is there anything else you can tell me about the anonymous caller?" Roberts asked.

"Yeah," the secretary said. "He spoke very fast and with a thick New York accent."

Kane and Roberts went to Boyack's Portsmouth law office the next day, Thursday, June 27, with some cassettes they had been given by Vicki Bader. The tapes were from her answering machine, on which she had recorded several conversations between herself and Seth. Within seconds of hearing the first tape, the secretary identified Seth's voice as identical to the anonymous caller's. The investigators also played the tape for the other employee who'd answered the phone. She, too, picked out Seth instantly, saying she was "absolutely sure" it was the same man she'd spoken to earlier in the week.

Why would Seth Bader start fingering other people for the pipe bomb? Kane wondered. *What is his game?*

SIXTEEN

Second Thoughts

On a June morning in 1996, three months into the pipe bomb investigation, Vicki took a phone call from a rambling Seth Bader, who bemoaned his tortured relationship with Mary Jean.

"It's on and off, on and off," Seth told her. "I'm walking on eggshells and I don't know what to do but she's really not in my life on any kind of full-time basis. Are you aware of how close Matt is to Mary Jean?"

"Yeah," Vicki replied. "I know he's been very close to her."

"He has crying fits at the thought of not seeing her. What do you want me to do? It gets to me. And Matt just goes into crying fits."

Vicki sighed and explained that Matt's pain over his separation from Mary Jean was the same that Sam would have if Seth continued to oppose her custody. Then Seth changed the subject.

"I wanted to be married to her. I wanted to have a child with her. I thought it was gonna last a lifetime. I am in love with Mary Jean and I haven't stopped being in love with her for a second." Then Seth's tone softened. "I'm sorry. You're not the right person for me to tell this to."

Vicki went on filling the kitchen coffeemaker on her end of the line. Her answering machine was recording the conversation, as was now her practice each time Seth called.

"I know it's difficult," she said.

"But I don't think she's capable of loving back. She's not capable of emotional intimacy or if she is, it's coupled with anger and hate. I complained about her temper and threw her out, and so she stopped with the temper, but she stopped giving me her love completely also." Seth began to weep. "I'm falling apart."

"You need therapy, Seth."

"I'm barely able to function. I'm up at 5:00 A.M. every morning. I'm not sleeping. I'm losing weight."

Vicki pressed Seth about whether Mary Jean was behind the pipe bomb and the other threats. He said he didn't know what to believe, that he was "wandering through a maze of mirrors."

Seth said he'd been to a counselor, who had told him he was attracted to sociopathic personalities, people who were more exciting and dynamic than normal people.

"Hitler, from all accounts, was an attractive and dynamic

person," he offered somewhat abstractly. "Charlie Manson, from all accounts, was attractive and dynamic."

"Maybe," Vicki said, "it will be easier for you if you joined a dating service or something like that."

"Don't be hurt by this," Seth cautioned. "I never had a passion for you to the extent that I have a passion for Mary Jean. I loved you, I cared about you. But you were not an obsession. I was never obsessively in love with you. I basically stopped loving you a year before the divorce. I didn't want the pregnancy with Sam. Matt coming into our lives was stressful. You were the right person at the right time. But I didn't have this obsessive, irrational passion for you."

Seth searched for his next words. "Mary Jean is more than a relationship. Mary Jean is an addiction," he said. "I'm addicted to Mary Jean."

If the words stung her, Vicki did not let on. "Seth, you have no friends outside of Mary Jean."

"That's true," he agreed.

"That's why you call me to talk to me, because you've got no one else to talk with." She added, "Seth, you're gonna collapse at this rate. I'm worried about you."

"I'm on the edge of collapsing."

Despite everything he had put her through, all the attempts to control and humiliate her, to bankrupt her and deprive her of her children, Vicki remained a kind and caring person. She suspected her ex-husband was involved in all sorts of dirty pool, breaking the law and still laboring to separate her from Sam. But in that one moment, Vicki Bader showed her true colors. When she stood at the edge, Seth tried to push her in; when he was standing at the edge, Vicki tried to pull him back.

"I honestly and truly am scared for you," she said. "You've never figured out who Seth Bader is or what Seth Bader wants. Okay? You need some time to find yourself before you jump into another relationship."

"Vicki, there is no Seth Bader," he moaned. "I'm hollow inside. There is no Seth Bader. There never has been."

She shushed him like an infant. "No, there, there is a Seth . . ."

"You know my parents ordered me around all my life. You ordered me around when we were together. And I needed it up to a point. You were good for me in a lot of ways, Vicki. You did a lot of good for me."

"And MJ ordered you around."

"Because," Seth then admitted, "I can't make my own decisions."

With each passing day, Seth felt more and more like Mary Jean Martin was slipping away from him. It wasn't just the financial pressure of providing for her. He felt something was amiss when she was away. He wondered if she was involved in prostitution or selling drugs. He also believed that Mary Jean had been collecting prescription pads from doctors for months and writing herself prescriptions for her migraines.

Seth didn't want to go to jail for the bomb attempt, nor did he want to find himself drained like a sponge with

his heart and wallet depleted by a bleached-blond temptress. With Vicki on the one hand and Mary Jean on the
other, Seth found himself in a Gordian knot, and he
needed an equally bold stroke to get himself out of it.

Within days of the anonymous calls placed to Heidi
Boyack's law office, anonymous letters were delivered to
the police in Stratham and Medford and to the federal
Drug Enforcement Administration. The letters each contained the same information: they accused Mary Jean
Martin of prescription fraud and of using and selling pain
pills via a list of local doctors, and claimed, "Mary Jean
has some hold over these doctors—I don't know if it is
sex or money or blackmail."

Any of those were possibilities, the letters intimated.
Their writer accused her of being "a psychopath, a liar, a
leech, and a slut."

The writer also freely admitted that he was one of Mary
Jean's many exes. "This is payback for some problems she
has recently caused me." He ended the letter by saying he
would deny everything if confronted, because he was
frightened of Mary Jean.

Days later, another set of letters arrived at the same
three agencies. The dot matrix font was changed, but the
difference was so subtle everyone concluded the correspondence was generated on the same computer printer.
Moreover, the second letter began, "Here is more on
Mary Jean Martin."

It went on to reiterate that Mary Jean was blackmailing doctors over insurance fraud, and it accused her of

corruption, prostitution, child abuse, and boasting about her "mob connections and hoodlum friends." Mary Jean "is in multiple relationships" and "is a monster and will do anything for money," the letter said.

The writer warned that Mary Jean had many connections in the dog-breeding world and could hide "underground" if she got a head start. Finally, the "concerned citizen" wrote that Mary Jean was "greatly feared by almost everyone close to her due to her explosive temper and her abilities at lying, manipulating, blackmailing and revenge," and closed with the dire warning that if she knew the writer's identity, he would not be safe.

It's not clear how Seth first heard about Mary Jean's ex-husband Brian Messenheimer's conversation with Vicki, whether it was declared in a meeting between attorneys Heidi Boyack and Barbara Taylor, or whether Mary Jean heard about it and threw it in his face. But Seth was now obsessed, nearly unhinged.

He knew that Brian Messenheimer had shared some sort of information with Vicki about Mary Jean—information that was slow in coming to Seth from his costly private investigator. Seth wanted to know what Vicki knew. He wanted to know what the truth was behind the woman who had moved into his home and spent all his money. And this time, Seth was willing to negotiate almost anything to find out.

Seth begged Vicki for days for a face-to-face meeting

until she finally capitulated. She couldn't take any more of his frantic telephone calls. They agreed to meet at a McDonald's where they could talk privately but still be in the public eye.

Vicki was flabbergasted when she saw Seth walk into the restaurant. He had dropped twenty pounds since the last time she saw him, but it was not the healthy kind of weight loss that comes from diet and exercise. Seth looked like he'd starved and sweated the weight right off his back.

"MJ is killing me," he said. "She charged fifteen hundred dollars on my American Express for concert tickets which she intended to sell. When I asked her about it, she blew up."

According to Seth, the person at the ticket outlet said Mary Jean was well known for ordering thousands of dollars worth of tickets. Seth tried to block the charge to his card, which spurred another screaming fit from Mary Jean. She told Seth he "should trust blindly" and that blocking the credit charge was costing her a nice profit.

"She's costing me more than six figures," a demoralized Seth confessed to his ex-wife. "I've decided to get rid of her."

"I don't know why you're telling me this."

"I'm scared of her, in light of all that I know." He said he suspected that Mary Jean might have been the one who put the pipe bomb in Vicki's mailbox, or that she might have hired someone to do the job for her.

Seth then told Vicki about the letters he had written to authorities regarding Mary Jean's prescription drug abuse. "She'll get fifteen to twenty years, but she could probably cut a deal for giving up the doctors."

Seth said he'd sent the letter to police in Stratham and Medford because if he'd sent the letter to Exeter police and they questioned Mary Jean, he would be in danger.

"There was this man who approached me at the library," Vicki said. "He was middle-aged and . . ."

". . . with a mustache? Sunken cheeks? That's Sebastian Caradonna." Vicki found it odd that Seth could finish the description and rattle off Caradonna's address and phone number off the top of his head. "You should leak his name anonymously to the police."

"No, Seth," she protested. "I'm not going to play your game of secrets."

Seth then confronted Vicki with the knowledge that Brian Messenheimer had visited her, and he wanted to know what was discussed. Vicki said Messenheimer gave no details or confirmable facts. She also said she had no way of knowing his motives or of contacting him again.

"I wanted to talk to you about all this," Seth then told Vicki, "in case things start to happen to me and I turn up dead."

When Vicki went to pick up Sam the following day, Seth offered her a Luger handgun for protection. She refused it. He explained that he'd gotten it in a private sale, which, although legal, meant there was no paperwork linking the firearm back to him.

"I've been thinking about giving you a thousand dollars so you can put an alarm system in your home." Although she didn't want to encourage him, the idea of a home security system was appealing. Vicki thanked Seth and said that she would feel better with an alarm.

"Someone called Heidi Boyack's office and said Caradonna threatened me," Vicki mentioned.

"Yeah, that was me," Seth fessed up immediately. "He hangs out at a place called Brighton Billiards. He has two 'muscle men' that do things for him."

Vicki went home and, knowing her memory would fail her, wrote out a memo to Boyack on her word processor. In it, she listed all of the things that Seth told her, but she seemed none the closer to any clarity about the situation.

I am very alarmed at this point. I don't know if Seth is trying to set up Mary Jean, if Seth is being set up by Mary Jean or what. I do know that Seth is genuinely scared at this point. He is carrying around a weapon at all times . . .

If something happens to me, I want my estate solvent. I'm afraid of what will happen if I do so before then. If MJ has access to these people, so does Seth. For all I know, Seth may have asked MJ to arrange the things that have happened to me and is afraid, if she links the drug leak to him, she will tell on him. I do not know. I just know that Seth is very worried. I have never seen him like this.

In the corner of the three-page document, Vicki added a handwritten note that said, "Seth told me he is on the verge of a breakdown. I believe it!" She finished up the letter to her attorney this way:

> You know, I can't win. I feel manipulated but if I didn't talk to him, I wouldn't get all this information. It's my own doing and I know that but I feel sorry for Seth in a way. Regardless of what he may have done, he has no friends. I don't know what to think and I'm worried about the effect of all this on the children.

The couple's attorneys, Barbara Taylor and Heidi Boyack, met in late June with the judge who would be presiding over the final hearing in *Bader v. Bader.* The Honorable Douglas Grey told the lawyers there wasn't anything mystical about this case. He suggested Vicki settle for alimony and insurance coverage for three more years, and that Seth should give the Exeter home to her outright. He said the guardian ad litem was preparing a final report, but he saw no reason why Vicki could not have regular unsupervised visits with Sam and resume joint custody of all three children. The attorneys said they'd go back to their clients and discuss the terms for a settlement offer.

For Seth, this meant he was about to lose all his leverage. And there were still things he wanted from Vicki.

* * *

"This is what I'm proposing," Seth said in another rambling telephone call to Vicki placed at 6:30 in the morning. He would give her alimony, unsupervised visitation, everything Vicki wanted, effective immediately regardless of the judge's ruling. "But I want to know everything you have on MJ, where it's coming from, what it is, nothing held back."

Seth claimed his private eye was gathering dirt on Mary Jean, but he was willing to give Vicki anything she wanted if she could trump the investigator's report. Vicki was noncommittal, her answering machine recording the entire call. She wasn't sure that what Messenheimer had told her was all that valuable, and she was likely to get the concessions offered by Seth within a few weeks anyway.

"I just don't think I want to make the information I have on MJ a bargaining chip," she said.

"She's pressing me for certain decisions. I'm . . ."

"What? Is she pressing you for when you're going to get married?"

"Other things," Seth said dismissively.

"So what you're saying," Vicki went on, "is you'd be willing to make a settlement offer and unsupervised visitation with Sam until the custody gets settled?"

"Yeah, but the exchange is that I want everything on MJ, nothing held back. I need to verify your source. I need things that can be checked. It has to be stuff that's traceable, verifiable."

Vicki said she wasn't convinced that Mary Jean was uninvolved in the pipe bomb. Seth passionately pleaded ignorance but slyly added that he might know the answer if Vicki shared all her information.

"I'm groping in [the] dark! I need a flashlight to guide me because I'm just groping in the dark! I can't make decisions on gut feeling and be confident in it!"

"I'm very much afraid," Vicki said, "that if I tell you this about Mary Jean, I'm going to have my house burned to the ground."

"In a few weeks, your information on MJ will be worthless," Seth said. He was prepared to give up everything he'd fought for over the past two years—give her near-unfettered access to Sam—just to learn the truth about the woman he was obsessed with. He put her above his kids and his money.

He would do *anything* to keep Mary Jean in his life.

SEVENTEEN

Unusual Suspects

On Monday, July 1, 1996, Exeter police lieutenant Richard Kane found Sebastian Caradonna's name in the Medford phone book and placed a call to the man. The reason for the call was his name's repeated appearance in the "anonymous" calls made by Seth Bader. Though the investigator didn't elaborate on why he wanted to talk to him, Caradonna agreed to have Kane meet him at his house the following day at noon.

"If this is the same as the death threat against me," Caradonna said, "I already reported that to the FBI."

Kane checked with the FBI agent who'd looked into Caradonna's complaint. The agent said it had sounded like a "love triangle" between Bader, Caradonna, and Mary Jean Martin. Whenever Mary Jean wasn't staying with Seth in Stratham, it seemed she was staying over at Caradonna's.

On Tuesday, July 2, Lieutenant Kane drove to Caradonna's home in the working-class suburb of Boston. Despite his promise to be there, Caradonna wasn't home. Kane tried calling him repeatedly but had no luck.

On Wednesday, July 3, 1996, Seth and his attorney Barbara Taylor came to the Exeter police station at Kane's request. When they all sat down to talk, Kane stated that Seth was not under arrest and could leave whenever he wanted.

"Would you like me to sign a release form saying I've been advised of my rights?" Seth offered helpfully. Kane said it wasn't necessary, that he was sure they understood what he had told them.

"Seth, what's the status of your relationship with Mary Jean Martin?"

"It's off and on," he said. "I have some concerns that MJ might be a prostitute."

"Why is that?"

"She's very secretive about where she goes and who she sees. She has a night job in Massachusetts at a place that is supposedly a dispatch center for plumbers." Then, acting very proud of his own craftiness, Seth said, "I had a private detective look into it. The place says she isn't an employee there. I think it's a front for some kind of illegal activity."

"Did you tell Vicki that you were going to turn Mary Jean in for prescription fraud?"

"I never said anything of the kind!" Seth protested, rubbing the top of his head.

Seth said that if Mary Jean ran, she could go underground and hide with her friends in the dog show circles. *Where have I heard that claim before?* Kane thought. *The thing about hiding out on the dog show circuit was in the anonymous letter!*

"So *you* sent those letters to the police about Mary Jean."

"I don't know what you're talking about." Seth rubbed his head again.

Holy shit. Kane's mind went racing back to all of the previous interviews and conversations in which he'd seen Seth do this very thing. *He has a "tell." Whenever he lies, he rubs the top of his head. He's lying right now.*

"The writer of the letters said it would be dangerous to show them to Mary Jean."

"I didn't write them," Seth protested some more. "Go ahead. Look for my fingerprints on them. Tell me if they're mine or not."

"We're not going to find your fingerprints on them because you wore gloves when you handled them. And you used water to seal the stamps and envelopes."

"You can't prove that," Seth said.

Kane opened his notes. "Somebody called Vicki's attorney with information on the threats against her."

Seth rubbed his head. "I wasn't aware of that."

"Do you know who the caller said put the bomb in the mailbox?" Kane asked with great flourish. "Mary Jean Martin!"

"She's dangerous. I wouldn't put anything past her," Seth agreed.

"Another thing, Seth," Kane went on. "The secretary said the caller had a New York accent and spoke so fast that she had to tell him to slow down twice." He said they'd played a tape of Seth's voice, and the woman had positively identified him as the phantom caller.

"A lot of people around here have New York accents," Seth feebly tried to explain away. "Or they can change up their voices . . ."

"Don't try to pass that one off on me, Seth. There is no one else in this case who would have all this information and be afraid to talk directly with Vicki's attorney because they were afraid her lawyer would recognize them." The lieutenant pointed a finger in Seth's face. "That's *you*!"

Kane told him there was no reason to lie about it any longer. He knew who put the bomb in Vicki's mailbox and said Seth should tell the police what else he knew. Seth sat with his arms crossed instead.

Kane showed Seth and his lawyer the charred Dixie cup found in Seth's trash and explained how testing showed that the powder in the cup matched the kind of powder used in the bomb.

"Anyone could have put that there!" Seth exploded. "MJ is over all the time. Even when I'm not there, she's been over. Caradonna's been to my house, too."

Seth Bader said that he was finished talking to the police and would instead talk to the prosecuting authorities and tell them what he knew in exchange for a deal.

Any Independence Day plans were scrubbed as of 8:30 the next morning, when Kane got a call at home from Seth Bader. The nervous New Yorker asked if he could talk to Kane more about Mary Jean's involvement in the case. The lieutenant told Seth to meet him in his office in half an hour.

When the two men sat down, Seth began sputtering at full speed. "It's just the tip of the iceberg, what I told you in regards to MJ! I think I should be treated as a hero for coming forward with this information."

Seth said he had learned the details of a conspiracy from a third party, an unnamed source who played pool at a hall outside of Boston called Brighton Billiards. Seth said that he spoke to Mary Jean the other night and she made threats against Vicki. He said she shook him down for money to cover legal retainers for all the other people she had caught up in the conspiracy.

"I want to come out of this a hero," he said again. "This will all probably look bad in my custody case, and maybe I'll lose my law license if this information gets out."

Seth said he wanted to cut a deal with the U.S. Attorney in Concord, New Hampshire. He would tell him everything he knew if they could just cut a deal. Kane said he'd talk to Inspector Moores and the U.S. Attorney about it and get back to him.

*   *   *

On July 5, an increasingly anxious Seth Bader returned to the Exeter police department with some of the blank prescription pads that Mary Jean had allegedly stolen from different doctors' offices and health clinics. Kane said they'd look into it.

Seth also brought a cassette tape he claimed incriminated Mary Jean Martin. Kane, Seth, and Barbara Taylor listened to the tape in Kane's office. It had obviously been made in the previous day or two. The recording consisted of Seth asking Mary Jean to repeat details from past conversations, including asking how much it would be for one of her associates to place a fifteen-foot snake in Vicki's home. Seth then asked how much it would cost for this associate to make a proper "package delivery"—hinting this meant another bomb—to which Mary Jean said somewhere between $20,000 and $30,000. The rest of the tape was about what they were going to do that weekend.

Kane followed up on the names left by the "anonymous" caller with the Brooklyn twang. There was a Sandro Stuto living in Medford, Massachusetts, who had a couple of minor charges on his record—receiving stolen property, traffic violations—but was otherwise clean.

When Kane reached him by phone on July 7, Stuto said he was about to leave for a week in New Hampshire's

Vicki Buzby grew up on Long Island to a middle-class family. She was described as a smart student with a kind heart.
Courtesy of the Buzby family

Vicki, shown here in 1991, was on the rebound from her first marriage when she met a talkative law student named Seth Bader, who seemed to understand her.
Courtesy of the Buzby family

Vicki and Seth Bader left Brooklyn, New York, for Stratham, New Hampshire. But after their marriage deteriorated, Vicki moved out, and Seth received custody of their three sons.
Courtesy of the authors

Though police found no evidence that Seth Bader had constructed the pipe bomb found in Vicki's mailbox, Seth did maintain a locked workshop in his basement, which contained all the materials necessary to build a similar pipe bomb.
Courtesy of the New Hampshire Attorney General's Office

Among Seth's supplies were large amounts of a common gunpowder that was also found inside the bomb.
Courtesy of the New Hampshire Attorney General's Office

Vicki was walking down this hallway in the Stratham home when a gun was put to the back of her head and the trigger was pulled.
Courtesy of the New Hampshire Attorney General's Office

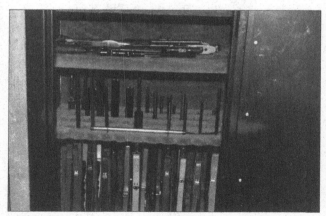

A firearms enthusiast, Seth Bader owned a cache of weapons, including a handgun with an interchangeable barrel, like the one found buried near Vicki's body.
Courtesy of the New Hampshire Attorney General's Office

Seth Bader, mobbed by reporters while entering a New Hampshire court. The brash attorney turned his divorce and custody case with Vicki Bader into a violent crusade. Bader claimed he was a patsy and not the mastermind of a criminal conspiracy to kill Vicki. *AP Photo/Jim Cole*

Mary Jean Martin, Seth Bader's girlfriend, outside the Rockingham County Courthouse. Mary Jean told police about Seth's plot to terrorize his ex-wife, but investigators suspected she played a larger role in the crime than she admitted. *AP Photo/Jim Cole*

Sandro Stuto, one of several people drawn into the conspiracy, testified how he shot out Vicki's windows to frighten her. Stuto, a wannabe gangster with a thick Italian accent, said he didn't expect to play an active role in the murder of Vicki Bader.
AP Photo/Jim Cole

Joe Bader (above) and his brother Matt were adopted by their cousin, Seth Bader, and Vicki. The children were used as pawns in a bitter court fight between their adoptive parents. Both eager to please and afraid to disobey, Joe said he did whatever Seth told him to do . . . including digging a shallow grave in a secluded forest.   *Courtesy of the New Hampshire Attorney General's Office*

When Vicki Bader disappeared in August 1996, her car was discovered abandoned, with the keys left inside, in front of the Leather & Lace adult store.   *Courtesy of the New Hampshire Attorney General's Office*

After Vicki's Cadillac was found, police searched the car for any evidence connected to her disappearance.
Courtesy of the New Hampshire Attorney General's Office

Seth Bader studied area maps ahead of time to find an acceptably secluded spot to dispose of Vicki's body.
Courtesy of the New Hampshire Attorney General's Office

Teenage Joe Bader, accompanied by police, pointed to the wooded area where he dug Vicki Bader's grave.
Courtesy of the New Hampshire Attorney General's Office

Maine State Police began the slow process of thawing the frozen ground to retrieve Vicki's body.
Courtesy of the New Hampshire Attorney General's Office

John Kacavas, now the U.S. Attorney for New Hampshire, led the prosecution team that sought justice for the slain Vicki Bader.
Courtesy of the U.S. Department of Justice

Mark Sisti was an aggressive defense attorney who stressed the prosecution had trouble with the forensics in the case.
Courtesy of the authors

White Mountains, but he would stop at the Exeter police department on his way north.

Stuto was very much at ease talking to Kane. He spoke to the detective with an Italian accent so thick it was almost comical. He said he was having a problem with the Commonwealth of Massachusetts about his driver's license, so he had been driven everywhere by friends. Kane asked how he knew Mary Jean Martin.

"She's a secretary for-a my attorney," he said. Stuto said they'd become friendly while he was trying to settle a personal injury case. Kane asked if he knew Sebastian Caradonna, too.

"Sure I know-a Sibby," he said. "He's a friend-a Mary Jean, too. We all plapal together."

Kane stopped taking notes, stymied by Stuto's accent. "You mean, *play pool*?"

"Yeah, *plapal*," Stuto went on. "We all plapal together."

"Where do you play?"

Stuto said they all played at a place called Brighton Billiards.

Lieutenant Kane and Inspector Moores discussed whether the U.S. Attorney's office was willing to meet with Seth Bader about an immunity deal. Moores said the federal prosecutors didn't want to jump ahead of the investigation, nor were they putting a lot of stock in Seth having information that would exculpate him. According to the U.S. Attorney, Seth should tell police what he knew, and if investigators felt the information was strong and useful, they would come back to the issue of plea deals.

Responding to numerous messages from Seth's lawyer, Kane told her that the U.S. Attorney was reluctant to offer a deal. She said she'd go back to Seth and discuss his options.

Kane considered how this case—which less than a month ago had seemed to involve only either Vicki or Seth—had blossomed into such an unusual list of suspects. Who were all these out-of-state characters connected to Mary Jean Martin? Was she directing them to harass her lover's ex-wife, or had Seth Bader been pulling the strings all along? And why was he so eager to sell out his girlfriend?

Despite the fact that he was trying to negotiate a deal to send her to prison, Seth took Mary Jean on a two-week vacation to Florida in mid-July. They brought Joe, Matt, Sam, and Courtney with them and spent most of the time at Walt Disney World's Grand Floridian. The rest of the vacation was in Naples, near the home of Mary Jean's parents.

Just before they departed, Seth received the final recommendation from the guardian ad litem, who'd found that there was no further reason for Vicki's visits with Sam to be monitored by a third party and who would be suggesting to the judge a full reinstatement of Vicki's parental rights. This, coupled with the knowledge the judge was going to rule in favor of alimony and other financial concessions for Vicki, enraged Seth. Instead of focusing on the vacation, he kept grumbling about how Vicki had screwed him over and how much she was going to cost him in the future.

In Orlando, the kids enjoyed the park, and Mary Jean bought more Disney collectibles. Later, they drove to Naples and stayed at the Ritz-Carlton, swam in the pool, and soaked up the five-star luxury around them. While splashing in the water Seth snapped a picture of fourteen-year-old Joe—now developing the frame and form of a young man—holding a bikini-clad Mary Jean in his arms. It would be a photo that would later haunt them both.

They had two adjoining rooms at the Ritz. All the children piled into one room, and when their bodies finally gave in to sleep, Seth and Mary Jean closed the door to their own room.

And there, lying in the quiet of the hotel room, the sky painted sultry indigo outside the balcony, Seth Bader told Mary Jean his plan for murdering Vicki Lynn Bader.

PART THREE

A Code of Silence

He's mad that trusts in the tameness of a wolf, a horse's health, a boy's love, or a whore's oath.

—WILLIAM SHAKESPEARE, *KING LEAR*

EIGHTEEN

Change of Plans

The morning of Monday, August 26, 1996, attorney Heidi Boyack called the Exeter Police Department to report Vicki Bader missing. One of Vicki's neighbors, Ellie Leclerc,* said she'd spoken with Vicki on Friday, but hadn't seen her since. The attorney told the desk sergeant she didn't want to raise alarm, but it was unlike her client to be out of touch for so long.

The Exeter desk sergeant recognized Vicki's name from the pipe bomb incident and phoned Lieutenant Richard Kane at home to bring him up to speed. Kane drove to work immediately and started making phone calls with the hope of tracking Vicki down.

---

* Denotes pseudonym

"She was in very good spirits when I talked to her last," Boyack said of her client. The only thing on Vicki's mind was a concern that the custody battle with Seth would drag on for another year, but Boyack had assured her it would be over much sooner than that.

Kane called the neighbor who had reached out to Boyack. Ellie Leclerc said she left several messages on Vicki's answering machine and that the weekend newspapers were still piled at the end of her driveway. Leclerc had let herself into Vicki's house with a spare key and saw signs that no one had been home for some time. She also discovered that Vicki's cat, Q-Tip, had been left outside and wanted to get in. Leclerc told the police that when she'd spoken to Vicki the previous Friday, Vicki told her that she planned to take Sam to spend the night with a friend in Franklin, New Hampshire. Kane called Vicki's friend and left a message.

The following day, Kane contacted Seth Bader. Seth said Vicki was supposed to have met him and Sam at a pediatric specialist's office in Portsmouth on Monday afternoon, but when he'd arrived with the child, Vicki wasn't there. The receptionist told him that Vicki had canceled the appointment weeks earlier but apparently forgot to tell him. Seth said Vicki was supposed to take Sam with her after the appointment and he had yet to hear from her about future visitations.

Seth said the last time he had seen Vicki was Saturday the twenty-fourth. She'd dropped Sam off around 4:00

or 5:00 then immediately left. He said there was nothing unusual about the handoff.

Vicki's not showing up to pick up Sam really troubled Kane. He called Ellie Leclerc back and asked if she would meet him at Vicki's house and let him in. When he arrived, he saw that Vicki's bed was unmade, but it didn't look like anything violent had occurred in the house. He asked the neighbor what she had moved or touched when she came in the first time. Leclerc pointed to the pile of mail and newspapers. She had also moved some dishes that had been on the table into the kitchen sink. They were covered with the scrapings of macaroni and cheese.

"It's her favorite meal," Leclerc told the detective.

Kane then checked Vicki's answering machine. It was filled with messages from Leclerc and other friends asking her to call them back. The lieutenant heard his own recorded voice imploring Vicki to call as soon as she got his message. There was also a message from Seth, left on Sunday night.

"I just want to let you know that I'm sending the young gentleman over with a long-sleeved shirt," Seth said on the tape, referring to Sam. "I apologize. I know it's not the best choice in this weather, but we're doing laundry here. The children's laundry is all being done, which has gotten a bit piled up the past few days . . ."

Kane took the cassette tape and replaced it in the answering machine with a blank one. The lieutenant also found a half-written letter in the trash by Vicki's desk.

"She always writes out her letters longhand in a first

draft before typing them on her word processor," Leclerc noted, seeing what Kane had discovered. The note was dated "8/26/96" and addressed to someone whom Kane presumed was Vicki's doctor. Did it mean she had been home that day—Monday the twenty-sixth—or was it postdated for future typing and mailing?

Leclerc insisted that Vicki would not leave for an extended period without letting someone know and without making arrangements for her cat. And, without a doubt, Vicki would not miss a visitation with Sam.

Kane thanked Ellie Leclerc and asked her to lock up the house and to enter only to feed the cat.

Lieutenant Kane was able to confirm that Vicki and Sam Bader had spent Friday night, August 23, 1996, at the home of Natasha Woolsey* in Franklin, New Hampshire. Woolsey said the visit hadn't been for any particular occasion, but that she and Vicki simply enjoyed each other's company. Vicki had brought a bottle of wine, which they never opened. The women stayed up late, talking about their lives. Mostly, Vicki was trying to brace up Woolsey, who was having relationship problems. But over the course of several hours, Woolsey was also able to ask some pretty probing questions of Vicki as well.

The bomb incident and recent string of vandalism threats weighed on Vicki, but Woolsey didn't feel that her

---

* Denotes pseudonym

friend was in nearly the same state of crisis she had suffered in 1995. Woolsey said she had confronted Vicki directly on the subject of suicide. Vicki said it had been more than a year since her last episode and seemed sincere when she said those days were behind her.

In fact, Vicki's friend recounted, Vicki had said she was looking forward to the future, planning for life once her custody case was finally settled. Vicki said she wanted to quit her job so she could spend more time with Sam. She said she wanted to sell the house in Exeter and move in with her neighbor Ellie Leclerc, all in an effort to improve her financial situation. Vicki also mentioned that she'd like to have more children at some point but didn't want the complications of another relationship.

Woolsey said they also spent a lot of time talking about Seth Bader. They both were certain he was behind the pipe bomb and other acts of intimidation.

Finally, the woman told Kane that she and Vicki had stayed up until 2:30 A.M. and then slept in as late as they could on Saturday morning. After a quick stop at Walmart to buy something for Sam, Vicki left for Exeter at 11:45 A.M.

"I don't think she had a lot of money on her," Woolsey said, "but Vicki usually didn't have a lot of money on her anyway."

On Saturday night, August 24, 1996—two days before Vicki was reported missing—Seabrook police officer Ted Anagnos was riding in a two-man patrol car, cruising Route

1, which cut through the town village and fed the roads in and out of Seabrook Beach and Hampton Beach. While swinging around in the Vachon Plaza strip mall, his headlights caught hold of a blue Cadillac Coupe DeVille. The sedan caught Anagnos's eye because it reminded him of a car his father-in-law had once owned. It was parked facing nose out toward Route 1, about five feet from the road. Its position—all alone at the far end of the parking lot—struck the patrolman as odd. But the primary tenant of the Vachon Plaza was an adult bookstore called Leather & Lace, and Anagnos mentally wrote the car off as belonging to someone who didn't want to park directly in front of the bookshop door for fear of being spotted by a nosy neighbor.

On Monday, August 26, Officer Anagnos was on another patrol in the area. When they passed Leather & Lace, the cop again noticed the blue Coupe DeVille in the lot in the same unusual parking spot. Still, Anagnos didn't find anything particularly suspicious about the car, so he didn't stop to inspect it or run the plate.

On Tuesday evening, August 27, Seabrook police were called to Vachon Plaza by the owner of Leather & Lace, who had reported an abandoned car in the store's lot. Anagnos spoke up, saying that he had seen the car there Saturday night, so it must have been sitting there at least since then.

Seabrook officer Dana Bedell was first to respond to the abandoned car call. When he pulled in, he was met by Ivan Eaton, the owner of Leather & Lace. Eaton was a big guy—close to three hundred pounds—who wore a leather jacket, had a grizzly beard, and drove around town on a Harley-Davidson. He brought a biker's sensibility to running an adult-oriented business in a conservative New Hampshire hamlet. Eaton did what he wanted to do inside his store for as long as he could, while the town and the county officials feigned shock at the rumors of what happened in the shop's peep show and video booths.

Bedell inspected the Coupe DeVille from the outside, careful not to touch it. He treated the car like it was radioactive. Eaton, however, hadn't felt the same constraints. He tossed Bedell the keys that had been in the car's ignition when he'd found it.

"I already went through it looking for an owner. I called a number on the insurance card and left a message," he told the cop. Eaton then jumped on his bike and rode off, but not before assuring the officer that the Cadillac "ran fine."

Bedell ran the Cadillac's plate and learned that the night before, the car had been listed on a BOLO, or "be on the lookout" bulletin out of Exeter, about four miles away from Seabrook. The dispatcher advised that they suspected the vehicle might be connected to a homicide and asked if Bedell could secure the car until a detective from Exeter could get there.

Five minutes later, Eaton returned to the parking lot on his bike. "Do you have any orange cones?" Bedell asked him. "The car may be tied to a homicide and I want to secure it." Eaton considered this for a moment and said that he thought he had some cones back at his house. Again, the portly biker chugged out of the Vachon Plaza parking lot.

Another five minutes passed, and Eaton pulled in driving his pickup truck. "I didn't have any at home, but I'll go to the town shed and get some."

The other establishments in Vachon Plaza were nearly as colorful as Leather & Lace. There was a head shop, a comic book store, a fireworks seller, and a pawnshop. While they waited for the Exeter police to arrive, the local Seabrook cops started going door-to-door to see if anyone knew anything about the Cadillac. One of the clerks said he'd seen it there over the weekend. Another said he'd seen someone from Leather & Lace get in and take some items out of the car.

While Ivan Eaton continued to zigzag across Seabrook, Sergeant Patrick Manthorn and Officer Ted Anagnos arrived and roped off part of the parking lot with police tape. The adult bookstore owner returned with some orange cones in the back of his pickup truck and an uneasy look on his face. The patrolman marched up to him and let him know he didn't want any bullshit story from him.

"Ivan, I need a statement from you about how long this car has been in your parking lot and exactly what you did when you went inside the car."

Eaton told Bedell that he'd taken three items from inside the Cadillac.

"They're right there," he said, pointing to them in the bed of his pickup. Bedell noted a duffel bag, a white pillow, and a black bag that looked like a camera case.

"I don't wanna get caught up in no fucking homicide case," Eaton said.

At about 8:00 P.M. on Tuesday, August 27, 1996, Lieutenant Richard Kane got a call at home from Seabrook sergeant Patrick Manthorn, who told him they'd found Vicki Bader's missing car but that she wasn't in the vehicle. Kane's mind started racing. He called Police Chief James Gilmore, who asked to be briefed on any developments in the case. Gilmore said he would go with Kane to Seabrook to check out the car. They met at the Exeter station, where Kane grabbed a 35mm camera, and sped to the plaza. After taking some pictures, they called for a flatbed to tow the Coupe DeVille back to the Exeter police station.

Sergeant James "Rick" Kelly of the New Hampshire State Police first heard Vicki Lynn Bader's name on August 27, 1996, the day her car was found. The commander of the Major Crime Unit, Lieutenant David Eastman, called Kelly in to brief him on a phone call he had received from a detective in Exeter.

"I want you to head up the investigation. It's a missing persons case, but of course, it's likely that Mrs. Bader is dead—either by her own hand or someone else's. Get over there right away and talk to local PD. There's quite a backstory to this one."

Eastman gave Kelly a copy of the state police report

on the pipe bomb incident from March. Since their unit had dismantled the device, New Hampshire State Police already had an interest in the case. Despite all the unusual activity that had previously surrounded Vicki, Kelly drew no opinion on whether or not she had met with foul play. Her vanishing act could just as well have been a desperate attempt to get away from her tormentors. But as time went on, it would become clear to him that Vicki Bader was never coming home.

Lieutenant Kane was glad to have Sergeant Rick Kelly's help, as well as that of the New Hampshire State Police, especially if they learned that Vicki was indeed a victim of foul play. State law was pretty clear on who had jurisdiction over a homicide case. Any murder prosecutions were the responsibility of the state attorney general's office. The attorney general almost always used the state police and its Major Crime Unit to do the investigative legwork. The police departments in a handful of large New Hampshire cities had the resources to do homicide cases, but Exeter certainly was not one of them.

Sergeant Kelly suggested they go back to Vicki's house and search for more evidence there. In the meantime, a patrol of Exeter and Seabrook cops went to every restaurant and hotel within two miles of Leather & Lace to see if Vicki had turned up in any of those places.

After getting permission from Lois Stewart, Vicki's mother, and Heidi Boyack, Vicki's attorney, the police went back into the house on Patricia Avenue. Detective Kimberly Roberts discovered ten different prescriptions for Vicki in the medicine cabinet. They had all been purchased within the previous six months—likely more failed experiments by her physicians to balance her psyche. The detective took one other item from the bathroom: a hairbrush. Roberts knew that if Vicki remained missing too long, her DNA might be the only way to identify her if her body was eventually found.

Roberts contacted all the banks at which Vicki had accounts. The bank security officers reported that Vicki had withdrawn $30 at the supermarket and $40 at an ATM on Friday, August 23, but that no other activity had occurred since then. Her debit and credit card accounts were then frozen, and the banks pledged to notify the police if anyone tried to access the money.

Sergeant Kelly was able to get the New Hampshire State Police helicopter to fly over the town of Seabrook and take some aerial photographs. There were thick woods behind Vachon Plaza, and salt marshes and tiny tributaries surrounded the rest of the area. Police search teams combed the woods looking for clues. A woman's T-shirt and jeans were discovered rolled up in a bog, but they were much too small to have belonged to Vicki.

Sergeant Kelly met Vicki Bader's mother at the Patricia Avenue home in Exeter. Lois Stewart had flown up from New York to wait for Vicki. She had been in such a rush to get to New Hampshire that she made one of her sons go to Long Island just to retrieve her car. Lois was a bundle of nerves, but to Kelly she seemed to be holding herself together well. There was a gentleness between them, the kind born of a lawman's compassion and a mother's resolve.

"Will you be all right?" Kelly asked the woman.

"I'll be fine for now," she said. "I'm going to stay here in Vicki's house and take care of things, wait for her to come home." They didn't acknowledge what "coming home" might mean in this case. Kelly promised to keep Lois informed of any developments, or if anyone reported they'd spotted Vicki. Lois was polite, but she had already made up her mind. She knew Seth Bader had had a hand in Vicki's disappearance. She didn't know where or how, but Lois knew in her marrow that Seth had killed her daughter.

Kelly gave her a business card with his contact information and told her not to hesitate to call him. Lois summoned a smile of gratitude as she walked the detective to the door.

"Do me a favor. If you make an arrest," said Lois, looking deeply into Kelly's eyes, "would you call me? Call me immediately. I want to hear it from you."

Kelly pledged that he would do that and he hoped he'd be able to make that call soon. He drove away and left Lois alone to ponder the fates of her daughter, her grandchildren, and herself.

Not long after Kelly left the home, Lois heard the front door click open. She rushed into the living room. *Vicki? Could that be you?* Her heart jumped into her throat.

Standing in front of her was Seth Bader. Without her

car in the driveway, Lois wasn't sure if he'd expected the place to be empty.

"What are you doing here?" he said.

"I'm here waiting for Vicki," she said pointedly.

Seth's beady eyes bounced around the room. "I'm still the owner of this house, not Vicki." He turned his back on the grieving mother and slithered out the door. "You can stay for one more week. After that, consider yourself evicted."

NINETEEN

Brooklyn Abridged

During the 1970s, the summer noises on Olean Avenue distinguished it from its Brooklyn surroundings. Rather than the car horns that blared on larger throughways, this street echoed with the sounds of children playing, laughing, or sounding a high-pitched roar at a solid hit in a game of stickball. Olean Street, a one-way that ran diagonally from Avenue N and Avenue O, was isolated from the bustle of the rest of Brooklyn's Midwood section. Slashing its way through the city grid, the street's geography allowed for homes with backyards and lush foliage on one-eighth-acre lots. When a breeze would blow, leaves would rustle along the tree-lined street, and in the autumn, the footfalls of families would crunch atop the leaves' browned and yellowed remains.

While the children of Olean Street took advantage of their summer reprieve from school, a teenager named Seth Bader sat quietly in his room. The sounds of cheers and insults from pickup games came through the open windows, but Seth didn't heed their call. Instead of engaging with the world around him, the boy was focused intently, funneling his vision at a speck just beneath the light on his desk. He worked with a soldering gun and circuit board. He was making a transistor radio, and every so often, tiny puffs of smoke would detach from the hot tip of the gun as he touched it to a bare wire.

"Seth?" called his mother. "Why aren't you practicing your violin?" The boy ignored her, hoping she would not press the issue further. He hadn't practiced either the piano or the violin in several weeks. Seth had finally given them up. It wasn't that he *couldn't* play them—he seemed to have inherited at least some of his mother's musical skill—but he refused to capitulate anymore. He was in high school now. He thought his silence would be enough of a signal that he had outgrown the instruments, that he now had other interests that were all his own.

"Seth?" A polite knock came from the door before it was slowly pushed open. "Why haven't you been playing your violin?" Yvette Bader asked.

"I don't want to," the boy said without looking up.

"But why? I love to hear you play."

"I don't want to."

"So that's that? After all these years you're just not going to play anymore?"

Yvette's tone was harsh, fueled by disappointment. Seth's mother was much older than the other parents on the block, and she had had a lot of time to imagine what kind of child she might have. As an accomplished musician, she never thought she'd end up with a son who had no interest in music at all. When Seth didn't reply, Yvette finally put her hands on her hips and exited the room in a huff.

The young man continued making his radio, unsure whether his mother would try another tactic to get him playing again. As far as the boy was concerned, he had stood up to his mother and won. Was she hurt? He didn't think about that. Only that his point was made.

Seth Bader was in charge of his own life now.

Seth Bader was born in 1959, the only child of Yvette and Abram Bader. The boy's father had two degrees in physics and had worked toward a PhD at Columbia in the 1930s. Abram Bader's faculty adviser was Isidor I. Rabi, the famous scientist who worked on the atom bomb and later won the Nobel Prize in Physics in 1944. But Abram never finished his doctorate. Wiped out financially during the Great Depression, Abram had dropped out of Columbia and took a teaching job at Far Rockaway High School in Queens, one of the largest secondary schools in the country.

Even as a young educator, Abram had an eye for academic talent. One day he pulled aside a student who had been bored and fidgety during Abram's hour-long physics lecture. The teacher recognized the young man as an extremely bright student who was left unchallenged by the pedestrian nature of the class. Abram drew on the blackboard an arc representing the path of a thrown baseball. Explaining the possible trajectories the ball could take, he began a one-on-one lesson about the principle of least action. The student, Richard Feynman, was taken by the logic and beauty of this principle. Soon, Abram Bader was lending Feynman thick secondary physics textbooks in order to keep his attention while he taught the rest of the class at a high school level. Before his graduation, Feynman queried Abram on whether he, too, should become a high school teacher. As Abram Bader would recall decades later, he laughed at the suggestion, saying it would be a terrible waste of Feynman's talent to stay cooped up in a classroom. A career in applied sciences awaited him.

Feynman obtained his PhD in 1942 and was a key contributor (along with Abram's mentor I. I. Rabi) to the Manhattan Project. Abram's star pupil would later work the principle of least action into his own theories about quantum physics, and when Feynman won the Nobel Prize in Physics in 1965, he told the press that it had been Abram Bader at Far Rockaway High School who had set him on the path to greatness.

Abram Bader was, of course, filled with pride and joy that his favorite student had achieved so much, and that he had played a role in Feynman's success. He read every article he could find about Feynman, including a profile that featured a photograph of the now-famous scientist posing with his young son.

"My own son is five years old and insists he's going to win the Nobel Prize himself," Bader wrote to Feynman in October of 1965. "He has already constructed a time machine with his Tinker Toy set and was somewhat disappointed when it did not send him back to World War II so he could join me in the Royal Air Force."

Abram's son Seth never did get that time machine working. Time itself was always something that seemed to be working against him in Midwood.

In the 1950s, Abram Bader had taken over as chairman of the physical sciences department at another public high school in Brooklyn. There, the school's music teacher caught his eye. Her name was Yvette Rudin. In 1951, she had won the Concert Artists Guild International Competition and played in the first violin section for the New York Philharmonic.

Yvette intrigued Abram. At the time, the bachelor was pushing fifty and Yvette was fourteen years his junior, but the attraction was intellectual as well as physical; Yvette already had four degrees, BAs and MAs in both English and music, and had nearly completed a doctorate in music from the Teachers College branch of Columbia. When they met, Yvette was working on her dissertation, entitled *An Analytic Study of Representative Literature on the Art and Technique of Violin Bowing*. Although the title suggests a rather bland, esoteric discussion of symphonic playing styles, its contents revealed the writer's appreciation of the art, not just her comprehension of the technique.

"The ability to produce a beautiful, expressive tone on the violin challenges any attempts at explanation," she wrote. For centuries, she noted, teachers and musicians had argued about the finest way to render a note. "It may be that some force in nature arbitrarily defines the limits of ordinary knowledge so that the ultimate solutions, like the fabled pot of gold at the end of the rainbow, remain tantalizingly out of reach."

By 1957, Abram and Yvette were married and had moved into a tidy home in Midwood. The Jewish neighborhood was somewhat of an obvious choice, as Abram's heritage meant everything to him. In later years, the Hasidim would overflow the traditional neighborhoods of Borough Park and Williamsburg and encroach on Midwood's Reform Jewish population. But in the late 1950s and '60s, Midwood was the ideal place for Abram and Yvette to settle down and raise their only child.

The Baders were perplexed by their son's uneven academic achievements. It was assumed by his parents that Seth would go to college and get an advanced degree. After all, it was in his blood. The teachers at school all knew his parents' professional reputations. This added to Seth's academic pressure; good grades were expected from him by *all* of the adults in his life. Yet it wasn't uncommon for the boy to bring home a report card with As and Ds mixed together. It was frustrating to his high-achieving parents.

"I don't understand how you can get As in science but Ds in social studies," his father would say. "Are you even *trying* in these other classes?"

Seth always denied that he was intentionally tanking certain classes. He'd explain it away as some kind of fluke of his ability to learn. Certain subjects grabbed his attention and concentration; others did not.

"Why can't all of these be As?" his father would ask.

"I don't know," Seth would shrug.

"What!?"

"I said, 'I don't know'!"

Abram was hard of hearing, so Seth constantly needed to raise his voice. To him, it felt like his whole life was spent yelling so that his father could hear him. Over time, the yelling was so second nature that it became the way Seth talked to everyone.

Seth Bader admired his father very much, but—unlike Abram's Nobel-winning protégé—he did not yearn to follow in his footsteps. This greatly disappointed Abram, who deeply regretted never finishing his own PhD. In his career he had been mentored by—and had mentored in turn—two Nobel laureates, Rabi and Feynman. He'd hoped to produce a third one in his son. But Seth had a passion for something other than physics. He wanted to study naval architecture and design ships.

Abram Bader would hem and haw with great distress each time Seth brought it up.

"Ehhh," he'd go on, "probably not for you."

He discouraged the thought of his son going into the shipbuilding trade. It was not a growing field, as airplanes had replaced luxury liners as the preferred method of oceanic travel, and the U.S. Navy was scaling back its fleet because of the air-related military needs of the escalating Vietnam War.

Seth Bader also suspected his father's lack of enthusiasm was colored by the idea of a Jew going into a trade. It was not the normal, Brooklyn, Jewish thing to do.

Seth Bader went to a private Jewish elementary school where he mostly kept to himself. He had some schoolyard rivals, but he never got into fistfights or shouting matches like other children. Seth's temperament always seemed cool, even when he was filled with rage. Despite the erratic pattern of his letter grades, it was clear to his parents that Seth was a gifted student. They hoped a more rigorous curriculum would challenge him and keep him focused on *all* of his classes.

So when Seth completed the eighth grade in 1973 at the religious school he had known his whole life, his parents pulled some strings and had him skip ahead to tenth grade at Midwood's public high school. There, the bookish loner very much felt the cultural and age differences between himself and his new classmates. He had gone from being one of a couple dozen Jewish kids in the same class to being the youngest face in the crowd at a multicultural public school.

But if Seth thought the size and scope of Midwood High would grant him some kind of anonymity among faculty, he was wrong. Here, too, the teachers knew his parents by reputation, and great things were expected of him.

In his mid-teens, Seth gave up the piano and violin lessons, much to the disappointment of his mother. Until then, he'd been kept on a rigorous schedule of lessons for both instruments, as Yvette yearned for her son to follow in her footsteps.

Much like higher education, a love of music was supposed to be de rigueur in this household. But Seth never thought of his rejection of music as a rebellion. He just thought of it as doing what he wanted to do. His disinterest in physics, his indifference to classical music—they were not acts of self-determination; they were simply necessary. Seth was driven by just one thing: getting what *he* wanted.

Seth Bader graduated from Midwood High School in 1976, after just three years of study. He scored in the 99th percentile on the SATs. At age sixteen, he enrolled in the State University of New York at Stony Brook to study engineering.

If he'd felt like a fish out of water at Midwood, Seth was practically a Martian at SUNY Stony Brook, a sprawling campus on Long Island's north shore, fifty miles from Brooklyn. The dorms there were notorious party spots with beer flowing and coeds wandering around at all hours, an atmosphere fueled by the school-sanctioned bars in the living quarters. The drinking age of eighteen was rarely enforced, not even against the adolescent freshman Seth Bader.

But Seth was like a lamb among the lions. The boy barely drank or smoked pot; he didn't gamble or enjoy popular music. He had enough trouble socializing with students his own age, let alone the college upperclassmen who ruled the dorm.

The cultural and social divide had become too pronounced to ignore. Seth Bader was becoming self-aware, seeing himself as the other students did: a short, loud Jewish kid who was perpetually on the outside; a stranger in a strange land.

Nicholas Goldstein* was a couple of years older than Seth Bader, but he liked hanging out with the kid anyway. Like Seth, Goldstein was an engineering student at SUNY Stony Brook. He was exactly what the young Seth Bader had been lacking: someone to look up to.

Seth hadn't had the kind of father the other kids in Midwood had; the kind who would show you how to throw a curve ball, rather than lecture on the ball's path of least action. Abram, who had been in his fifties when Seth was born, had been elderly for as long as his son could remember, and he was always too serious, too intellectual to have time for sports. Like all sons, Seth was

---

* Denotes pseudonym

a born follower, eager for male leadership, but he didn't find any men he could relate to until he met Nicholas Goldstein at Stony Brook.

Seth was completely fascinated by Goldstein's hobby of collecting firearms, and on weekends, Goldstein would take Seth to his Long Island home and show off his armory. Goldstein's father was also a serious gun enthusiast. He would show the weapons to Seth and point out certain aspects of each one, such as a shorter than normal muzzle, the unusual calibers of the ammunition, or the deep grain of a wooden stock.

Seth was spellbound by the weaponry. A gun embodied all of his interests—history, physics, and engineering—in one small package. For him, a rifle was more than a rifle. It was a fantastic machine of incredible power.

One might think Seth's elderly academic parents would see his interest in guns as another form of rebellion, but if Abram and Yvette Bader veered from their neighbors in any way, it was politically. Far from liberal, they were conservative Democrats who became full-fledged Reagan Republicans by the 1980s. And unlike other urbanites in Midwood, Abram was comfortable around guns, having done some competitive shooting before his own service in the war.

At age seventeen, Seth Bader was still too young for a New York rifle/shotgun permit. Seth approached his father and suggested *he* get a permit.

"I've been thinking about getting a gun for a while,"

Abram said aloud, perhaps to convince himself. "There have been too many burglaries around here lately."

Abram Bader purchased, at Seth's choosing, a Winchester Model 94/22 rifle. It was a small-caliber version of a classic lever-action rifle, like the kind Chuck Connors used to dispatch desperadoes in the opening credits of *The Rifleman*.

"It was a handsome item of classic design," Seth Bader would later say about the Winchester. The rifle itself wasn't terribly accurate and was not a good choice for a burgeoning target shooter, nor was it practical to defend against home invaders. But now, on breaks from college, Seth and Abram Bader would drive east of the city limits to a small indoor range in Nassau County. His father may have been too old to throw a baseball around or show him how to put a perfect spiral on a pass, but Abram could shoot with his son. And Seth loved it.

Seth continued to question his own career path. He considered a job in law enforcement, but he was too short to be a cop. His friend, Nicholas Goldstein, had enrolled in law school, so Seth contemplated likewise enrolling at Hofstra University to pursue a legal degree.

For an undergraduate college assignment, Seth wrote an ambitious paper about the rifles chosen by armies and what they revealed about those nations. Seth's fascination with the mechanics of weaponry was continuing to blossom. He saw the design of every firearm as a compromise between weight and accuracy, ammunition caliber and magazine size, and scores of other factors that made each rifle unique. For example, Seth postulated that the overly mechanic nature of the Russian Kalashnikov, which borrowed liberally from European and American automatic weapons, demonstrated the Soviet lack of creative thinking. The paper went on for nearly one hundred pages, several times more than what the professor had assigned. Even Seth later admitted his conclusions were simplistic and the whole exercise was self-indulgent, but at the time he considered the work his magnum opus.

"I could turn this into a doctoral thesis," he told his parents, excited at the thought of equaling them in academia. Seth gave his notes to his mother to type. She had a musician's fingers on the typewriter and had transcribed all of Seth's assignments since high school. She dutifully took the handwritten pages into the other room and ratcheted a clean sheet of paper into the carriage.

Yet when she returned the incomplete manuscript to him, Seth noticed that the pages were sullied with typos and spelling errors. It was not like Yvette to make such mistakes; her typing had always been flawless. Abram chalked it up to his wife being fatigued from crunching out so many pages. Seth Bader suspected something worse, and he was right. This incident would later be noted as the first sign of his mother's Alzheimer's disease.

Both Seth's parents' health declined rapidly, and in concert. Abram would soon be diagnosed with cancer.

With her husband ailing, Yvette would be placed in a nursing home to deal with her swift onset of dementia. Abram died in October of 1989; Yvette passed away four years later.

Neither of his parents were there to see Seth graduate from Hofstra or marry Vicki Lynn Buzby in the spring of 1991.

TWENTY

Worse Than Her Bite

Following Vicki Bader's disappearance in August 1996, life inside the home on Doe Run Lane did not get better for anyone. Though she was gone, Vicki was still very much a part of Seth Bader and Mary Jean Martin's lives. It didn't help that they had both been interviewed about her disappearance on numerous occasions.

Mary Jean was vacillating between love and hate for Seth. Despite his ex-wife's disappearance, Seth's money situation was none the better. The court ordered him to put all of Vicki's alimony into escrow in case she returned. Mary Jean couldn't believe that even with Vicki out of the picture, Seth was still spending money on her. It did little to bridge the emotional gap between them.

One evening, a TV crew knocked on Seth's door

asking for an interview, questioning where his ex-wife was. Seth asked if he could have a moment to shave and put on a clean shirt, as it had been a long day and he wanted to look presentable. The crew waited out on the front stoop for several minutes before the door opened again.

"I'm ready," Seth told them. Once the videographer turned on his bright light, they noticed something quite curious. Seth's cheeks and neck were speckled with tiny droplets of blood.

He cut himself shaving, the cameraman thought. *He's as nervous as all hell and can't steady his hands.* The next day, the reporter called the state police and offered them a copy of the video.

Seth was now living hand-to-mouth, waiting for client fees or settlements to replenish his bank account. In quite the reversal of fortunes, he even took a loan from Mary Jean in the amount of $70,000. Seth wrote her a promissory note for the full amount and made a pledge to pay after the New Year, when his home equity loan would be approved. Ironically, Seth was likely borrowing money Mary Jean had either taken from him or raised by selling items he'd given her.

Seth decided to bury the hatchet with Sibby Caradonna, convinced by Mary Jean that the man was gay and had no romantic intentions toward her. While cruising the boardwalk in Mary Jean's Trans Am in August, Caradonna had been ticketed by a cop at Hampton Beach for having his stereo too loud. "It's a bullshit charge!" he ranted to his friends. In November, just before his court date, Caradonna called Seth and asked if he would help him fight the ticket. They hadn't ever socialized, but the Stratham lawyer decided to take the case.

"What the fuck are you doing?" Mary Jean roared when she found out. "Why are you going to be his lawyer?"

"Sibby's a good guy. I want to do it," Seth told her. Mary Jean wasn't calmed by this explanation. Seth was beginning his own friendship with Caradonna, independent of Mary Jean. It annoyed the woman, though she wasn't sure why. The more she thought about it, the more suspicious she became of Seth's motives.

In the meantime, Seth also reached out to Sandro Stuto for some help moving furniture. An elderly aunt, a distant relative of Seth's, was moving to a nursing home on New Hampshire's seacoast. Seth wanted to get some of the aunt's items to the new facility and bring the rest of the furniture to his place.

"Sure, I can-a do it," Stuto said. He drove to Stratham and met some of the other friends Seth had hired for the day. When they were done moving furniture, Seth offered Stuto a cold drink for his trouble. Stuto tossed his leather coat aside, and when they were alone, Seth asked him a hushed question.

"Hey, how much did Mary Jean give you for the pipe bomb?"

Stuto swallowed hard. "Nothing. I didn't a-do the bomb."

Seth looked surprised. He said nothing else about it.

* * *

The same November weekend that Seth was moving his aunt's furniture, Mary Jean packed up her van with dogs and supplies and drove to Texas for a national show. The ride back on Tuesday was a particularly long drive on busy highways, with the final eight hours in darkness. It was election night, and she hit traffic on the George Washington Bridge coming through New York, which made the drive even longer. The dogs were itching to get out of their crates and run around, and Mary Jean, tired of smelling exhaust fumes and canine urine, wanted to get out, too.

Sometime after midnight, an exhausted Mary Jean dragged herself into Seth's home. He had watched her daughter Courtney while she was gone, and now all four children were asleep upstairs. Mary Jean wanted to go to bed very badly but couldn't just dump the dogs in the garage. She needed to get them out of the van, cleaned up, walked, and into clean crates.

Of the eight dogs she had left behind in Seth's garage, she discovered five were covered with feces from their own crates. The remaining three looked dirty and unfed. Seth had purchased several bags of dog food for her, but he'd piled them on the floor where she was going to unload the crates from the van.

Mary Jean shook Seth awake and asked for some help moving the dog food. He rolled over, saying he had a big case in the morning and he'd left her a note on the refrigerator. Mary Jean left a snoozing Seth under the covers and retrieved the note.

MJ,

> *WELCOME BACK!*
> *Dogs are done*
> *Sandro's leather coat is on the glass table—please take to work & give it to him*
> *Please prepare grocery list*
> *Sibby called—[his dog] is dying—can you help him?*
> *I must leave early tomorrow for court—will you make sure Matt leaves on time & switch my dogs?*

> *Thanks—love you!*

Mary Jean didn't know about Stuto's job that weekend, helping move furniture. She freaked out. *Why had Sandro Stuto been in the house? Why was Sibby Caradonna leaving messages with Seth?* Mary Jean wondered if Seth was trying to create an alliance with Stuto and Caradonna, leaving her on the hook.

After taking care of the dogs, an exhausted Mary Jean finally lugged herself up the stairs to the bedroom, tossed her clothes on the floor, and rolled into bed next to Seth. She heaved a deep sigh, ready to give herself over to slumber, but Seth had other ideas.

"Let's make love, MJ," he whispered into her ear.

Mary Jean grumbled. "I've spent all day in the car and

I wanted nothing more than to go to sleep, but you stayed up here while I took care of the dogs. And *now* I have to get up early to make sure your son gets to school and take care of *your* dogs, too."

"Come on, MJ." He tried sweet-talking her. "I haven't seen you all weekend."

"No. We're not having sex."

Seth rolled on top of her, playfully trying to kiss her neck, spreading her arms wide. "Come on, baby." He grabbed her wrists and tried to hold her down. He used his knee to pry her legs open.

"No!" Mary Jean tried to kick him in the crotch but was slightly off mark. Seth got the message, though.

"If you're not paying rent and you're not making love to me," he said, "then you can sleep someplace else."

Mary Jean grabbed a pillow and blanket and prepared to sleep on the couch, but Seth insisted she leave his home. Mary Jean pleaded with him to let her go to sleep on the couch. Seth grabbed her by her T-shirt and pulled her down the stairs. He tried to shove her outside dressed in nothing but a shirt and socks.

"I'm not leaving my daughter here with you! I'm not leaving my dogs here!" she yelled, pushing back. "You're a murderer!"

To escape his hold, Mary Jean bit him, breaking the skin. Seth howled while Mary Jean slipped back into the kitchen. She grabbed a bar stool and waved it at him like a lion tamer. She then reached into the drawer and pulled out a steak knife. She pointed the tip at her lover.

Seth changed tactics. "I'm calling the police. They'll make you leave." Seth went to the living room telephone and dialed the Stratham police. He told the dispatcher he had been assaulted by his girlfriend and that he would wait in his office for the police to arrive.

Corporal David Pierce, the same officer who'd investigated the burns on Sam's buttocks, arrived on the scene with another patrolman. They separated the couple and quizzed them about what had happened. Seth said that the fighting had been going on for some time. He had a nasty bite on his right forearm. He pointed to a broken living room lamp he claimed Mary Jean threw at him. He also showed Pierce a bruise on his chest, along with a scar on his leg he alleged he'd gotten when Mary Jean had once previously cut him with a high-heeled shoe.

Mary Jean admitted to Pierce she'd bit Seth in order to get away. She claimed he had attacked her in the past, trying to push her out of the car, and one time he'd locked his son Matt out of the house so he could abuse her uninterrupted.

"There was no way I was going to leave my daughter here," she said. "I think Seth killed his ex-wife."

Pierce asked how she knew that. Mary Jean just said it was a feeling.

Instead of hauling Seth Bader away for murder, the police told Mary Jean Martin that she would be charged with breaking the state's domestic violence law. A restraining order against her would likely be put into place, and she was not to have any contact with Seth. Mary Jean was issued a summons and was then allowed to take her daughter somewhere else for the remainder of the evening.

The supposedly big case that Seth needed his sleep for was Sebastian Caradonna's noise complaint defense. Seth met Caradonna at the Hampton district court the next morning, and they entered the courthouse together. Caradonna wore a suit and sported a diamond tie tack in his necktie. Seth discussed the violation with the town prosecutor and decided fighting the ticket would be folly, so he opened his wallet, paid the $60 fine for Caradonna, and escorted his new friend from the building.

Corporal Pierce called Lieutenant Richard Kane at Exeter Police and told him how, during her arrest, Mary Jean Martin had said some peculiar things about the ongoing missing persons case. Kane had been patient, waiting for clues in Vicki's disappearance to turn up. *This might be our chance.*

Kane greeted Mary Jean and Courtney at the Exeter police department the following day, asking the girl if he could talk to her mother in private. He then asked Mary Jean to repeat some of the statements she made to Pierce about the mystery of Vicki's whereabouts.

"Several times in August, around the time Vicki went missing, I noticed Seth's Jeep was covered in mud," she said. "He said he had gone to Maine. I thought he might have gone off-roading."

Kane took down the notes. When pressed for specifics, Mary Jean ducked questions. It didn't seem like Mary Jean was going to give him facts; just her feelings.

"I know in my *heart* that Seth killed Vicki," she said. Mary Jean pointed to the $70,000 debt Seth owed her and implied the money might have paid for the killing. She also said that Seth had already sent a fax to her workplace saying that despite their fight, he wanted to get back together with her.

Kane found talking to Mary Jean very confusing, as she tended to jump from subject to subject. She was noncommittal, and every one of her assertions was speculative. Mostly, Mary Jean seemed to be choosing her words very carefully, thinking for such a long time about each answer she often forgot the original question. *She knows more than she's saying.* Kane was sure of it.

"Do you ever recall speaking to Seth about how to kill Vicki with a bomb?"

"No. Not really."

Kane reached for a tape recorder on the table. "Because your boyfriend gave us this."

As he pressed the play button, Kane noticed Mary Jean's eyes flash. She had no idea what was coming next. It was obvious that Seth neglected to tell her that in the month before Vicki's disappearance he had had many conversations with Kane in which he tried to divert attention away from himself and onto her. Seth had given Kane this tape of a recorded phone call, made in between the

July 1996 interviews Seth had with Kane seeking immunity to testify against Mary Jean.

Seth Bader's voice came from the speaker. "Are you on a cell phone?"

"Uh, no. A pay phone." It was clearly Mary Jean on the other end of the line. For a moment they talked about plans for their weekend, such as what movies the children might like to see. There was a bit of negotiating over whether Mary Jean would go out to dinner with him and whether she would stay the night. The woman in the room gazed at the cop, not apparently recalling what her recorded voice was going to say next.

"I'll speak very carefully," the electronic Seth intoned. "I was just thinking long and hard about what you told me the other night when we talked. Uh, with regard to that . . . you feel a certain problem ought to be made to go away if you were going to give me the lifetime commitment that I want. I just wanted to know, is our fifteen-foot friend still available?"

In the interrogation room, Mary Jean said nothing and betrayed no hint that she knew the "fifteen-foot friend" was Danny with Tattoos's python.

"I don't know," the recorded Mary Jean said in response to the solicitation.

"Now, you told me it was like seven or seven and a half. That was the cost of the thing?"

"I don't know. I'll have to check again. I don't know if he's available."

"Okay," Seth said. "The other thing is with regard to

the Christmas present for a gentleman that will make him ecstatically happy. Am I expected to pay for this?"

"Um, maybe chip in depending on what it runs."

"One other thing that you've mentioned to me in the past, that someone you're acquainted with could make a package delivery that was *properly made*. You know what I'm talking about?"

Kane nodded along. He was quite sure he knew that the package that needed to be properly delivered to Vicki was another bomb.

"There's no guarantees with that," the Mary Jean on the tape replied.

"But at least it will be a properly made package?"

"Yeah. From twenty to thirty, I would think."

The rest of the conversation was more small talk about their lives together. Seth said—or attempted to say—"I love you" three times; each time, Mary Jean ignored it.

"I don't recall having that conversation" was all Mary Jean said in response to hearing the tape. It was clearly her voice, but she had nothing more to say. She got up from the table and left the police station with her daughter in tow.

"Wait, Mary Jean!" Kane chased her outside. They stood face-to-face on the sidewalk in front of the police station, the winter wind blowing the flag's grommets into the pinging metal flagpole. Kane had nothing to hold her on, but he couldn't let her go.

"This case isn't just going to go away, you know."

Mary Jean looked daggers at him. She wasn't going to break.

"Seth told us that *you* were the one who placed the pipe bomb in Vicki's mailbox. You were driving around, putting flyers for a yard sale in everyone's mailbox . . ."

"You didn't find any flyers," she interrupted. "Did you?"

"No," Kane said. "But how would you know we didn't find any flyers?"

Mary Jean turned on her heels and walked away.

Later that week, Mary Jean called both the Stratham police and the SPCA to report Seth Bader for animal abuse. She was angry that Seth still had several of her dogs. No evidence of neglect was found by either agency.

On the Saturday night after they arrested Mary Jean for domestic violence, Corporal David Pierce and his partner responded to a burglar alarm at another home on Doe Run Lane. After a few minutes it was clear that the alarm had been tripped accidentally and the homeowners were safe. The officers took a moment to enjoy some idle chit-chat and remind themselves that not every house in the neighborhood was filled with drama.

Before they left, they noticed two headlights coming from deep in the woods between the houses. There was no road there, so the cops wondered who might be using the undeveloped property as a shortcut. Within seconds, from the edge of the Bader property line, a blue Jeep burst into the clearing and zoomed up the street.

The officers followed the vehicle and witnessed it make two turns without signaling and then roll through a stop sign before they switched on the light bar and pulled the Jeep over. Pierce approached the driver's side carefully and was surprised by who he saw behind the wheel. It was Mary Jean Martin. And Seth Bader was in the passenger seat.

"Miss Martin?" he said. "Can I have your license and registration?"

While Mary Jean passed him her license, Seth retrieved the registration from the glove compartment. The officer observed that Matt, Courtney, and Sam were all in the backseat.

"Miss Martin, I know you were arrested for domestic assault last week and you are in violation of the restraining order."

"No I'm not," Mary Jean said matter-of-factly.

"To the best of my knowledge, you are," Corporal Pierce replied.

Mary Jean told the cop that Seth had written her a letter saying he was going to withdraw the order as soon as court opened on Monday. Pierce pointed out that regardless, it was now Saturday, and the order was still in effect. Seth was silent throughout this exchange.

After conferring with his partner, Pierce told Mary Jean he was placing her under arrest for violating the restraining order and asked her to exit the vehicle. Mary Jean refused, repeating that she had a letter proving she hadn't broken the order.

"I'm *not* going to be arrested," she said.

Pierce reminded her that there were children in the car and there was no need for them to see the police physically remove her from the Jeep. The woman did not respond. Pierce tried to open the door but it was locked. He reached in through the open window and fumbled for the lock. From the passenger seat, Seth reached over and unlocked Mary Jean's door for the officer. With the door open, Pierce again requested she get out. She continued to refuse and even moved her hands to the center of the car, away from Pierce. He was able to get one handcuff on her left hand but couldn't drag her out. The other officer called for backup, then tried to help Pierce pull Mary Jean from the Jeep.

"If you do not exit the vehicle and consent to the arrest, I *will* pepper spray you," Pierce threatened, though he knew that realistically, with the kids in the backseat, using the spray would not be an option.

"Seth!" she pleaded while kicking the patrolmen. "Help me, goddamn it!" But Seth did nothing to interfere with the arrest.

The cops forced Mary Jean out of the Jeep, double-locked the cuffs, and tossed her in the backseat of their cruiser. When the squad car pulled away, Mary Jean glared through the rear window at Seth. As they drove off to bring her to the Stratham police station, it looked to the officers like her lover didn't even care.

Mary Jean Martin was atypically quiet as she waited to get booked. Before he uncuffed her, Pierce checked her handbag for any weapons. Among the items she was carrying was a pill bottle from a pharmacy in Medford, Massachusetts. The label said the medicine was for her daughter, Courtney, but the tablets inside were huge, far too big for a child to swallow.

"Those are my daughter's," Mary Jean insisted. "She needs to take one every day."

When the bail bondsmen arrived at the station, they discussed giving Mary Jean personal recognizance bail. Overhearing this, Pierce laid out some concerns. He said Mary Jean was already out on personal recognizance from her last arrest—less than a week earlier—and one of the conditions of her previous release had been good behavior.

Corporal David Pierce took some pleasure in informing his suspect that she'd be fingerprinted, photographed, and taken to the county jail. He also promised to get the pills back to her daughter.

"No, her father has the other half of the prescription," she said. "Those pills can come with me."

Half? he thought. *There are 65 pills already in this vial.* Worried that the medicine might truly be for the little girl and the dad could have misplaced them, the cops decided it was best to hold on to the bottle. They shipped Mary Jean off to the Merrimack County jail without the medication.

At Pierce's request, Courtney's father, Brian Messenheimer, drove from Massachusetts to pick up his daughter. A female officer had transported the girl to the police station after her mother's arrest. They asked Messenheimer if he knew anything about the pills that Mary Jean was carrying with his daughter's name on the bottle. He said he wasn't aware of any illness or condition that required the girl to take any medication. Then they showed the bottle to Courtney and asked if her mom ever made her take the pills. She said she took a daily vitamin, but no other medicine.

While they spoke, a woman phoned the Stratham police station looking for Messenheimer. It was his mother in Charlestown, Massachusetts. She said Mary Jean had phoned her from jail and asked her to pass a message along to Messenheimer, demanding that he take with him the pills supposedly meant for Courtney.

Instead, Corporal Pierce took the pills to a local drugstore and showed them to a pharmacist. "What kind of medicine is this?" he asked.

The pharmacist double-checked the label with the letters on the pills. The medicine was a combination of butalbital, acetaminophen, and caffeine. "It's prescribed for very bad headaches, like migraines."

"Is this something a six-year-old girl would be prescribed?"

He handed the bottle back to the cop. "Definitely not."

Between the blank scripts that Seth had given them in July and now this false prescription, Pierce had stumbled onto some important information for his colleagues investigating the disappearance of Vicki Bader: Mary Jean was clearly abusing prescription medicine. Could that be used to their advantage?

TWENTY-ONE

Left Cross, Double Cross

Mary Jean Martin planned to stay away from Seth Bader, but once the restraining order was dropped, they agreed to see each other again. The next time she saw Sandro Stuto, however, her paranoia about a double cross returned. Stuto was driving a new Toyota and had bought his girlfriend a ring. *Where did he get the money for these things?* she wondered.

"Is Seth planning to kill me?" Mary Jean asked Stuto. "Is he paying you to kill me?"

Stuto shook his head and frowned. "No. I've just been-a helping him move the furniture and all."

The next big dog show Mary Jean planned to attend was in West Springfield, Massachusetts, in late November

1996. Only two hours away, it was close enough that Seth could meet her there with the kids. On the Friday before Thanksgiving, Mary Jean loaded her dogs into her van and took Matt with her to the show. They checked into the Holiday Inn, and then on Saturday, Seth, Joe, and Sam drove down and went out with them to dinner. After dinner, Seth took Sam back to New Hampshire but let Joe stay with Mary Jean and Matt to finish the dog show.

When Mary Jean and the boys returned home Sunday night, she and Seth fought again. Sometime during the weekend, two of the dogs at the house had been injured biting each other and another had developed an eye infection. Then the adults started yelling about things not being done around the house—that the house perpetually smelled like urine and never had any food in its cupboards.

Joe became increasingly angry listening to the fight. He blamed Seth for the dogs' injuries. Joe took care of these dogs on his own almost all the time, and the one day they were left alone with Seth they'd gotten hurt. Joe held his tongue, as usual. But when he walked into the kitchen where Mary Jean and his adoptive father were arguing, it looked to Joe like Seth was about to strike Mary Jean.

Joe acted preemptively. The first punch he landed, a left to the right side of Seth's head, came as a complete surprise. Seth tumbled backward and landed sprawled out in the hallway.

Seth jumped up and charged his son. He grabbed Joe's sweater and tried to punch him back, but he telegraphed it so much that Joe easily ducked out of the way. This time, Joe struck Seth dead center in his face. Seth wound up again to return the punch, but Joe decked him a third time, making his nose bleed. The man let go of the boy's sweater and crumpled to the kitchen floor, fully conscious but utterly unable to act.

It was the first time Joe had ever struck anyone in anger, let alone his father. It was the first time he had shown any sign of insubordination at all. Now fourteen, Joe had a young man's build, and he towered over Seth.

Seth did nothing but lie there and bleed from the nose. He stared blankly at the kitchen ceiling. Life resumed in the house as if he weren't even there. TVs switched on, dogs barked, a door slammed. For nearly fifteen minutes, Seth lay on his back and said nothing. Eventually, he rolled over on the tile and shuffled into his office. He called his attorney, Barbara Taylor, and asked her to come over.

Taylor brought her husband with her to the Bader home, unsure of what kind of scene she was walking into. She stopped and took a moment to remove her earrings before ringing the doorbell. She was afraid something violent would happen and they might be ripped from her lobes.

When Taylor arrived, Joe left to walk the dogs. The adults huddled in Seth's office. The boy knew when he returned from his chore there would be trouble; maybe even the police would be waiting. That Thursday would be Thanksgiving. A year earlier he and Matt had run away, but this year Vicki would not be waiting in her home for them with Steak-umms. She'd been gone for nearly three months.

When Joe returned, he was ready for expulsion from the home. Would they send him to juvie? Would they send him back to his relatives in Brooklyn?

Barbara Taylor did the talking. She told Joe that he was a very troubled boy, that he needed help, and that they would provide it. After Thanksgiving, they were going to commit him to the juvenile psych unit at Portsmouth Pavilion, the same facility where Vicki had been treated. Seth's reasons for committing Joe to a psychiatric hospital were clear: to punish him for getting out of line and to paint his son as an unstable person whose claims were not reliable.

While Joe endured his two-and-a-half-week committal at the psych facility in early December 1996, Mary Jean Martin drove to Cleveland for yet another dog show. She talked with her breeding partner about whether she ought to move closer to their new kennel in Virginia.

What Mary Jean didn't know was that a New Hampshire judge had recently signed a warrant for her arrest for prescription fraud. It took investigators several days to track her to Ohio, so state police asked if officers in Cleveland could make the arrest and hold her. Their orders were to pick her up for the drug violation and not to mention the possible homicide investigation until they could fly out from New England.

Two Cleveland police officers went to the dog show and approached a woman who fit the description, telling her that they were looking for Mary Jean Martin. The blonde gave them a fake name. But the cops had a copy of Mary Jean's jailhouse booking photo with them, and they placed her under arrest, wanted in the state of New Hampshire for two counts of felony prescription fraud.

John Kacavas was a dashing, athletic young man. He had JFK's looks and his sense of optimism. The grandson of Greek immigrants, he grew up to working-class parents in Manchester, New Hampshire, and worked his way into Saint Michael's College on a scholarship. Kacavas was interested in public service and earned a master's degree in international relations from American University in Washington, D.C., before going to Boston College Law School. Though he quickly found a job as an associate at his hometown's finest law firm, Kacavas wanted to do more public service. When a position opened in 1993, he joined the New Hampshire Attorney General's office prosecuting homicides.

While Kacavas and his colleagues were elbow-deep preparing for current murder trials, there had been a rumor around the office about a state police missing persons case to keep an eye on. It had been floating in the air for months. When Sergeant Rick Kelly called him on a Saturday asking if he'd fly to Ohio with him to question Mary Jean Martin, Kacavas figured he'd use the flight to get up to speed on this phantom case.

Kacavas and Kelly found Mary Jean waiting for them in a Cleveland police station interrogation room. Her eyes immediately locked on the assistant attorney general. Kelly asked her if she was "okay," but she didn't respond. He repeated the question several more times.

"Why do you keep asking me that?" she finally said, turning from Kacavas.

"Because you look like you're in a daze," Kelly said. He told her they weren't really interested in the drug charges; the two of them were looking into the disappearance of Vicki Bader. Kelly said he knew she had information that would help their case.

They were throwing Mary Jean a lifeline, and she knew she needed to grab it. The dilemma for her was exactly *what* to tell them.

When Sergeant Kelly called his house, Seth Bader asked him to hang on a second. Kelly then heard some clicks on the other end of the phone before Seth excused himself and the conversation resumed. Kelly told Seth he wanted to talk to Joe about Vicki's disappearance. Seth said his son had gone to live with his relatives in New York.

Kelly then spoke with Seth Bader's attorney, Barbara Taylor. She told the authorities that Seth had been living in fear of Mary Jean Martin, whom he said had been cavorting with underworld types in the months leading up to Vicki's disappearance.

"Why won't Seth let us talk to Joe?" Kelly queried.

Taylor admitted that Joe had just been released from Portsmouth Pavilion and Seth worried he was too unstable to answer questions. She described Joe as a "violent kid" who had beaten his little brother badly (though there was never any corresponding evidence of that claim). "His eyes look right through you when you talk to him."

Taylor offered the investigators a hypothetical situation involving Joe and Mary Jean. "Suppose you had a young man with hormones running rampant in the same house with a woman of low moral character. Can you just imagine what might happen?"

Kelly asked Taylor point-blank if she had any proof of a relationship between Joe and Mary Jean. She said it was "women's intuition."

On Sunday, December 15, 1996, Joe Bader finally submitted to an interview with Sergeant Rick Kelly at the state police barracks. The boy was aware that Seth and his lawyer were watching him on the other side of the two-way mirror. Joe said he didn't know anything about Vicki's disappearance, even though he was among the last people to see her on August 24, 1996.

Joe had been released from Portsmouth Pavilion on December 11, 1996. He had spent his entire time in the hospital wearing a robe and slippers, doing inkblot tests and talk therapy, telling anyone who would listen that he didn't belong there. Seth had visited him twice, both times saying Joe could come home only if he promised not to yell or fight and did everything that was asked of him. Joe was more than ready to leave by Seth's second visit, so he agreed to the terms.

Unlike the previous times they'd talked to the Bader clan, the police were now armed with some inside information. Mary Jean had agreed to tell what she knew about the conspiracy to make Vicki disappear. While an immunity deal still needed to be worked out, she had shared enough details to make investigators believe they could get other people to fold. And the softest target was Joe Bader.

"If I told you that Mary Jean told the police certain things," Sergeant Kelly asked, "do you think Mary Jean would have told us the truth?"

Joe said yes.

Kelly proceeded to tell him how Mary Jean claimed Joe was part of a conspiracy to kill Vicki in Seth's home, and that Mary Jean had not been allowed in the home while the conspirators removed Vicki's body and cleaned up the house.

Joe said that was not true. Seth watched through the mirror.

Kelly asked Joe if he had a sexual relationship with Mary Jean. Joe shook his head no. Kelly asked if there had been any type of physical relationship between them, and again Joe shook his head no. The detective noted that

Joe had responded with a verbal "yes" or "no" to all of the other questions, but gave nonverbal responses to these questions.

Joe admitted writing angry notes to Vicki but denied ever threatening her with a baseball bat. "If Mary Jean said you confessed to killing Vicki that would be a lie?" The boy said that it would. Kelly further noted that throughout the entire interview, Joe showed little or no emotion.

In another room at the barracks, Matt Bader watched Patriots football on television with his little brother Sam and New Hampshire State Police corporal Richard Mitchell. Matt introduced himself to Mitchell as a nine-year-old fourth grader and said his three-year-old brother Sam didn't talk much.

"I don't like my little brother. I wish when babies were born, they'd come from the hospital already potty trained." Mitchell asked about Joe, and Matt said his older brother could be mean, but that he never hurt him.

"Do you know what happened to Vicki?"

"I don't know," Matt said. "But I hope she's dead."

"Why would you wish such a thing?"

"I didn't like Vicki. Nobody liked Vicki."

"Did Seth or Joey like Vicki?"

The boy looked at the trooper like he was stupid. "*No one* liked Vicki."

Mitchell asked Matt if Vicki had been a help to Seth

when she was around, and Matt made a face like Mitchell was completely nuts. Then the child proceeded to tell the investigator about a long list of people who pissed him off.

The next month, January 1997, Mary Jean sued Seth for the $70,000 he still owed her. She also filed a domestic violence petition against him, alleging all types of physical and emotional abuse. Seth countered with his own tales of her bad behavior. The court reluctantly ruled that while there was plenty of evidence of a troubling relationship, it didn't meet the threshold required for injunctive relief.

After working out her deal with the attorney general's office, Mary Jean Martin moved to Ruther Glen, Virginia, in order to be closer to her partner's breeding kennels and to get away from Seth Bader once and for all.

Seth was arrested on an unrelated charge on January 4, 1997, in Hooksett, New Hampshire, for endangerment of a child. He had parked in the lot of Riley's, one of the state's largest firearms dealers. A woman who recognized the blue Jeep with the yellow stripe as the car that had just been tailgating her approached the parked vehicle to discover a three-year-old boy sitting alone in the backseat. The engine was not running, and it was in the mid-thirties outside. She called the police, and the officer who responded found the Jeep's door locked. The boy in the backseat was yelling and wouldn't calm down for the officer.

The cop went into Riley's and asked for the driver of the blue Jeep. He found Seth Bader in the book section in the back of the store. Seth said he'd only been in the store five minutes and had forgotten anyone else was in the car. When the cop told Seth he'd been there for at least twenty minutes, Seth didn't argue. The officer wrote him a summons and referred the case to the DCYS.

Seth threw himself into another romantic relationship immediately after his breakup with MJ. He'd originally met Debbie Rich the same way he had Vicki and Mary Jean—through an ad in the dating pages. He'd placed this ad in May of 1994, right as he broke up with Vicki. Although he had chosen Mary Jean as his romantic ambition, he'd remained friends with Debbie throughout the years.

Once Mary Jean moved to Virginia, Debbie Rich visited the Bader house often. She believed his boys were well behaved. Only twice did she see any tension between Seth and Joe. One time, Joe wanted to use the stove and Seth gave him some grief about it. Joe yelled, "Go fuck yourself," and left the kitchen. Seth spoke to Joe privately then made him return to the kitchen and apologize to Debbie for his poor behavior.

Another time, Debbie saw them quarreling over Joe's report card, then Seth told Joe to go change Sam's diaper.

Again, Joe said, "Go fuck yourself," and walked out of the room. Later, Seth asked Debbie what she thought he could do about Joe's behavior.

"You're not going to like my answer," she told him. Debbie told Seth he was simply a bad parent who wasn't taking care of the needs of his children. He needed to cook, clean, supervise, and support, and he wasn't doing any of it.

On Sunday, March 31, 1997, Seth was in a hurry to get out of the house and go to Debbie's place. "You stay home to babysit and take care of the dogs," he told Joe. Although there were only three dogs in the house with Mary Jean finally gone, this was not something Joe was willing to do any longer.

"No way, I want to go see my friends."

Seth said no and Joe stormed off, slamming the door at the bottom of the staircase before marching up to his third-floor bedroom. Seth ran to the foot of the stairs and started yelling. "You're gonna put a hole in the wall!"

Joe bounded back down the stairs and swung open the door, slamming it into the wall and putting a hole in the Sheetrock. Enraged at this act of defiance, Seth put both his hands around Joe's throat and began to choke him.

"Let me go," Joe said calmly.

"I'm not going to let you go," Seth replied.

Joe clenched his left fist and landed one devastating blow to the side of Seth's face. The pudgy man fell backward, flattened by the single punch. Seth rebounded, though, and reached behind him, pulling out a black Browning 9mm handgun from his belt holster. He pointed it in Joe's face.

Joe knew Seth had been carrying the semiautomatic in the brown leather holster on his belt for weeks now. The previous month, Seth had agreed to defend a man accused of child pornography, and since taking the case, he'd been extra sensitive about his personal safety. Joe knew Seth liked to have the Browning already cocked with the safety on. He had no doubt there was a round in the chamber. From the corner of his eye, he could see his brother Matt watching the tableau from the bathroom down the hall.

"I'll kill you!" Seth yelled. He was breathing heavy, eyes wide, the gun waving just inches from Joe's face. "I'll shoot you in the head!"

Joe said, "Go fuck yourself."

Seth stuck the weapon back in its holster, spun around, and marched away. Relieved, Joe went back up to his room, closed the door, and switched on the stereo. He sat in his chair and wondered how to get out of this mess.

Moments later there was a rumble of thunder as Seth charged up the stairs to Joe's bedroom. Joe stood on the top step, waiting for his father to reach him. Seth had his right hand down by his side, away from Joe's line of sight.

Seth drew his hand upward and pointed a canister of pepper spray at his son. Red foam shot out and coated Joe's face. He fell immediately to his knees, coughing and trying to rub it out of his eyes. He staggered into the bathroom and searched for the shower faucet.

Seth turned around and roared as he went back down the stairs. "Next time it'll be the gun, motherfucker!"

That Monday at school, Joe's homeroom teacher couldn't help noticing that the teen's face was inflamed and his eyes were severely bloodshot. When they remained so on Tuesday, the teacher suspected that Joe had come to school high on drugs, and he was sent to the principal's office. Joe denied accusations that he'd used drugs and was sent back to class. On Wednesday, his face still inflamed, Joe was approached by the school nurse. Finally, he told her that he'd been pepper sprayed by his adoptive father.

Matt was pulled from his elementary school, and both boys were taken to the police station for questioning. With some reluctance, Joe told his tale to representatives from the Stratham police, the state police, and DCYS; Matt confirmed the story.

It was quickly determined that Seth Bader would be charged with criminal threatening and criminal assault, and the boys would be removed from the house. Joe and Matt asked if they could stay with Seth's girlfriend, Debbie Rich. As long as they felt safe there, both Debbie and the authorities agreed.

New Hampshire State Police sergeant Rick Kelly looked into Joe's eyes for a long time. "Is there anything else you want to tell us about?" The boy shook his head. Kelly gave Joe a business card with his home number and told him to call anytime, day or night, if he wanted to talk.

Seth Bader was arrested on Thursday, April 4, 1997, for his assault on Joe and was held on $500,000 bail—a staggering amount for the listed crime. But reporters remembered that Seth had publicly identified himself as the last person to see his ex-wife alive. The circumstances seemed suspicious, and the otherwise mundane arraignment soon became a media circus.

In addition to the media, the gallery at the district court was filled with police from multiple agencies, all there to watch Seth Bader. Stratham was represented by the police chief, Michael Daley. New Hampshire State Police sergeant Rick Kelly was there with two other plain-clothes troopers. Lieutenant Richard Kane, Detective Kimberly Roberts, and three other members of the Exeter Police Department took up a whole row of seats. "Just interested in the case" was all Kane would say when reporters asked about his presence in the courtroom. Despite the media interest, the law enforcement officers downplayed any connection between the assault case and Vicki Bader's unsolved disappearance.

At the arraignment, the judge reduced Seth's bail to

$5,000 personal recognizance, and the accused stepped outside to speak to a mob of reporters.

"The facts of the case are as follows," Seth said. "I have a fourteen-year-old son who is unfortunately taller and stronger than I am, and he became physically abusive to me. It's not the first time this has happened. I had to use pepper spray to subdue him." Seth denied using a firearm or threatening the juvenile. "My son has a history of violent outbursts. He has been hospitalized in the past for his emotional disturbances."

Seth walked away from the bank of microphones smiling and calm. He seemed completely in control, defiant, and almost happy with all the attention.

A week later, Sergeant Rick Kelly spent the day celebrating his daughter's first birthday. Police officers do not often get an uninterrupted day to celebrate a family milestone as many of the rest of us take for granted. Kelly had just climbed into his bed and switched off the light when the phone rang.

"Sergeant Kelly?" a halting voice asked. "This is Joe Bader."

The teenage boy and his brother had been living independent of Seth Bader for a week now. Did he finally feel comfortable? Did he finally think he could speak the truth without retribution from his father? Kelly prayed this was the moment they'd been waiting for.

On the other end of the line, Joe said, "I think I want to talk now."

Kelly leapt from the mattress, put on a suit, and drove straight to Debbie Rich's house. After more than seven months, he was finally about to learn what happened when Vicki Bader disappeared.

TWENTY-TWO

The Italian Job

The planned harassment of Vicki Bader had fully transitioned into her planned assassination as soon as Seth and Mary Jean returned from their Florida getaway. Sandro Stuto and Danny with Tattoos were laughing over beers and a game of nine ball in Brighton Billiards in early August 1996 when Mary Jean Martin sashayed in and asked whether they knew anyone who could get a gun with a silencer. The two guys offered no help. Then Mary Jean, tan from her recent trip, asked if they'd be interested in killing "the lady."

"'The man' is willing to pay twenty-five thousand dollars for both of you to do this job," she said. "Half now, half later."

Danny with Tattoos was skeptical and said he needed

time to talk to Stuto privately about it. Neither of them was thrilled about doing a murder, and they were about to turn Mary Jean down flat. Then Stuto came up with another idea.

"We'll do it for fifty thousand. Half a-now, half a-later."

Mary Jean said she'd check with "the man" and get back to them. When Danny with Tattoos asked what the hell he was doing, Stuto said they'd take the $25,000 up front then tell "the man" to go screw himself. "The man" wasn't going to report a rip-off to the police.

Two days later, Mary Jean tracked Stuto down at Brighton Billiards and said "the man" didn't want to pay that much money for the job. There was no counteroffer.

Ever since she'd called him about seeing the pipe bomb on the news, Stuto didn't like talking to Mary Jean on the phone. She called him on August 21, 1996, and spoke just long enough to arrange a face-to-face meeting. They got together at Bambino's, an Italian restaurant across from Stuto's mother's house. They sat in a booth and read from giant plastic menus.

"How would feel about driving the car away?" she asked.

"What-a you mean? Drive whose car?"

"The man is going to shoot the lady himself, but he has to get rid of her car. Can you drive it away and dump it somewhere?"

Stuto pondered it. If the woman was already dead and

someone else had pulled the trigger, he figured there was no harm in stashing her car. He assumed he wouldn't even see the body. Stuto asked for $10,000 to do the job, and Mary Jean said he'd get $8,000.

Sandro Stuto woke up Saturday, August 24, 1996, and went shopping. The day before, he'd visited Mary Jean at her legal firm. She gave him $6,000 in hundred-dollar bills. She explained the payment was less than $8,000 because Stuto had borrowed some money from her in the past and this would clear his debt.

Stuto went to Caldor department store and bought a pair of black leather gloves. He wanted to do this job like a professional and not leave any fingerprints behind. Stuto then went home and put on a pair of black jeans and a black ball cap. He also layered on two plaid shirts, a blue one and a green one, and shaded his eyes with a pair of dark sunglasses. His plan was to throw away the hat, gloves, and top shirt once the deed was done, then go to work at his uncle's pizzeria that afternoon.

Mary Jean picked Stuto up in her Astro to drive him to New Hampshire. She took him through some small seacoast towns where they scouted places to dump Vicki's Cadillac. The plan called for them to park Mary Jean's van a short distance away so Stuto would have transportation back to Massachusetts. Seth was on his way to rendezvous with Mary Jean and Stuto, to bring them both to Stratham once they planted the van.

"There he is." Mary Jean pointed to a red Trans Am on the side of the road. Seth had been pulled over by a cop who was running his license. Seth motioned to them to keep driving and that he'd catch up. Stuto noted that Seth's Trans Am looked just like Mary Jean's, but not nearly as new.

Seth took his summons for a moving violation, then signaled Mary Jean to follow him into a bagel shop. Inside, Seth and Stuto met for the first time. Mary Jean ordered a cup of coffee while Seth got a bagel with cream cheese. Stuto could not pull his eyes away from the way Seth ate his bagel. He made smacking noises with his lips and got cream cheese all over his face and cheeks. *He is a disgusting little man*, Stuto thought.

Stuto himself was too nervous to eat anything, but somehow he was the one who got stuck with the bill.

Mary Jean and Seth huddled up over an unforeseen complication. "Sandro is never going to find his way back to Massachusetts from here. There's too many little highways and side streets. He'll get lost."

"Let's have him drop the car in front of the porn shop in Seabrook. Leather & Lace," Seth said. "It's right off the interstate. Someone's bound to steal it from there."

"Where are you gonna put-a the body?" Stuto asked.

Mary Jean sneered. "There are a lot of woods in Maine," she said, cutting off the discussion.

On the ride to Stratham, Mary Jean wrote out directions to Leather & Lace and passed them to Stuto in the backseat of Seth's Trans Am. Her Astro had been safely deposited in a supermarket parking lot near the porn shop. Seth eased the red Pontiac into his driveway, and the three of them piled out. Joe Bader, wearing black shorts and a white T-shirt, was sitting quietly on the outside stairs. Mary Jean disappeared into the house. Stuto looked around for the blue Cadillac he had vandalized six months earlier. The only other vehicle in the driveway was a Jeep.

"Hey, what's a-going on here?" Stuto was suddenly jumpy. "Where's her car?" Seth didn't answer. He simply walked into the house. Mary Jean came back outside with young Matt in tow. They got into the Trans Am and left without saying another word.

Stuto and Joe followed Seth down to the gun room in the basement. The lawyer pulled out a black double-barrel pump-action shotgun with a brown wooden handle and passed it to the Italian. Stuto's head started to spin.

"Well, this is what's going to happen," Seth said. "Vicki's not going to be here until 4:00. I'm going to shoot her. But in case I miss, I need you to be my backup."

It was already after 3:00. "Whoa, whoa. That's not what you hired me for! She's already a-sposed to be dead! I'm just-a driving the car," Stuto protested.

Seth then pulled out his own handgun and began gesturing with it. Stuto wasn't sure if he was being threatened or not. Seth told Stuto he was to wait inside the office and listen for a shot. If Vicki was still alive, his job would be to block her escape out the front door.

"Make sure if I miss that you put the barrel of this shotgun right up to her chest. Don't make a big mess."

Stuto went into the kitchen to smoke a cigarette. He flicked the ashes into the sink and put the stub of the cigarette in his pocket. He didn't want to leave anything behind. Stuto wandered into the other room and stared at the dogs crated there for a long time, wondering if he would be called upon to pull the trigger. He thought about running from the home, just bolting down the driveway, but he convinced himself he'd be shot in the back before he got away.

Without a word, Seth summoned Stuto to follow him back to the office. He pulled the window shades and left Stuto alone in the office with the door closed.

The Thompson Contender was not the prettiest handgun Seth Bader owned. It was a pistol with an interchangeable barrel. It had been configured with a very long .22 caliber barrel that made the weapon look more like a rifle. Seth planned to swap out the barrel after the shooting. He told Joe he didn't want the rifling marks on the bullet to show that his gun had been used.

Seth and Joe stood on the stairs leading to the second floor because it gave them a vantage point out the small windows on the front door. Vicki's blue Cadillac appeared in the driveway at 4:00, and Seth ran to take his position.

Through the blinds in the office window, Sandro Stuto watched the blue Coupe DeVille pull up to the house. He moved to the office door and leaned against it, listening hard. Stuto made out the footfalls of a woman in the front doorway before the dogs started barking. He was still able to hear the woman walk past the home office and down the hallway that would lead her through the kitchen and into the living room. Stuto waited for his cue.

Vicki pulled her car right up to the entrance of the house. She was wearing green shorts, white canvas shoes, and a flowered shirt. Joe stepped outside and purposely left the front door open. He reached into the back of the car and took Sam out of his car seat.

"Seth wants to talk to you in the living room."

Suspecting nothing, Vicki took her purse and walked toward the front door. As soon as she made it to the entry, a cacophony of pit bull barks emanated from the house.

For Joe, it was done. He had betrayed Vicki for the final time. *I should tell her to run. I should warn her,* he thought. *But what would happen to me if Vicki just drove away?* Joe couldn't look, so he turned away from the house. He carried his three-year-old brother in his arms and walked to the dog pen in the side yard. There, the fourteen-year-old waited.

Vicki Bader never said good-bye to Sam. She had every reason to believe she would catch him on her way out the door. The worst she could have feared was that Seth had summoned her inside to reveal another legal stall tactic to delay her inevitable custody victory.

Vicki could have gone through the dining room to get to the living room, but the door was closed and a pack of pit bulls was howling in there. She naturally went to the right, passing the closed door to Seth's office, unable to hear the nervous breathing of the Italian man with the shotgun.

Vicki walked down the hallway toward the kitchen and passed two doorways across from each other. The bathroom was to her left, the laundry room to her right. She walked along with her purse over her shoulder, unaware that her ex-husband's eyes were tracking her every step.

The laundry room door quietly opened as Vicki passed by and Seth materialized with the Thompson Contender. He reached out with the long barrel of the handgun and pointed it at her head like a bony, malevolent finger. The tip of the firearm lay suspended in the air, just a whisper away from Vicki's right ear. Seth had practiced this. He had wrapped an apple inside a towel and placed it in a coffee mug to simulate a skull. He tested different caliber bullets this way. Seth knew precisely what would happen when he fired this .22.

From the position of the wound, it's unlikely that Vicki heard anyone behind her. She didn't seem to have turned her head in the least. It's unlikely Seth ever hesitated. He pulled the trigger and she dropped to the floor right in the hallway. Vicki was dead before she hit the floor.

TWENTY-THREE

Hide Your Love Away

Sandro Stuto caught his breath after he heard the shot. He opened the office door and walked out with the shotgun pointed up in case a wounded Vicki was rounding the corner. Instead, he found the woman lying in the hallway on her left side, her arm stretched out underneath her head, which was on the threshold of the bathroom door. There was some blood on her right temple. Stuto looked away quickly; he didn't want to see her face.

Standing over the body was Seth Bader, a smoking gun literally in hand. Seth was wearing a pair of large red headphones, the kind of ear protection one might have at a firing range. Stuto couldn't help but see the scene as a detached viewer might: the two men looked like a tragicomic couple, Stuto with his shades and nouveau-gangster gloves, and Seth with his beady eyes, sweaty face, and giant crimson earmuffs.

"I'll be right back." Seth dashed down the stairs to the basement, then came up with a new barrel for the Thompson Contender. "Go get Joey."

Stuto ran to the front door and called for the kid. Joe was walking nervously by the outside dog pens with Sam. He never heard the shot. As Joe went past, Stuto thought, *this kid has got a little baby's face.*

Joe carried Sam straight up both sets of stairs and into his own room on the third floor. There was a baby gate he used to keep Sam out of his things. Now he used it to contain Sam in the third-floor bedroom while they removed the body of the baby's mother.

Joe descended the stairs and found Stuto pacing back and forth in the hallway. There was no smell of gunpowder in the house, only the usual odor of canine excrement. Stuto led Joe around the corner to view the body in the hallway. Seth was squatting over his ex-wife, the weapon and new barrel in his hands. He was examining her lifeless form as if to make sure she was really dead.

Joe gritted his teeth. A rush of grief came over him when he first saw Vicki lying there. He was angry at Seth for killing her. He was angry at himself for taking part.

Seth looked up at Joe. He was breathing heavily. "Get the stuff from under the sink and start cleaning up the blood. Then wrap her head in a trash bag."

Despite the up-close shot to the head, the crime scene was remarkably clean. The bullet had not been powerful enough to exit the skull. There was only a small pool of blood that oozed from the entry wound. Vicki had died before her heart had had time to pump out much blood, and most of what had seeped out was apparently sopped up by her hair.

Joe pulled out a bottle of Formula 409 and some paper towels from the cabinet under the kitchen sink. He put on a pair of rubber yellow Playtex dishwashing gloves and went to work. Seth took the shotgun from Stuto and returned it to the basement while Stuto helped Joe clean up the blood on the white tile floor. They both moved hurriedly. Joe picked up Vicki's head with his left hand and slipped a green drawstring garbage bag over it. He cinched it tightly around her neck.

Seth came back from the basement to find his accomplices scrubbing the floor. He had with him the barrel he'd used to fire the fatal shot. Seth gave his car keys to Joe. "Back the Jeep up to the front steps and open the hatch." When he got to the Jeep, Joe put the spare tire, the toolbox, and the shovel in the backseat to clear room in the hatchback for the body.

Seth told Joe and Stuto to bring the body to the door. Since the house was gated, bordered by rich trees, and set back from the road, there was little chance a neighbor would see what they were doing. Each of them grabbed one leg and began to pull the body down the hallway. But Vicki was too heavy to drag out easily.

"Please-a Mister Bader?" Stuto gestured for Seth to lend a hand. Joe took the body by the shoulders and Stuto wrapped his arms around Vicki's waist. Seth had her feet under his right arm and led the group. They got to the front steps, but before they could lug Vicki into the Jeep, Seth had them put the body down.

Vicki's premonition had come true: she was, in fact, too heavy for Seth to easily dispose of her dead body.

"Come on, come on. Give-a me the keys already." Stuto wanted the keys to Vicki's Cadillac so he could get the hell out of there.

Seth handed over Vicki's pocketbook, and Stuto dug through it for the car keys. Joe put the soiled paper towels and rubber gloves in another trash bag. Seth picked up the kitchen phone and placed a call.

"Everything is all set, MJ. You can come back now."

At Seth's instruction, Joe washed the front steps down with the garden hose even though there was no blood on them. The boy watched Stuto jog by with the keys to the Cadillac, start the car's engine, and drive away.

Joe and Seth paced in the sunken living room waiting for Mary Jean to return. They double-checked their path for any blood. There were no visible splatters on anyone's clothes. It took another five minutes for Mary Jean to show up with Matt and some bags of groceries. As she and Matt brought the food in the house, Joe dashed up the stairs to retrieve Sam from his room. Without any other words, Mary Jean gathered Sam and Matt and put both boys back in the Trans Am. She revved the engine, then disappeared past the gate at the end of the driveway.

Seth and Joe got into the Jeep and drove the route they'd traveled earlier in the week. They made one stop on the way. They pulled into a strip mall with a Kmart and a Strawberry music store. Seth stopped the Jeep behind the stores and told Joe to toss the bag with the bloody paper towels and rubber gloves into one of the mall's trash cans.

Joe could remember saying only one thing the entire trip. "Where are MJ and the boys going?"

"The Burlington Mall." It was in Massachusetts, over an hour in the other direction. Mary Jean would do some school shopping and occupy Matt and Sam while Joe and Seth did their dirty work.

Seth took some roundabout routes, hoping to confuse Joe and make it difficult for him to find his way back. It took more than two hours to travel fifty miles. Seth needn't have bothered, as Joe shut his eyes and tried to fall asleep. When he was stressed about something, he could close the world out and drift off. He stayed this way—either asleep or just with his eyes closed—the entire ride there. But having driven this way two days earlier, Joe already knew the final destination: a secluded section of woods in Maine near a fire tower.

Counting a tenth of a mile from the fork in the dirt road, the Jeep powered its way up an abandoned hiking trail.

Seth stopped near the hole they'd prepared for Vicki's body. Joe removed the sticks he'd used to camouflage the shallow grave.

They opened the hatchback and slid Vicki's body out of the Jeep. Joe lifted her by the head and shoulders while Seth gathered her legs in a bundle. Joe walked backward the fifty feet to the grave. Seth kept getting winded and dropping the legs out of exhaustion. When they got to the edge of the grave, they rolled her body into the hole.

Seth withdrew from the Jeep the small shovel and the barrel from the Thompson Contender. He handed the spade to Joe and told him to start covering Vicki up. Not only had he forced Joe to dig his adoptive mother's grave, he was going to force him to bury her body as well.

Seth walked along the pebbled path that by spring would be a flowing stream. In late summer, however, it was nothing more than a dry bed. Seth placed the gun barrel nose-down in the soft ground and stomped on it. He pushed down with his foot until it disappeared below the mud. He also had a .30 bullet, which he stomped underground as well.

It took an hour for Joe to fill the grave, and by then twilight was falling. He tramped his sneaker on the mound of dirt to flatten it out. Seth told him to place some logs on top of the site so animals wouldn't dig up the body. He placed a call on his car phone to Mary Jean to let her know this part of the plan was completed, too. Seth drove up the path to find a place to turn around, then picked up Joe. The teen thought he'd never visit this place again.

* * *

When he sped away from Seth's house in the blue Coupe DeVille, Stuto passed Mary Jean in the Trans Am coming the other way. He didn't bother to wave.

The directions she had written out for him on how to return to Leather & Lace were not particularly accurate. Stuto drove through the same tollbooth twice looking for the right exit. He rolled down his window and asked another driver if she knew where a big supermarket might be, as this was the place they'd stashed the Astro van. She signaled him to follow her. Leather & Lace and the Vachon Plaza were on the left this time, not the right, so he'd obviously come from the wrong direction.

Stuto pulled up to the front of the plaza and parked at the far end of the lot facing the road. He unrolled the windows and left the keys in the ignition. Seth had instructed him to touch nothing, to take nothing. He dumped the car and walked away. Stuto found the van right where he had left it. By now it was 5:30 and he was late for work at the pizzeria.

Stuto raced the forty miles from Seabrook, New Hampshire, to Malden, Massachusetts, but he didn't want to pull into work late driving someone else's van. When he finally got to DiPietro's, Stuto stashed the van around the corner, apologized profusely to his uncles, then excused himself to wash up. He took off his outer shirt and the cap, gloves, and sunglasses and threw them into the restaurant Dumpster. He covered the clothing with some boxes and other refuse. Stuto then worked until 11:00 P.M. Mary Jean would be by the next day to retrieve the van.

On the drive back from the woods, Joe noticed a drop of blood on his shorts, which he probably got while moving Vicki's body into her grave. The stain was on his right thigh. He told Seth, who said nothing.

After crossing the border from Maine, Seth drove to the Fox Run Mall in Newington, New Hampshire. He bought the boy a pair of green corduroys, a tan shirt, and a new pair of shoes. Seth also bought himself a new pair of jeans from the Levi's store. They changed in the mall and threw the clothes they had been wearing all day into a trash can outside of Sears.

It was nearly 8:00 P.M., and neither of them had eaten for hours. Seth drove the Jeep to Portsmouth and parked in the downtown district. They went to The Library, one of the city's swankiest steak houses.

Seth said that Mary Jean would be home soon and that she'd put the little kids to bed. He told Joe that the next morning he'd have to wash the Jeep and hose down the tailgate and floor mats. Other than that, the father and son ate in silence, pushing pricey slices of meat through the red juice on their plates.

TWENTY-FOUR

Remains to Be Seen

Corporal Richard Mitchell and Sergeant Rick Kelly of the New Hampshire State Police picked up Joe Bader at Debbie Rich's home on the morning of April 10, 1997. It had been seven months since Vicki Bader disappeared. The trio drove to the state police barracks in Exeter, where Joe signed a form acknowledging his Benoit rights, the state's juvenile equivalent of Miranda. The three of them then went to Stroudwater Books in Portsmouth to buy a detailed map of the state of Maine, one that Joe insisted should include back roads and fire towers.

"The map Seth showed me was black and white," Joe told the investigators. "It may have been a photocopy, I don't know."

After purchasing the map, Kelly pointed his car north

on Route 1, toward Maine. Joe was certain Vicki was buried southwest of a fire tower, on a dirt path off of a country
road, and he circled the spots on the map that most closely
matched what he remembered. He told Mitchell that he
and Seth had traveled there twice that week in August,
once to dig the grave and once to bury the body.

At 11:00 A.M. the car pulled into the tollhouse parking
lot in York, Maine, where they were met by Detective
Sergeant Jeff Linscott of the Maine State Police. After
conferring with the Maine officer, the four set off toward
the first potential site Joe had identified on the map, an
area known as Mount Agamenticus in York. When they
arrived at the spot, though, Joe shook his head.

"This isn't it."

The foursome then headed toward Waterboro in Kelly's state-issued vehicle, stopping for lunch at a roadside
restaurant. At 1:40 P.M., they resumed traveling westward
on Route 202 in Alfred, Maine, toward Waterboro. A few
miles later, they passed a police barracks.

"I remember that Seth and I drove by that," Joe said,
unsolicited. A few minutes later, he asked the men to turn
around after Sergeant Linscott mentioned they'd passed
Straw Hill Road, also known as Ossipee Hill Road. Linscott explained that it wasn't uncommon for roads to have
more than one name in Maine, and that who called them
what often depended on what generation was making the
reference. After turning up the lane and driving nearly
two miles, the car approached an unpaved road used for
carrying supplies, also known as a tote road. Joe requested

they pull in and walk down. After walking a hundred yards or so, the path finished at a dead end.

"This isn't the place," Joe said. When they returned to the car, however, he indicated that they should continue driving up Ossipee Hill. Something about the place, it seemed, rang a bell in Joe's memory of the two trips he'd made to Maine with Seth Bader.

The car continued up the country road, stopping at each turnoff and fork it offered them. Each time, Joe asked if the men would walk with him down dirt lanes, and each time, he'd say the same thing. "This isn't the place."

At just over the four-mile mark from their turn off of Route 202, Sergeant Linscott stated that they'd just passed McLucas Road on their left. Joe whipped his head toward the officer. "That's it. McLucas Road. That's the name!"

Sergeant Kelly hit the car's brakes, made a U-turn, and quickly covered the short distance to the right turn onto McLucas Road. After 150 yards, the road turned to dirt, passing two small ponds on either side and a campground on the right, containing a couple of dozen camping trailers and motor homes. The campground was closed for the season.

"This is it. That's the trailer park. The road is going to fork up there." The boy, who had slouched down in his seat most of the day, was now leaning forward and scanning the road ahead. Joe was clearly excited to be on the right track, and the officers likely wondered if he realized exactly how grim the task they were on truly was.

At the 5.8-mile mark, the car came to a fork in the road and slowed to a stop. Joe was once again quiet. He pointed to the dirt trail on the right side of the fork.

"It's one-tenth of a mile down that way."

Corporal Richard Mitchell, Sergeant Rick Kelly, and Joe Bader got out of the car and walked down the roadway. The woods of New England are nothing but mud in the spring, deep enough to suck a loafer off the foot of a plainclothes detective, so Sergeant Linscott stayed with the car, making notes and readying himself to call for more investigators to come to the scene. It was 2:30 in the afternoon when they reached the spot in the road where Joe indicated they should stop walking.

The place had changed. The dry summer bed that had run parallel to the road was now a rushing spring stream, fueled by the melting snow from the mountains. There were still patches of snow in the shadows where sunlight had trouble piercing through.

"This is it. The gun, bag, and gloves are buried right under that stream," Joe said. Then the teenager swallowed and pointed toward a small mound just off the path. "Over there," he said, indicating Vicki's grave. "That small pile."

Mitchell examined the mound. While the ground had not completely thawed from winter, there were several small holes in the pile, likely dug by mice. He peeked down one of those dark holes and could just make out something green-colored at the bottom.

Kelly asked Joe several times if he was sure this was the right spot. "Yes," he said, "I think so."

"Who put those logs there?" Kelly asked.

"I put them there." Joe continually looked back and forth from the brush pile to the stream. The sergeant noted that the teen seemed anxious.

"Are you okay?" Kelly asked the boy.

"Yeah," he said, swallowing loudly.

"Want to go back to the car?"

"Sure."

Maine's medical examiner, Dr. Henry Ryan, was not in any rush to drive to Waterboro to exhume a body. "The ground is still too frozen," he told Sergeant Linscott. Where the ground wasn't already mud, they would need a jackhammer to punch through the turf. Ryan suggested they try to warm the ground around the grave to cause it to thaw. It was the only way to dig down to the body without damaging it.

The Maine State Police erected a tent made of green plastic tarps over the burial site, then placed a few space heaters in the tent. They also laid two-by-fours on the ground right over the body, believing the wood would conduct the heat and focus it right where they wanted to dig. Dr. Ryan was pleased, and he told the cops to call him in a day or two.

While they waited for the ground to thaw, Corporal Richard Mitchell was frustrated that the Maine State

Police had yet to find the gun barrel that Joe said had been buried in the waterway. It had been a long day. He was cold and splattered with mud. The New Hampshire detectives had come all this way to find a body; why couldn't the Maine police just locate the gun?

What was really getting under Mitchell's skin was the way the Maine troopers were scanning the stream. They were using a metal detector to skim the top of the water, but the device never registered a signal noise.

"But it's buried under the stream," he tried to explain. "You have to put the detector *in* the water, on the floor of the stream bed."

The Maine troopers wouldn't hear of it. "This is a brand new metal detector. It could short-circuit if we put it in the water."

Mitchell rolled his eyes. He'd plead his case to someone else, but he could tell the officers were not about to sacrifice their newly appropriated equipment for a piece of evidence in a New Hampshire murder.

Once dusk fell, Mitchell waited for his chance. While the Maine troopers huddled to discuss crime scene logistics for the coming days, Mitchell picked up the metal detector and brought it to the edge of the stream.

"Hey, hey!" someone shouted at him. "No, no. Don't do that!"

Mitchell pushed the coil through the surface of the water and onto the pebbles below. Immediately, the device let out a squeal, which died as soon as an angry Maine state trooper pulled the metal detector from Mitchell's hands. The officer tried to get the equipment to work again, but it wouldn't make a peep.

"You shorted it out!" he accused the New Hampshire detective.

The other troopers examined the device and discovered that the magnetic coils were fine. Mitchell had just jammed the handle; that's why the detector shut down.

"It didn't short out," Mitchell said sheepishly. "So why not give it a try underwater now?"

The Maine trooper eased the metal detector's base back into the water and made a pass or two. Nothing registered. Then it began to get a reading. The trooper moved a step or two and heard the detector squeal. He had placed the coil in the exact same spot as Mitchell's mutinous scan. Miraculously, Mitchell had haphazardly placed the metal detector directly on top of the object they had been searching for. They had found the barrel to the murder weapon.

"I'd rather be lucky than good," Mitchell would later say.

By April 11, 1997, the process of slowly heating the ground around Vicki Bader's body had been successful enough that Dr. Henry Ryan believed they could begin the tedious process of exhuming her remains.

Ryan and forensic anthropologist Marcella Sorg began by determining the limits of the grave, delineating the edges of the hole. They dug into the undisturbed soil around it and worked their way inward to the looser, previously shoveled ground in the center of their search grid. They began with trowels, and when they finally came to Vicki Bader's head, they switched to camel's hair brushes.

Ryan and Sorg transported Vicki Bader to Augusta, Maine, where they were able to make a positive identification using dental records. The autopsy showed there was a small hole in Vicki's skull, low behind her right ear. Ryan measured it as around seven millimeters, but the condition of the corpse made it nearly impossible to determine the exact diameter. Anything smaller than a .32 caliber bullet could have made the hole. X-rays of the skull showed no bullet, but there were traces of fine, gray soft metal consistent with lead inside her head. There was no evidence of an exit wound.

On April 12, 1997, Seth Bader was at an expensive seafood restaurant on Boston's waterfront when he received a message to come to the state police barracks in Epping, New Hampshire, to discuss "something important." Sergeant Rick Kelly watched for Seth's Trans Am. He later said it appeared to have been doing 100 miles per hour when it screeched into the parking lot.

At 9:00 P.M. on the day of the autopsy, April 12, 1997, Sergeant David Kelley (no relation to Sergeant Rick Kelly) of the New Hampshire State Police Major Crime Unit sat down with Seth Bader at the state police barracks. The sergeant, who had never previously had any interaction with Seth, told him that he had important information to share about his ex-wife's disappearance.

"Is this about the children?" Seth asked.

"It's about both the children and Vicki," Kelley replied.

Once he established that Seth was settled into the interview, Kelley began talking.

"I've been monitoring the case of your ex-wife's disappearance, and though I haven't been directly involved, I've heard a lot about it, and I've heard that you've been under a lot of strain."

Seth nodded vigorously, as if relieved that the sergeant was empathetic to the pressure he'd been living with. "I've had nothing but bad luck since I've moved to this state," he replied, "and have been under all sorts of stress since I married Vicki."

"Well," Kelley said, "one thing I know about you is your propensity for talking . . ."

"I have to defend my reputation!" Seth interjected. "With the press, and what's been going on with Joe . . ."

Kelley held up his hand to silence Seth. "I'm not interested in talking about that," he said. "Just be quiet for a second and listen to me. What I'm about to tell you is very sensitive in nature."

Seth leaned forward and nodded. The sergeant had learned enough about the man to know he'd be drawn in by the idea of being privy to something important.

"There's one thing I've learned as an investigator, Seth,

and that is that everything happens for a reason. As an investigator, answering the questions of the *who*, *what*, and *where* something happens is pretty easy to figure out, through interviews and evidence and such. But figuring out the *why*, now that's the real challenge."

Seth nodded solemnly.

"Take someone who commits suicide, for example. When you arrive at the scene, it's pretty obvious what happened, right? But the key is finding out *why*. That's where the real answers are.

"Now, Seth, the reasons aren't always apparent. As investigators, we gather evidence, and theories about the *why* start to emerge. It's a picture, of sorts, of what really happened. Take your life for the past year. The custody litigation, the problems with Joe, Vicki's disappearance, that's a lot to have happened to one person."

Again, Seth nodded. Kelley took advantage of the man's silence and continued.

"I want to share something with you, and I want you to keep in mind everything I just said to you. I—we—the investigative team have been talking to a lot of people. People who know you. We've talked to Mary Jean Martin, Danny Payne . . ."

"I don't know any Danny Payne," Seth interrupted.

Unfazed, Kelley continued, "Sandro Stuto . . ."

"Oh, yeah, I know him."

"How do you know him, Seth?"

"He helped me move some furniture," Seth replied.

Kelley made a note before continuing, "And Sebastian Caradonna?"

"Yeah, I know him really well. I met him through my girlfriend, Mary Jean."

"Well, we've also talked to your son Joe. And what you need to know is that all these people have painted a very clear picture for us of an end result. Let me show you what that end result looks like."

Kelley reached into a manila folder sitting on the table between him and Seth Bader. He pulled out a photo of a dirt path flanked by trees.

"Is that my backyard?" Seth asked.

"No," Kelley replied. "That trail is in Waterboro, Maine."

"I don't even know where that is," Seth replied, rubbing his head.

Kelley pulled out a second photo of a hole in the ground, in which was sitting a long .22 caliber gun barrel. He asked Seth if this type of barrel would fit a particular gun Seth owned, a Thompson Contender.

"The Thompson Contender has interchangeable barrels," Seth confirmed. Kelley nodded, pulling out a third photo of a pair of muddy sneakers.

"Do you know who was wearing these sneakers?" Kelley asked Seth.

"No."

Kelley pulled out a final photo and tossed it on the table between him and Seth.

"This is the end result, Seth." He was pointing to a photograph of Vicki Bader's unearthed body.

Seth responded in a way Kelley would later describe as forced and unemotional.

"Oh my God," he said. "Is that body Vicki?"

"Yes. That is your wife."

Seth paused, then said, "She wasn't my wife. She was my ex-wife."

"Seth," Kelley said calmly, "I'd like to give you a chance to tell me your side of the story."

"Am I under arrest?"

"No, Seth, you're not."

Indignant, Seth rose to his feet. "Well, if you have all that information, why aren't you charging me?"

Kelley left the room for a moment, then returned with another officer.

"Seth Bader," Kelley said, "you're under arrest for first-degree murder." When Kelley was done reading him his rights, Seth Bader stared at the sergeant and asked him just one question.

"Can I have a candy bar?"

PART FOUR

On Trial

The law hath not been dead, though it hath slept.

—WILLIAM SHAKESPEARE, *MEASURE FOR MEASURE*

TWENTY-FIVE

Building the Case

When Seth Bader was arraigned in Exeter District Court for first-degree murder on Monday, April 14, 1997, his demeanor was far different than it had been just ten days earlier when he'd faced assault charges against his son Joe. Then, he'd been defiant, certain he would be walking out of the courtroom. This time, however, Seth would not be going home—he'd be returning to his jail cell in the Rockingham County House of Corrections.

Only a handful of details about the crime were revealed in open court. The state said that Seth and several "co-conspirators" had murdered Vicki Bader and buried her remains in Maine. The prosecutor also noted that the children had been removed from the house before the shooting.

"I'm pleading not guilty, and I have no further comment

at this time," Seth told reporters as he was escorted into the courtroom. Sitting next to her client in court, Barbara Taylor was in shock, unable to believe how the divorce case she'd taken on three years prior had led to this day. She was not alone at the defense table. On Sunday, Seth had hired attorneys Mark Sisti and Paul Twomey to represent him in the homicide case. Sisti and Twomey ran the best criminal defense firm in New Hampshire and had been stars of some of the state's biggest trials. Their presence signaled two things to the prosecution: Seth had money to spend, and he wasn't looking for a plea deal—he was playing for an acquittal.

Paul Twomey's full head of white hair made him look like a patrician lawyer on a TV courtroom drama, but his upbringing was far more blue-collar than blue-blooded. He was the son of a disabled World War II army vet from Worcester, Massachusetts, one of eleven children. When he graduated from high school, Twomey wanted to join the armed forces and go to Vietnam, but his mother—whose father had also been a disabled vet, from World War I—convinced him that coming home wounded was no way to live his life.

Instead, Twomey got a scholarship to Yale as a political science major. His roommate was a young man named Howard Dean, and the pair enjoyed taking the type of antiestablishment classes so popular in the early 1970s. Dean would later graduate from medical school, serve six terms as governor of Vermont, and become a leading figure in the Democratic Party. Twomey also had ambitions of public service. A college service project required him to accompany disadvantaged minors into New Haven, Connecticut, courts, where Twomey first saw public defense as a noble undertaking.

After graduating from law school, Twomey moved to Wisconsin, where he represented local Indian tribe members, then eventually he and his wife—also an attorney—moved back to New England. He and fellow public defender Mark Sisti worked on fifty homicide cases together before striking out on their own in private practice.

Sisti and Twomey became legal celebrities when they defended Pamela Smart in 1991. The high school teacher had been accused of seducing a student and convincing him to murder her husband—a story later fictionalized in the Nicole Kidman film *To Die For.* The fourteen-day trial was among the first to be seen live on television by millions of people. Despite ultimately losing the case, Sisti and Twomey became forever cemented in the minds of the public as Northern New England's premier defense team.

Twomey was already juggling several homicide cases when Seth hired him. The more he observed his client, the more intrigued he became about the crime. He perceived Seth as completely socially inept, unable to take care of his children or himself. Everybody had taken financial advantage of him. Seth Bader, Twomey thought, was the perfect fall guy to set up for a murder.

On Friday, April 11, 1997, the same day that pathologists were meticulously digging Vicki's body from the frozen Maine woods, Massachusetts State Police investigators paid a visit to Sandro Stuto at his new job selling cars at a Toyota dealership. Stuto said he was busy but would be happy to talk to them on Monday. As soon as the cops left, Stuto phoned Sibby Caradonna and Seth Bader in a panic, seeking legal advice.

On April 14, the same day that Seth was arraigned for the homicide, Stuto showed up at the Massachusetts State Police Detective Unit as requested. Instead of talking, Stuto handed a trooper the business card for his new criminal defense attorney and walked out of the building.

A state police forensics unit scoured the Stratham house for any trace of Vicki Bader's blood. They examined all rooms without any luck. They were also unable to find anything in Seth's Jeep.

The autopsy determined that Vicki had been shot with a small-caliber bullet that did not exit her skull. But despite Joe Bader and Mary Jean Martin having told investigators that Vicki was murdered inside the home on Doe Run Lane, the team was unable to turn up any splatter or trace evidence of blood pools anywhere.

A neighbor also told the team that the previous September, sometime after the murder, Seth had had his home's floors resanded.

Vicki Bader's mother, Lois Stewart, had asked Sergeant Rick Kelly for only one favor: that he call her immediately if an arrest was made in her daughter's case. He did so on Saturday night, minutes after they cuffed Seth. She was heartbroken to hear about the discovery of Vicki's body, but grateful that Kelly had kept his word to her.

Immediately following Seth Bader's arraignment, Heidi Boyack and her legal partner John Lewis filed a wrongful death suit against Seth on behalf of Vicki's children. They did so at Lois Stewart's request. Later that week, the registry of deeds attached two million dollars against Seth's assets.

On April 24, 1997, Sandro Stuto and Sebastian Caradonna were arrested in Massachusetts for the pipe bomb incident. The charge was possession of an "infernal machine" and reckless conduct. Arraigned the next day, the two said they would fight extradition to New Hampshire.

Mary Jean Martin had gotten her own lawyer after her Ohio arrest and eventually agreed to tell prosecutors everything she knew about the murder of Vicki Bader. If she were to answer truthfully, her deal stated that she would receive immunity for anything she told prosecutors. Approximately a week before Seth pepper sprayed Joe, Mary Jean met with Sergeant Kelly to tell him what she knew.

Mary Jean told Kelly that Seth, Joe, and Stuto pulled off the murder in Seth's home while she was innocently out grocery shopping with Matt. Stuto had taken her van, without her knowledge, as part of his mission to dump Vicki's Cadillac. The day of the killing, Mary Jean said, Seth mysteriously banned her from the house until after Vicki had left, and afterward, she took Sam and Matt back-to-school shopping at a mall in Massachusetts fifty miles away. She said she had no idea that Vicki was walking into a trap and didn't learn what really happened until Joe confessed to her in November, when they were at the dog show in Western Massachusetts.

Kelly wasn't convinced. He showed Mary Jean her bank statements, which detailed large deposits coinciding with each harassment of Vicki Bader. There were also canceled checks from Mary Jean to Sandro Stuto. Mary Jean said the money had come from Seth and was supposed to pay for yard work and other jobs around his house.

"Did you know you were paying him money to help kill Vicki Bader?" Kelly asked. Mary Jean said she did not, but later in the interview she said that at the time she'd "had a feeling" that it might be used to hurt Vicki.

"But it implicates you," Kelly continued, "because you know you're the middle man for the money."

"I didn't feel I was," she responded.

Mary Jean then said that Seth had told her during their Florida vacation that he wanted to murder his ex. Seth detailed a plan where he would shoot Vicki in the head, and Mary Jean would be the backup shooter who would only have to fire if Vicki tried to escape. Mary Jean said she had cut Seth off in the middle of telling her his plan. She said she told him she didn't want to hear anything about killing his ex-wife and didn't care if Vicki "lived a hundred more years."

After his arrest, Sibby Caradonna agreed to a plea bargain but exhibited limited memory for details of his own participation in the crimes. Mostly he told prosecutors about the times he'd refused Mary Jean's solicitations for murder and the fact that she'd brought a pipe bomb to his house. He also said he'd been bedridden with the flu the week of the killing, which he said accounted for why Mary Jean hadn't included him in the final plot.

Sandro Stuto got the same deal from prosecutors as Caradonna, but he was more than willing to spill everything about the conspiracy and its members. He freely dished on the many times Mary Jean had asked him to commit various petty crimes, even chauffeuring him and Caradonna to Vicki's house and workplace. Stuto refuted Mary Jean's claims that she didn't know he took her Astro van the morning of August 24; he said she'd helped him pick the supermarket parking lot in which to leave it.

These revelations were troubling to Assistant Attorney General John Kacavas. If the hired muscle in this plot was to be believed, Mary Jean Martin wasn't just a witness to a murder conspiracy. She was an active participant, perhaps even an instigator. And he had already cut her an immunity deal.

On May 1, 1997, Mary Jean and her lawyer, Richard Foley, were summoned for a follow-up meeting with Senior

Assistant Attorney General Michael Ramsdell, the head of the Attorney General's Homicide Unit and Kacavas's boss. Ramsdell laid out the problems with Mary Jean's statements from March 1997 and how they weren't jibing with what Stuto, Caradonna, and Joe Bader had told them.

Ramsdell pushed hard on Mary Jean, but she wouldn't back down. She insisted that she had had no knowledge that Vicki would be killed on August 24, 1996. Ramsdell said Joe claimed she took Matt from the house to go grocery shopping specifically because she knew Vicki was going to be murdered.

"That's not true," Mary Jean exclaimed. "I'll even take a lie detector test to prove it."

On May 7, Ramsdell watched as state police polygraph technicians quizzed Mary Jean. The test focused only on two issues: whether Mary Jean participated in the pipe bomb incident and whether she knew "for certain" that when she left Seth's home, Vicki was going to be killed.

The tech reported that when asked these questions, Mary Jean displayed "significant physiological responses." It meant her body was contradicting what she was saying. On the polygraph scale, anything below a -6 would be considered "deception." Mary Jean's scores for both questions were -23 and -16. She'd failed the polygraph by every standard.

Later that month, Mary Jean Martin was arraigned on felony bomb conspiracy charges, but she was released on personal recognizance. Later in the summer, she would be indicted by a grand jury for conspiracy to commit murder.

*   *   *

In early May 1997, Seth's attorneys Sisti and Twomey filed a motion for a bail hearing. Normally, bail was denied for those charged with a homicide, but they pointed to an obscure law that said bail shall be denied "where the proof is evident or the presumption great." Twomey argued that such proof was not evident, and he wanted to argue it in open court.

"It's really an interesting little motion," Twomey said. The loophole in the law had been discovered by his client, Seth Bader, while scouring the inmate law library.

On May 15, 1997, the parties appeared before Judge Walter Murphy, a former varsity football coach and chief justice of the superior court. The state was represented by Ramsdell. The bail hearing essentially required Ramsdell to lay out the facts of the case before trial. It wasn't unlike a probable cause hearing, but the evidentiary rules were different. The burden was not to prove guilt beyond a reasonable doubt, but simply to show that the preponderance of evidence was enough to deny Seth Bader bail.

Ramsdell told the court that much of the state's evidence had been provided by Joe Bader. He'd led them to Vicki Bader's body, and the now fifteen-year-old told them that he had agreed to take part in the murder. Joe had told the cops that after Seth shot Vicki, he and a man he didn't know had helped remove her body from the house, and that Joe had buried her in the grave Seth had made him dig in advance. Ramsdell said the state's evidence was consistent with the story Joe told them.

Defense attorney Twomey complained about the state's case.

"Almost all the evidence offered by the state is offered exclusively by Joseph Bader!" he argued. He then described Joe and Matt's difficult upbringing, saying the brothers were "damaged goods." Twomey said that letters written by Joe would prove the boy hated Vicki Bader, and that Joe had recently been hospitalized for violent outbursts.

Ramsdell objected. "I don't think it's this court's function to make a credibility finding." But Twomey countered that the evidence used to deprive Seth Bader of his liberty was being provided by a juvenile with a "major mental illness." Twomey asked the judge to compel Joe to testify.

Judge Murphy pondered the legal dilemma before him. He told the attorneys he'd hear arguments from them the following week on whether or not Joe should be compelled to testify before concluding the bail hearing.

The defense strategy was clear: to force the state's hand and compel their star witness to testify before trial. If they could impugn Joe on the stand, force the teenager into contradicting himself, it could be fatal for the prosecution before a jury had even been selected.

After weighing the risk/reward of putting Joe on the stand at this stage of the game, the prosecution withdrew its objection to bail for Seth Bader. The courtroom gallery was stunned at the thought of a homicide defendant walking around free; it was without precedent in New Hampshire. Judge Murphy set bail at $750,000 cash. Seth smiled broadly at the thought of being released, considering it a victory. But Twomey and Sisti left the hearing uncharacteristically quiet.

Seth made arrangements to secure the money and go home. But when he tried to access his funds, he was denied. The attachment in the pending civil wrongful death suit brought by Vicki's relatives had effectively cut him off from his money. Seth had won, but he had also lost. He would have to stay in jail for as long as a year before his trial.

Sisti and Twomey were not the only lawyers trying to outflank the attorney general's office. Richard Foley could not believe that his client, Mary Jean Martin, had been charged with conspiracy to murder by prosecutors, effectively reneging on their immunity deal.

The state claimed it was able to independently obtain the facts for their indictment after interviewing Joe Bader. The document they disclosed listed Mary Jean's illegal solicitations of Sandro Stuto. The problem, Foley realized, was that at the time Joe talked to police, he didn't know Stuto's name. There was no way the prosecutors could have gotten those details without Mary Jean.

Foley asked Judge Murphy for a hearing to argue that Mary Jean's right against self-incrimination had been violated and that her immune statements could not be used against her. Ramsdell, arguing for the state, said that the information used to indict Mary Jean hadn't come from her own statements, but from independent sources and investigation unrelated to her interviews. Foley countered by asking Judge Murphy to compel the state to prove Mary Jean's statements were not the basis of her arrest and indictment.

Gathering documentation at the attorney general's office, Ramsdell came to a distasteful realization: the indictment against Mary Jean Martin was fatally flawed. Of the ten material facts offered in the indictment, the state could only prove seven of them could have been obtained without Mary Jean's statements.

In court, the state admitted it couldn't satisfy the defense's request. As a result, Ramsdell, Kacavas, and prosecutor Joseph Laplante all recused themselves from the case against Mary Jean Martin. Judge Murphy said he had no choice but to throw out the indictment against Mary Jean.

Foley, seizing his chance, asked that the indictment be dismissed with prejudice, meaning the charges could never be filed against his client again. The state instead moved that the charges be dismissed *without* prejudice, preserving the chance of prosecuting Mary Jean down the road. Murphy said he would wait to determine the status of the dismissal until after the murder trial of Seth Bader, at which time he would hold a hearing on possible prosecutorial misconduct.

This was a major blow for the prosecution. Without either an immunity deal or an indictment against Mary Jean, she was not likely to be a cooperative witness at trial.

Moreover, there was a chance that a key conspirator in this murder could walk away scot-free.

The defense won some other important motions that would shape the nature of the trial. The state would not be allowed to present evidence of neglect or abuse of the children, nor could they discuss any of Seth's previous "bad acts," including his prostitution arrest. Peculiarly, both sides and the judge agreed to allow Mary Jean's polygraph results to be admitted as evidence (the first and only time anyone associated with the case can recall such a move). Both sides believed her deception bolstered their arguments, so Judge Murphy allowed it. Other motions were pending, such as presenting testimony that Sandro Stuto had bragged to other detainees that he was mob-connected and a "bone-breaker." And everyone knew a blistering cross-examination awaited the simmering, sulking teenager who was the state's star witness.

Despite being outmaneuvered by Seth's defense team in the opening round of the case, the prosecution had gotten a peek at Sisti and Twomey's cards. The defense was going to focus on discrediting Joe Bader, and they would use the specter of an absent Mary Jean Martin to sow the seeds of doubt in the minds of the jury. After all the indignities that Seth had put Joe through, he was going to add one more to the list. He was going to blame the murder of his ex-wife on their adopted son.

TWENTY-SIX

Criminal Lawyer

When Seth Bader arrived at the Rockingham County House of Corrections to await trial, he immediately tried to resume his law practice. This time, though, his prospective clients were fellow inmates who were themselves awaiting trial, or who had been convicted of crimes with sentences at the county jail. The unit where Seth was assigned housed nine other men.

Brian Gumbs* was only a year into his three-year sentence for misdemeanor theft. A recovering alcoholic, Gumbs was an electrician by trade, but he spent his days in the unit reading and researching law and had become popular by helping his fellow inmates with their motion

---

* Denotes pseudonym

writing. Seth, upon hearing Gumbs was doing this work, tried to befriend the man right away, giving him advice about the motions.

"You know much about the Pam Smart case?" Seth asked Gumbs, who was already wishing the overly talkative little man hadn't landed in his pod a few days ago.

"Sure, everyone knows about that."

"Did I tell you that my fiancée, MJ, went to that trial every day?"

"Uh, really?" After only a few days, Gumbs had already learned it was often easier to just let Seth talk.

"You know Pam Smart slept with the kid who did the killing, right? She was stupid, though, I could have done that crime way better."

"What do you mean, you could have done the crime better?"

"Well, she fucked the guy who killed [her husband] just like MJ fucked my son Joe."

Gumbs didn't like the way Seth talked about women. His liberal use of the word "cunt" and his constant bragging about his sexual exploits were becoming offensive to even the most hard-boiled inmates in the pod. But this was too bizarre to just let lie. "Wait, you're saying your son had sex with your girlfriend?"

Seth nodded. "Yeah. Joe has all sorts of problems. He's crazy. I even put him away once. There was another time he threatened me, and I had to pull a gun on him. A little pepper spray in the face finally made him back off, though."

Gumbs was even more taken aback. "Are you saying your son was the one who killed your wife?"

"Ex-wife," Seth said casually as he rubbed the top of his head. "You know, the little fuck is probably going to get immunity, and then I'll really be screwed."

A few days later, Gumbs and a few other inmates were watching TV when Seth walked into the common room. A rerun of *Law & Order* was playing, and Sam Waterston was talking to the jury about the ballistics evidence in the case he was trying.

"They always get it wrong on these fucking shows," Seth said loudly. "Anyone who knows anything knows you can make it so they don't know what the fuck kind of gun someone got shot with."

As he usually did, Seth had found a way to dominate the room, despite the men's attempts to ignore him. Gumbs motioned Seth over to the table where he sat and asked if he wanted to play cards. Seth had told Gumbs that aside from Seth himself, he was the smartest guy in here.

"I know you really get what I'm trying to tell you," Seth had told Gumbs repeatedly.

Two other inmates from the pod came over to join the card game.

"What did you mean by that gun thing?" a man named David Nash* asked. Nash was being held while awaiting trial

---

* Denotes pseudonym

for felony burglary. When Seth found out that Nash used to be married to a woman who worked for the New Hampshire department in charge of welfare, he'd tried to make friends with him, too, pumping him for information about how the agency kept records on minor wards of the state.

"The cops found a .22 long gun barrel by my ex-wife's body," Seth said. "But that was just a decoy. They can't even determine the type of bullet that was used, because once it went in her head, it just disintegrated." Seth made a motion with his hands to demonstrate an explosion. "You want the job done well, you use a small-caliber bullet like that."

Gumbs and Nash looked at each other. It never got any less bizarre to them that Seth would talk about his untried case so openly, and with so little emotion.

"So, your son knew what he was doing?" Gumbs was having a hard time keeping up with all the versions of events Seth had laid out for him.

"Well, I put him up to it. You know, after I had him roast the birds. You know that her house was just a mile from Joe's school, right? He was able to walk right over there and put those fuckers in the oven, and then just walk away." Seth smiled. "That's what the bitch gets for costing me so much damn money."

Seth looked down at his hand.

"Gin," he said, laying his cards on the table.

Dave Nash was reading a magazine in his cell when Seth Bader walked in.

"Hey, you still talk with your ex-wife?"

Nash shrugged. "Sometimes she picks up when I call to talk to the kids."

"I need you to do something for me. I need you to get her to find out where my son Joe is."

"I don't think she'd do that. Besides, you know I don't have a lawyer right now. I can't get messed up in your shit. I don't want it to screw up my case."

"Here's the thing," Seth said, "I know a lot of lawyers, and I can get you a real good one, on me. I just really need to find out where Joe is, and I know you can help me with that."

"Why do you need to find him so bad?"

"So I can have him taken out."

"I don't think I can help you," Nash said to Seth the following day in the TV room. "I don't really talk to my ex-wife anymore."

"You only need to talk to her twice," Seth said. "There's a special computer that has all the names of state wards and witnesses. All she has to do is type in the name Joe Bader, and then tell you where the computer says he is."

"I'm in a lot of trouble, and I don't even think one of your lawyer friends could help me. I'm up on charges in Maine, too."

"Maine," Seth shook his head. "It was so stupid to bury Vicki's body in Maine."

Nash asked Seth where in Maine his ex-wife had been buried.

"Waterboro," he said. "Fucking stupid. Way too easy to find."

"I used to live in a trailer in Old Town, Maine," Nash said. "Anywhere north of that would have been a good place. There's nothing between where I was and Canada."

"Yo, Bader," another inmate said over his shoulder, "this bring back memories for you?" He was pointing at the TV, where another episode of *Law & Order* was playing. This time, a man was shown beating his wife.

The other men in the room laughed at the joke being made at Seth's expense.

"Nah," Seth just said, shrugging. "I didn't beat her. I just put one behind her ear."

"I've hired a private investigator," Seth told Gumbs one day. "He's tracked down a bunch of Joe's friends, found out they are willing to say certain things."

"What kind of things?" Gumbs asked.

"That Joe had a gun before Vicki got shot. That he bragged about shooting her, that kind of thing."

"Does Joe know about guns, too?"

"Sure. I used to take him shooting from when he was nine, ten years old." Seth was smiling as if making a fond father-son remembrance. "He knows almost as much as I do."

"So, you think you're going to get off?"

"My lawyers say that now that the PI found those wit-

nesses, there's a money-back guarantee of an acquittal."
Seth paused. "You know, MJ was the one who bought
the barrel they found."

"The decoy?" Gumbs was having a hard time keeping
Seth's stories straight.

"Yeah, I told her to go pick one up at the Hooksett
Trading Post." Seth frowned. "You know, I spent over
two hundred thousand dollars on that bitch. Gave her a
four-carat diamond that now nobody can find."

"That's got to be rough."

"You know," Seth said, rubbing his head. "I'm really
only guilty of one thing, and that's getting involved with
Mary Jean in the first place."

Seth Bader thought he'd made friends in the jail with
like-minded men who empathized with his situation.
What he didn't realize was that some of those men,
including Brian Gumbs, were cooperating with the New
Hampshire State Police.

"He's researching all sorts of obscure laws to try and
get released," Gumbs told Corporal Rich Mitchell on the
phone. "He says if three grand juries sit and he's not
indicted he'll be automatically acquitted."

Mitchell asked Gumbs if he still believed that Seth was
planning to hire someone to kill Joe.

"He talks about it all the time, says he's trying to get
some grenades from a guy in New York. 'If you can shoot
it, I want it,' is what he said."

"What do you think Seth's overall attitude is about his ex-wife's murder?"

"That's the worst part. He laughs about it all the time. Makes jokes about it. Tells anyone willing to listen that he put his son up to it, or that he did it, that she had it coming, on and on."

"And he talks about the shooting itself?"

"Yeah," Gumbs replied to the detective. "He talks about the gun, that he used a hollow point bullet so it would disintegrate. Also, why it was smarter to shoot her in the head."

"Why's that?" Mitchell asked.

"He says she was so fat that a body shot might not have reached one of her vital organs."

"So, you no longer believe that Bader had his son do the shooting for him?" Mitchell asked.

"No," Gumbs replied. "I'm absolutely sure—and he has admitted it himself—that Seth Bader shot his ex-wife himself."

Gumbs didn't know it, but two other inmates had told Mitchell the same thing. By October 1997, the state police had also interviewed Dave Nash, by then serving time at the state prison in Maine, about his county jail conversations with Seth. A third inmate had provided more than just hearsay statements to police. He'd actually worn a wire inside the prison and had gotten Seth on tape saying many of the same things Gumbs and Nash had reported. The police referred to that man as "CI-1" in their reports, shorthand for "Criminal Informant."

It's unclear if Bader ever made any progress in locating

Joe in an attempt to intimidate or harm him; it's also hard to judge whether the plans were jailhouse braggadocio or diabolical steps with the intention of action.

In the year Seth Bader spent in the Rockingham County House of Corrections awaiting his trial, he should have had every reason to believe his fellow inmates might be ratting him out. As a lawyer who'd worked on criminal defense, he was certainly aware of the way police used inmates to collect evidence against suspects in advance of their trials. Yet Seth never stopped talking about the case, spilling countless details about the crime, nor did he cease bragging about his certainty he'd be acquitted.

"You know, I've got all these women fighting with each other over who will get to spend the night with me first when I get out."

"Oh yeah?" one of the other inmates asked.

"When I get out of here I'm going to have a steak and a beer," Seth said. "Then, I'm going to get a blow job and right after, throw the woman out. My first night home, I'm going to sleep with my dogs."

Seth smiled, as if he were looking forward to the best night's sleep of his life.

TWENTY-SEVEN

Cold-Blooded

On March 24, 1998, a yellow school bus carrying fifteen jurors, Judge Walter Murphy, a court reporter, and several court officials barely squeaked through the narrow opening of the fence surrounding the Bader home on Doe Run Lane. The driveway was covered with a blanket of snow. Tracks from two previous vehicles laid a path for the bus to follow: one driven by the prosecutors and one driven by a deputy sheriff, who had brought the defense team and Seth Bader to the home shortly before the bus's arrival. As the jurors stepped off the bus, they saw Seth standing to the side of the entryway.

It was the second day of the trial of Seth Bader. It had taken close to two weeks to seat the jury panel, in part because of the intense media coverage of the case. The first two days of the proceeding were "the view" of the crime scene and other locations. The view took place even before opening arguments. The Stratham home was the third destination for the jury, who had on the previous day been shown the impounded vehicles being presented as evidence in the case: Vicki's ten-year-old blue Cadillac Coupe DeVille and Seth's navy Jeep Cherokee. They had then been escorted to Vicki's house on Patricia Avenue in Exeter, but because it was occupied by new owners, they weren't able to enter.

The jury was divided into two groups to tour Seth's home. While the first group entered, the second stood outside, taking in the home's tall stucco exterior and many-angled roof. Through the windows they could see gleaming hardwood floors and light streaming in through French doors on the rear of the house. There was a grand piano visible in the home's living room.

When the second group of jurors had completed their tour, they filed past Seth and his defense team. He and his lawyers had also been permitted in the house, but not at the same time as the jury. Seth now stood in a relaxed fashion, watching the jurors board the bus like a host bidding farewell to guests after a holiday party.

The bus driver roared the diesel engine to life, using the home's large paved parking area to reverse direction before slowly heading back down the driveway. The home wasn't the last stop of the jury's grim field trip. They'd also been asked to pack winter footwear and heavy coats for their tour of Vicki Bader's grave site, fifty miles away in Waterboro, Maine.

*   *   *

Assistant Attorney General Joseph Laplante had been a late addition to the prosecutorial team. Kacavas had asked for his assistance because he was prepping for three murder cases back-to-back, all of them against the formidable defense attorneys Mark Sisti and Paul Twomey. Laplante wasn't just a colleague, he was a regular at Kacavas's weekly poker game and was his closest friend in the legal world.

Like Kacavas, Joe Laplante was the first member of his family to go to college. When he graduated law school, he and Kacavas started on the same day at the same firm. When there was a job posting for new prosecutors in the attorney general's office, both Laplante and Kacavas applied unbeknownst to each other. They were both hired and, again, started their new jobs on the same day.

In his early thirties, Laplante was known as a fireplug, with ginger hair and a bulldog's tenacity. The Nashua, New Hampshire, native had originally wanted to join the FBI after college but failed to meet the medical requirements, so he chose Georgetown Law instead, spending several years handling white-collar crime cases for a private firm before joining the New Hampshire Attorney General's office.

Laplante enjoyed all kinds of sports and got interested in judging boxing matches. One evening the referee didn't show up, so Laplante volunteered to get in the ring and referee the match himself. If there was one thing Laplante appreciated, it was a fair fight.

* * *

Opening arguments were one of Joe Laplante's specialties. Laplante set aside one hour every evening until trial preparing to cross-examine Seth Bader if he ever took the stand, but laying out a compelling case for the jurors in the opening moments of the trial was even more important. He welcomed the jury that morning and spoke directly to them, standing directly in front of the jury box. Laplante brought them back to their visits to the Baders' respective homes and to Vicki's burial site in Waterboro, Maine.

"When you folks stepped out of those vehicles . . . you were at the top of that hill, on the dirt road, and you walked down the street and you took a look around you, what you were looking at was not some peaceful patch of Maine woods; what you were looking at, as you know now, was the site of a grave."

Laplante paused, making sure he had the jury's full attention before continuing.

"And it wasn't the type of grave you see in a cemetery with manicured grass and a nice fence. It was a ditch . . . it was the grave of a thirty-five-year-old woman. And you wouldn't know her name; there was no marker or headstone to tell you her name. But she had a name. Her name was Vicki, Vicki Bader. And Vicki Bader didn't *lay* in that grave peacefully on her back in a shiny coffin with her hands folded, because she hadn't been *laid to rest*. She was *thrown* in that hole, *dumped* in that hole by that man right there, her ex-husband, the defendant, Seth Bader."

Laplante then laid out Seth's motive for the killing, describing the custody case, Seth's disdain at having to pay Vicki support, and finally, his involvement with Mary Jean Martin. Laplante made no attempt to soften the tone of conspiracy and Seth's calculated actions against Vicki. He described Seth's advantage over Vicki after their divorce and how he used their adopted sons against her.

"He poisoned the boys' minds against Vicki, and the way he did was by lying to them. He told the oldest boy, Joey . . . that Vicki had tried to kill little Sammy by poisoning him with drugs . . . He even had Joey write hate mail to Vicki, terrible, terrible letters . . . calling her awful hurtful names and telling Vicki that he didn't love her."

Laplante promised the jury that they'd see the letters as evidence, assuring them that they would know that a child could not have composed them. He also promised that they would have a complete picture of Mary Jean Martin and her influence on Seth's actions after viewing the trial evidence.

"What Mary Jean wanted, Mary Jean got," Laplante said. "People heard the two of them talking about Vicki, how their lives would be so much better if Vicki would just go away . . . They wanted to get rid of her, not to kill her . . . not yet. The killing came later."

Laplante then detailed Seth and Mary Jean's campaign of terror against Vicki, describing how Joe had been enlisted to kill Vicki's birds, and then how Mary Jean's shady associates had been hired to commit increasingly troubling crimes designed to intimidate her, culminating in Mary Jean herself placing the pipe bomb in Vicki's mailbox.

"Now, the Exeter Police Department . . . didn't do a very good job," Laplante said. "They didn't treat the defendant like a suspect or like the criminal that the evidence in this case will prove that he is. He fast-talked them off his trail . . . first—if you can believe this—he pointed the finger at Vicki herself. You know what? The Exeter Police Department bought it.

"But Vicki didn't bomb herself. Vicki knew who did it . . . the only enemies Vicki Bader had lived [on] Doe Run Lane in Stratham: the defendant, and Mary Jean."

The prosecutor then laid out the details of how Seth flipped on Mary Jean. He said that at this point, Seth was beginning to realize that "MJ" was only with him for his money. He pointed police toward his girlfriend as a suspect, and when she wasn't arrested, he acted later as if he'd never done even that.

"He went to *Disney World* with a woman he said had planted a bomb in the house of the mother of his three little boys." Laplante shook his head incredulously. "He created the danger and then he used the danger against his ex-wife. That's how far he went to win. But he *didn't* win."

Laplante then told the jury how the custody case between Seth and Vicki had begun to turn Vicki's way, describing the conditions the court-appointed guardian reported after seeing how the Baders lived and how young Joe had been forced into caring for his baby brother.

"In July of 1996, the guardian made his recommendation. He reported to the court that Sam should be removed from the defendant's custody and be allowed to live with Vicki.

"Well, now [Seth Bader was] desperate . . . He had gone so far to win . . . had pulled every dirty trick in the book, and he was going to lose. He couldn't stand the idea of losing, not to Vicki. And he knew . . . he'd lose Mary Jean as well. Because for Mary Jean . . . it all came down to dollars and cents. If this defendant was going to have to start paying more money to his ex-wife, he wasn't going to be worth her time.

"So that summer of 1996, the defendant and Mary Jean made a decision. They realized they couldn't beat Vicki fair and square . . . and they realized they couldn't beat her into submission . . . so they decided to kill her.

"The defendant just stood and watched while Joey dug the hole, a four-foot shallow grave while he did what he was told. He watched while Joey just [threw] shovel after shovel on top of the body of the woman, the mother of his own natural son."

Laplante then described what happened after Vicki was reported missing, including Seth's phone messages on her answering machine, which he called thinly veiled attempts to throw police off his trail as a suspect. He described how the plan almost worked, summer turning into fall, and then fall into winter. Seth almost got away with it, Laplante said. Almost.

The prosecutor told the jury how the conspiracy began to fall apart "in the way conspiracies always fall apart; the conspirators started to turn on each other." First, he said, Seth and Mary Jean's relationship began to crumble, and then when Seth couldn't maintain his control over Joe, the subsequent altercation blew the lid off the plot. After social services removed the boy from Bader's house, Laplante said, Joe confessed everything, taking police to the site of Vicki's body, coming clean. Seth reacted by then turning on his son, Laplante said, denying any knowledge of the crime he'd orchestrated.

"Ladies and gentlemen, this case is not a complicated one. There might be a few players involved and there might be a few events to keep track of—bombings, tire slashings and the like—but the picture you see emerging will not confuse you. The picture you will see emerging will be very clear; it's the picture of a lawyer, a lawyer who could not stand to lose to his ex-wife, who turned a custody battle into a real battle, a war, a war complete with guns and bombs and his own personal army. And when his wife wouldn't surrender, he and his greedy girlfriend decided to kill her. It's as simple as that.

"At the end of this case we're going to return to you. We're going to ask you to tell us what you see in the form of a verdict, a unanimous jury verdict. It's the only verdict that the evidence in this case will support, a verdict of guilty, that this defendant is guilty of conspiracy and that he is guilty of first-degree murder."

* * *

Attorney Mark Sisti stood up from his place at the defense table, giving the court and the jury a full view of his ill-fitting suit. Though Sisti had a formidable reputation in print, his in-person impression left a lot to be desired.

Unlike his partner Paul Twomey, Sisti did not look like the kind of well-coiffed, dapper lawyer who strolled around movie courthouses, dazzling juries with charm and charisma. He looked more like a used car salesman, and it was this unexpected image that worked devastatingly well for him. Mark Sisti might not look like a slick legal eagle, and that fact often disarmed juries and opposing counsel alike. Because if Mark Sisti was anything, he was slick.

Sisti grew up in Pittsburgh, Pennsylvania, and his father worked in a steel plant. Sisti put forth great effort to get into college and eventually become a lawyer. He loved being a defense attorney. "There's not a more patriotic thing you can do," he was quoted as saying, "then provide a defense for a person accused of the crime. It's what makes us Americans."

"Good morning, folks," the attorney began. "You're going to laugh. Stay tuned. I know you don't believe that, but it's going to happen."

It was Sisti's signature style to begin a case brashly.

The jury may have been surprised by his glib delivery, but the judge and prosecutors were not. He pulled several mounted photographs from behind the defense table and brought them to a series of stands set up in front of the jury.

"This is an interesting cast of characters here. I've got quite a bit to say about these folks, so I'm going to put 'em up over here and we're going to draw a different picture, if you will."

Sisti smiled as though he was privy to an inside joke that the prosecution hadn't been let in on. He picked up a photograph mounted on poster board.

"This is a picture of 'poor little Joey Bader' and Mary Jean Martin. And that's where we're going to start right now." The picture showed an adolescent Joe Bader in a Florida swimming pool. In his arms was a sexy, bikini-clad Mary Jean Martin. The scene looked tawdry.

"Let's talk about Mary Jean. Mary Jean Martin is a gold digger. Mary Jean Martin is a vicious human being. Mary Jean Martin sucked Seth Bader dry. Mary Jean Martin hated Vicki Bader. Mary Jean Martin wished Vicki Bader was dead. Mary Jean Martin had friends in Boston. Mary Jean Martin had money to pay them. Mary Jean Martin drove them to New Hampshire. Mary Jean Martin had them terrorize Vicki Bader. Mary Jean Martin gave them handfuls of cash to do it. Mary Jean Martin was a manipulating human being.

"This, ladies and gentlemen, is the very foundation of the prosecutor's case. Mary Jean Martin—the well of truth—Mary Jean Martin—who came in to talk to the police and the attorney general's office and told an eight-hour tale of woe. And you know what Mary Jean Martin did for eight hours? She pointed the finger at that guy right over there! *Seth Bader!*"

Sisti swung around, gesturing at the man who now sat rapt behind the defense table.

"And you can just imagine how enthralled the state of New Hampshire was to have somebody singing and telling them all about a murder, giving them details, and being on their team. You can just imagine how wonderful that was."

Sisti swept his eyes over the jury. He'd barely taken a breath during his harangue. He then turned to the other person involved in the prosecution's conspiracy theory.

"Joe Bader, 'Joey,' as the prosecution wants to call him. Ladies and gentlemen, you're going to have a living, breathing fifteen-year-old take the stand in the course of this case who is as cold-blooded as a North Atlantic cod. You're going to see an individual that doesn't have *one ounce* of remorse in his body. You're going to see one cold-hearted kid is what you're going to see. And the prosecution is selling the premise that Joey Bader did *everything* that Seth Bader told him to do, but you're going to know that is *absolutely ridiculous.*

"When Joseph Bader takes that stand, you keep in mind a couple of things . . . that kid could take Seth Bader and break him in half in the blink of an eye, 'cause he has done it in the past, and he would do anything in order to get his butt out of the slammer . . . It's the save-your-own-butt theory at any cost. Joey Bader will do not one second, not one second of jail time."

"Your Honor, may we approach?" Joseph Laplante was already on his feet behind the prosecution's table.

"Yes," Judge Walter Murphy assented.

Laplante spoke in hushed tones at the bench. He was clearly worried about the implications of Sisti's rhetoric. He felt the defense was implying that the state needed Joe's testimony so badly to make their case that they wouldn't care if Joe lied. "I don't know how to interpret that last statement, when he says we are supporting perjury, [that] we are buying perjury . . ."

Defense attorneys Mark Sisti and Paul Twomey spoke at once, and the judge raised his hand to silence the argument.

"I'm going to leave it alone."

"Thank you," Sisti said, resuming his normal volume. "If I may, Your Honor?

"Joseph Bader, Sandro Stuto, the two of them run down parallel lines to one particular focused point, and that's Mary Jean Martin. They've both got their own reasons, they've both got their own desires, they've both got their own problems. Joseph Bader's a nut. Joseph Bader is a sick kid. And Joseph Bader *wasn't* pushed into cooking Vicki Bader's parakeets. He plucked them from the cage himself, he placed them into an oven all by himself, he turned on that oven all by himself, and he burned them to death. And that doesn't faze him.

"Let there be no question Joseph Bader was involved

in the death of Vicki Bader. And let there be no question that Sandro Stuto was involved in the death of Vicki Bader. And let there be no question that Mary Jean Martin was involved in the death of Vicki Bader."

Sisti turned toward the prosecution and looked directly at Laplante. He raised his voice so that the jury wouldn't have to strain to hear him.

"Now, about ten minutes before the prosecution ended its close . . ."—Sisti smiled and shrugged as though he'd misspoken by accident—". . . its *opening*, he apologized for the Exeter Police Department." The lawyer then faced the jury once again.

"Folks, the evidence will show that they should be apologizing to the survivors of Vicki Bader, *not* for the Exeter Police Department. Months, *months* before Vicki Bader's disappearance . . . Seth Bader, the odd man out, Seth Bader, the guy who they've been pointing the finger at, Seth Bader went to the police and Seth Bader said he was really, really worried . . . He made it known to the police and to Vicki's lawyer to watch out for Mary Jean Martin, watch out for Sandro Stuto . . . watch out for a guy by the name of Sebastian, watch out for these people because they could spell death for Vicki Bader.

"Not only was he afraid for himself, but he was afraid for Vicki. And, ladies and gentlemen, you will hear and you will see, during the course of this trial, that Seth Bader not only gave names and gave reasons, but he gave names and reasons to Vicki Bader herself. It's ridiculous to even conceive that you are *planning* a murder or being involved in a conspiracy . . . *before* the disappearance of Vicki. It's *absurd*."

Sisti paused for effect, then continued to list more flaws in the prosecution's case, including what he described as the "immaculate homicide."

"You're going to have a story brought to you, folks, where there's supposedly a killing in a house, and no one hears a gunshot, no neighbors. Where there isn't a speck of blood recovered at any time, where there's no evidence and no witnesses testify to this dragging of a body. Not only will there be absolutely *no* physical evidence at the house; there will be *no* physical evidence in Seth's Jeep Cherokee. Nothing. Zero. Absolutely *nothing*. And when you hear the stories from Joey Bader and Sandro Stuto, you'll know there's no substance, either."

Sisti had reached the heart of the defense's case. The prosecution, he argued, had pieced together an implausible chain of events based on circumstantial evidence and a motley gang of increasingly unreliable witnesses. Seth Bader, according to his attorney, was the convenient suspect, because in the end, it was easier to prosecute one person, despite the evidence pointing to a far more convoluted—and therefore more difficult to prove—truth.

"Folks, this case is riddled with reasonable doubt, *riddled* with it . . . and it's because the prosecutor's case doesn't have the stuff to put it over the hurdle of proof *beyond* a reasonable doubt."

Sisti stepped back from the jury box. He lowered his

voice, looking each of the members in the eye as he concluded his opening statement.

"Ladies and gentlemen, Seth Bader and Paul Twomey and I are relieved that, finally, *finally*, we're in a trial by a jury and not a trial by media or a trial by accusation. This is where we want to be and this is where we want to show you that the prosecution has failed. Thank you."

TWENTY-EIGHT

Star Witness

After opening arguments on the afternoon of March 31, 1998, Dr. Henry Ryan, Maine's chief medical examiner, described the results of his autopsy of Vicki Bader in open court. He testified that her death was the result of a gunshot wound from a small-caliber bullet that entered just below her right ear.

Vicki's attorney, Heidi Boyack, was the prosecution's second trial witness. She laid out a timeline of the campaign waged against her client by Seth Bader, testifying that Vicki's history of mental illness and suicide attempts were not only caused by Seth, but that her fragile state had been leveraged against her in court, resulting in $18,000 in legal bills, which precluded Vicki from being able to pay her other bills, or even buy groceries.

By the end of her testimony, tears were streaming from Boyack's eyes.

"Vicki's mother, Lois Stewart, came to New Hampshire after my client disappeared, and stayed in her daughter's Exeter home. Shortly after she arrived there, she received a letter from Seth Bader, ordering her to vacate her daughter's house by the end of the month so he could get a paying tenant."

In the first few days of Seth Bader's murder trial, the jury heard testimony from Seth's former housekeeper, who'd quit working for him shortly after the pipe bomb incident. She told the court that Seth had mentioned to her several times that he'd be better off if his ex-wife were dead.

When the prosecutors asked the housekeeper about the general state of the Bader home, Twomey objected. In one of several pretrial hearings, Judge Murphy had sided with the defense, ruling any evidence of neglect or abuse of the children by Seth would be prejudicial and therefore barred from the trial.

On Friday, April 3, 1998, Joe Bader was slated to testify against his adoptive father. Photographs, sketches, and video of Joe by the media had been banned by the judge, but despite the absence of some members of the media, the courtroom was packed for what was anticipated to be a key moment in the trial. Even the attorneys' wives were present.

Rapping his gavel to restore order, Judge Murphy surprised the courtroom when he announced that the proceedings were to be halted.

"You are dismissed for now," he told the jury, instructing them not to discuss the case with anyone. "You will return at 1:30 on Monday, unless you are notified of a further delay." On Monday morning, the jurors were notified that they were not to come into court that day. They received the same notification the following day. The press, as well as the public, began to speculate about why the trial was being delayed. Finally, on Tuesday night, a source close to the defense team issued a statement.

"The prosecution is having a problem with witnesses, and the case is melting down."

On Wednesday, April 8, Judge Murphy called to order a hearing in front of the jury and public that served to answer questions about the delay in the trial. Both legal teams needed to examine new evidence about Joe Bader and Sandro Stuto, he told them. Also, the defense had requested certain information that the prosecution had objected to, on the grounds that the documents would reveal the whereabouts of Joe Bader.

Assistant Attorney General Joe Laplante addressed the court, saying that the prosecution was in possession of police reports documenting that Seth Bader had been trying to find his son in order to "take him out."

"My understanding is that this means the defendant

wants to permanently eliminate this witness, his son Joseph Bader."

Seth's legal team objected to this characterization of their client.

"He is no threat whatsoever," Paul Twomey said to the judge. "If anything, it is others at liberty who pose a threat." Twomey went on to explain that certain reports, especially one that might include an incident where a knife had been found hidden under Joe's bed while he was in foster care, were critical to their claim that it had been Joe, and not Seth, who had killed Vicki Bader.

When Judge Murphy finally called the jury into court to give them an update, he explained that issues of documentation about Joe, things like school, police, or medical records, had been further complicated by an objection from the New Hampshire Division of Child and Youth Services, who represented the interests of Joe Bader while he was in their custody. The jury was again dismissed while further arguments could be made outside of their presence.

DCYS's concern was for Joe's safety, but also for privacy concerning their modes of protecting children and families in cases such as these. Ultimately, the judge ordered that Joe Bader's records be turned over to him, and that upon reviewing them, he'd decide which ones to turn over to the defense.

On Monday, April 14, 1998, after a week of wrangling over documents and evidence related to the fifteen-year-old, it was finally Joseph Bader's turn to talk.

* * *

Joe's attorney, James Boffetti, was an ordained priest as well as an attorney with the public defender's office. Around the time of the Bader trial, Boffetti was finalizing his separation from the Congregation of Holy Cross, the order that founded the University of Notre Dame, where he'd received his master's degree. He remained a priest with the option of returning to the church, and he saw public defense as an extension of his humanitarian mission. In court, Boffetti wore a suit and tie, just like the other attorneys; he also supplied Joe with sport coats and neckties from his own closet, items he knew the boy didn't own and couldn't afford to buy.

"You'll be okay, Joe," Boffetti told his client when he was called to the stand. The lawyer had spent a great deal of time with the teen in the year leading up to this day and had come to believe Joe was an exceptional person. He patted him on the back before Joe walked to the front of the chamber.

Joe looked neat in the clothes Boffetti had lent him. His dark hair was slicked back in place. He glanced nervously around the courtroom, his gaze avoiding the defense table, his focus finally settling on prosecutor John Kacavas, who was ready to question his star witness.

"Good morning, Joe."

"Good morning."

"Are you ready to tell us your story?" Kacavas asked his witness.

"Yes," Joe said. And in a soft monotone, he began to talk.

*   *   *

Joe said that the weekend before her murder, Vicki had dropped her then three-year-old son Sam off at the home on Doe Run Lane on a sunny August afternoon. Seth had greeted her at the door and asked if she'd come in. On the rare times Vicki stayed longer than it took to simply hand Sam off, it was for five or ten minutes because Seth had some topic to discuss. This day, though, they conversed about nothing in particular. Joe, who had been in the kitchen, walked into the hallway and joined the conversation. Seth then suggested they all go for a walk together behind the house and to the river. Vicki agreed.

It had been a long time since Vicki had wandered around the back side of the Stratham property. Matt joined them, and they all strolled down to the far end of the yard.

Seth and Vicki chatted pleasantly. They had little reason left to fight. Their lawyers were about to settle their custody battle after two long years.

Joe tossed some rocks in the water, and Matt tried to match his brother's throws. They played on a floating dock in the waterway. Sam still didn't talk, but instead voiced his pleasure in squeals as he flattened the untamed grass with his feet.

After an hour, Seth escorted Vicki back to the house and her car. The kids waved good-bye to her as she got inside the Cadillac and drove away. Once she was gone, Seth asked Joe to meet him in his office.

"I wanted to keep Vicki around for an hour to see if anyone is checking up on her when she drops Sam off," he explained. "Because next week when she comes I'm going to kill her."

Joe showed no reaction. Inwardly, though, he was stunned. Seth was so calm telling him these things. Joe didn't know how to take it or how he was supposed to react.

"We're going to have to start looking for places to bury the body," Seth said.

Halfway through the week, Seth and Joe drove to Maine in search of a place to dig a grave. Seth already had a potential site circled on a map. He thought burying Vicki out-of-state would complicate the search. It wasn't until they were on the road—putting the plan into action—that Joe said he truly understood Seth was serious.

The location he'd marked with an X looked isolated on the map, but the din of cars in the distance spooked Seth. They went home, and drove north again the next day to Waterboro, where Seth had selected a new spot. He watched while he made Joe dig the grave for his adoptive mother.

Although he said nothing, Joe was deeply confused by Seth's plan. Seth had told him so many things about Vicki that he wasn't sure what was true anymore, and he wondered sometimes if that was all designed to keep him off balance. Seth reminded Joe that Vicki had tried to poison

Sam and that this was what she deserved. He said she was crazy and dangerous. Joe believed him, but he wasn't sure killing her was the answer.

Joe showered as soon as the two of them got home. After he got dressed, Seth summoned him to the office again.

"On Saturday, your job will be to greet Vicki and tell her to come inside the house." Seth also said Joe would later clean up any mess, help put Vicki's body into the Jeep, and bury her in the grave he'd just dug. Seth then said he still had to hire one other person to get rid of her car.

"Joe, when the defendant says he's going to hire someone, does he mention any names?" Kacavas asked.

"No, he doesn't."

"Does he mention Sandro Stuto?"

"No, he doesn't."

"How do we know you didn't shoot Vicki Bader?" Kacavas asked Joe.

"Because I'm telling you Seth shot Vicki Bader."

"Are you telling us the truth when you say that?"

Joe pulled his shoulders back and said in a clear voice, "Yes, I am."

Kacavas nodded, hoping he had done enough to prepare both Joe and the jury for the pointed cross-examination that was going to rain down next. "Nothing further, Your Honor."

TWENTY-NINE

Bader vs. Bader

Fifteen-year-old Joe Bader had been on the stand for a day and a half telling his side of things, and defense attorney Mark Sisti had to acknowledge that he'd been an effective witness for the prosecution. To that end, the attorney got his niceties out of the way quickly. He didn't want to waste any time before dissecting Joe's credibility.

"Good morning, Joe," Sisti said.

"Good morning."

"How are you?"

"Doing all right."

"Did you sleep okay last night?"

"Yes."

"Are you well rested and ready to go, then?"

"Yeah, I guess so."

"Okay. Those last couple of questions that the prosecutor asked you, I guess they depend a lot on believing you, right?"

"Yes."

"So believing you is critical here, right?"

"Well, I guess so."

"Because you got a deal with the State of New Hampshire, right?"

"Right."

Sisti began by going over the list of all the people Joe had acknowledged lying to before he confessed his involvement in Vicki's death to Sergeant Kelly. A firm believer in the power visual cues had with a jury, Sisti kept track of the names on an easel. Every time Joe admitted to lying to someone, or admitted he'd told someone he'd had no clue where Vicki Bader was, Sisti would stride to the easel and write the name down with a flourish. The list included relatives, court-appointed guardians, and the police.

Joe told Sisti that he'd lied because he didn't want to be separated from his brother Matt and because Seth Bader had threatened to send him back to the psychiatric hospital if he told anyone about the murder.

"Seth told me what to say," Joe said many times during Sisti's questioning. And when Sisti asked him about killing Vicki's birds, Joe said, "I wanted to do what Seth wanted me to do," denying that he'd wanted to kill the birds at all.

Sisti also tried to use his questioning to distance Seth Bader from Sandro Stuto and Sebastian Caradonna. Joe admitted that the day of Vicki's shooting was the first time he'd seen his adoptive father with Stuto.

"But you lied to police about [your] ever having seen Sandro Stuto before."

Joe admitted that he had. On one occasion, he said, he and Matt had gone with Mary Jean Martin to work, and they'd stopped by Brighton Billiards before returning home to Stratham. Sandro Stuto had been in the pool hall that night.

"And your knowledge of guns?" Sisti listed dozens of models of handguns, rifles, and shotguns that Joe had testified he had fired.

"Seth taught me to shoot them," the boy replied.

On his second day of cross-examination, Mark Sisti hammered Joe Bader with a list of inconsistencies between his testimony in court and his prior interviews with police.

"Why didn't the police find the items you mentioned in your testimony, including the plastic bag you claimed you put on Vicki's head?"

"I think the presence of the gun barrel where I said it would be says a lot about my credibility," Joe replied.

"Now, there's another problem with the story you told in April of 1997, and that has to do with this four-hour ride to Maine you told the police it would take to where this body was buried, right?"

"Right."

"Four hours is a pretty significant period of time, right?"

"Right."

"But there's a problem, Joe, because Waterboro, Maine, is not a four-hour ride, right?"

"Yes."

"You know the difference between four hours and ninety minutes, right, Joe?

"Well, Seth had told me it was four hours."

"And in order to cover for that inconsistency, what you told the jury was that you fell asleep in the car, right, Joe?"

"I'm not trying to cover for anything. That's what happened."

"You fell asleep right after a murder in your own house, after loading the dead body of your adoptive mother into the back of a Jeep, you fell asleep and didn't know where you were going, and that's why you may be off a couple of hours on the trip, right?"

"That's right."

If Sisti was unrelenting, Joe was equally patient. After nearly four days on the stand, his voice remained steady and quiet as Sisti recounted every part of his testimony, comparing it with police reports taken when he'd told them his story a year earlier. There were inconsistencies in every single part of Joe's story, Sisti pointed out, including his insistence that he'd told Vicki that Seth was waiting for her in the living room on the afternoon of her murder. Joe also pointed out that during the first police interview, when he denied any knowledge about Vicki's disappearance, Seth and his lawyer had been watching his interview from the adjoining room.

"They weren't there when I talked to the police last April," he said, referring to the evening he called Sergeant Kelly and finally opened up. "I felt it was safe to tell the truth."

"Joe, there's no question that you were involved in the murder of Vicki Bader, right?"

"No."

"I mean, you're a cold character, aren't you?"

"No."

Sisti gestured toward the jury. "And you told these people yesterday that when you grow up, you want to be a nice guy and go to college, right, Joe?"

"Yes."

"But the fact of the matter is, your ambition, your *life's* ambition, has been to be a Marine sniper, right?" Sisti pressed.

"No . . . well . . . I had thought at one time . . ."

"What, Joe?"

". . . of joining the military."

"Because in your own words, you would be a good Marine sniper, right?"

"No."

"In your own words, Joe," Sisti said, "you'd be a good Marine sniper because you could kill somebody and just forget all about it, right?"

"No," the teenager said, shaking his head firmly.

*   *   *

"Permission to redirect?" Kacavas asked after Sisti had finished his cross-examination.

"Go ahead, Mr. Kacavas."

The prosecutor walked toward Joe calmly and looked him in the eye.

"Joe, what's this about wanting to be a Marine?"

"Seth had talked to me about going into the military because it would help pay for college, and his father was in the military."

"Did you ever express interest in being a Marine Corps sniper?"

"Yes, I did."

"Why?"

"Because Seth brought it up to me, and it seemed like something I could do."

"How'd you get interested in guns and shooting, Joe?"

"Through Seth."

"How old were you when he turned you on to this?"

"Nine years old."

"Had you ever touched a gun before you met him?"

"No."

"Joe, there's no question that you were involved in the murder of Vicki Bader, right?"

"No," the boy responded.

"Did you shoot her?"

"No, I did not."

THIRTY

Legal Theater

When the jury filed into their box on Friday, April 17, 1998, after a lunchtime recess, Sandro Stuto was already sitting on the witness stand.

When prosecutor Joe Laplante began to question him, it was quickly evident that Stuto's manner of speech would make him an entertaining witness.

"Mr. Stuto, do you want to explain to the court why you were already sitting there when the jury came in today?"

"Well, I'm-a, I'm-a being held at the Rockingham-a County Jail."

"You're in jail?"

"Uh, yes-a."

"Mr. Stuto, I'm going to have to ask you to keep your

voice up. Try to pull up to the microphone and speak a little more slowly, because you have a bit of an accent, okay?"

"Sure."

"Why are you in jail?"

"For, for-a being part of the Bader murder trial case."

"For being part of the case or part of the murder?"

"Both-a."

"What was your involvement, what did you do, generally?"

"Well, there were-a different things that I did: cut-a her tires, shot-a BB guns through her-a windows, I helped-a carry the body, I dispose of the car . . ."

Laplante held up his hand. Stuto's accent made him almost comical, even when he talked about Vicki Bader's murder. He wanted this witness to be taken seriously by the jury if the testimony given by Joe Bader was to be believed.

"Mr. Stuto, you've said a number of things. I'm going to ask you about them one at a time, okay?"

"Sure."

Unlike the kindly way Kacavas spoke to Joe, Laplante wore his disdain for Stuto on his sleeve. Over the next two days, Laplante walked Stuto through the story of how he was drawn into Mary Jean Martin and Seth Bader's world, how he harassed Vicki Bader for money, and how he helped to move Vicki's dead body and then disposed of her car.

"The only person I feel-a bad for is Mrs. Bader," Stuto said at the end of direct examination, "'cause she's the one that-a lost her life. And I could have prevented it, but I was-a too selfish for myself, to save-a my own ass."

Defense attorney Paul Twomey's cross-examination of Sandro Stuto began on the afternoon of Tuesday, April 21, 1998. Like Mark Sisti had done with Joe, Twomey chipped away at Stuto's credibility, focusing on the deal he had struck for a reduced sentence, his convoluted history with Mary Jean Martin and Sebastian Caradonna, and his motivation for participating in Vicki Bader's murder.

"Is the six thousand dollars you received more important than a human life?" Twomey asked Stuto.

"No. The human life is-a more important, but at the time I didn't think of it. It-a didn't go through my mind," said Stuto. "At the time six thousand dollars was important to me."

"Would someone who thinks that way commit perjury, Mr. Stuto?"

"I can't-a lie," Stuto said. "If I do, I go to-a jail on all the other charges."

Stuto was referring to his plea deal. Originally, he had been facing a potential sentence of thirty-seven years. Instead, he'd pleaded guilty to two counts of hindering apprehension and was looking at a sentence of just five to fifteen years.

"You got a pretty good deal, didn't you, Mr. Stuto? I mean, you could have been charged as an accessory to murder, and that could have meant a *life* sentence."

* * *

The jury wasn't privy to the real legal fireworks surrounding Sandro Stuto. On Monday, April 20, 1998, following Stuto's first day of testimony, the trial had been delayed for yet another hearing, this one focused on Stuto's activities *after* he'd been arrested for the conspiracy to kill Vicki Bader.

The defense wanted desperately to introduce evidence that Stuto had told people in jail he was a "bone breaker" and connected to the mob. More important, to undermine his credibility, they wanted to present evidence that Stuto had tried to escape from jail. Judge Murphy halted the trial so he could hear the facts and decide whether they would be relevant to the jury.

The incident happened in early March 1998, less than a month before the trial began. The defense contended Stuto plotted with another inmate to injure a cell mate and then use the ambulance that would transport him to the hospital in their escape, leaving a dummy behind as a decoy. Corrections officers testified that a clothes-stuffed figure was found in another cell, but many of the guards thought the dummy had been part of a prank.

When questioned about it at the hearing, Stuto said the dummy wasn't his.

"It was like a muhnett."

"A muhnett?" Laplante had struggled all trial with Stuto's broken English. "Do you mean a 'Monet'?" he said, referring to the famous painter.

"Yeah," Stuto said. "It was like a Monet. It looks-a good from far away, but once you get up close . . . fuhgeddaboudit." The response brought howls of laughter from both Laplante and the defense team.

At the daylong hearing, Judge Murphy also allowed the prosecution and defense to question the witnesses connected with the escape plot before he ruled the evidence inadmissible to Seth Bader's trial. All this was done out of the presence of the jury, a fact that likely made the judge say something to the lawyers he probably would not have said in open court.

"This is the most complicated case I've had in probably thirty-six years of practicing law. And it's very, very difficult to be sitting right now with all these questions, with you, being the prosecutor, and you, being the defendant . . ."

"Yeah," Mark Sisti interrupted, "but *you're* still the judge."

On April 23, the trial of Seth Bader came to a halt once again, when defense attorney Mark Sisti claimed he saw prosecutor Joe Laplante making a hand signal to Sandro Stuto's attorneys during Paul Twomey's cross-examination of Stuto. Twomey had just asked Stuto to comment on conversations he'd had with his lawyers about other figures in the case when Stuto's legal team, sitting in the gallery, objected, which Sisti claimed Laplante had signaled them to do.

The bench conference was tense.

"Your Honor, Mr. Laplante clearly signaled these two attorneys to make the objection, and he signaled it with his left hand and he signaled it by extending all five fingers of his left hand. I think it's absolutely incorrect."

"It is inappropriate to do any kind of signaling . . ." the judge began before Laplante broke in.

"That may be, Your Honor, but I was on my way up, anyway . . ."

"As I was saying," the judge continued, "I didn't see it."

Defense attorney Twomey chimed in, "Just wait a second, I want to know . . . I didn't see if Mr. Laplante did or didn't do that . . ."

Laplante interjected again. "What *Mr. Laplante* did was put his hand up because I wanted to rise up and make the objection. That's all I did. It certainly *wasn't* a signal for him to make the objection at all . . ."

"Look, I mean . . . I don't," Sisti sputtered, "I mean, I don't mind having a hearing on this, judge."

"Excuse me?" Judge Murphy was incredulous. *Another hearing?* Mark Sisti was certainly living up to his reputation as a defense attorney who'd try anything.

Someone gestured to the TV crew in the corner who had been recording all the testimony. Murphy would be able to get an instant replay.

"Okay" he said, "I'm going to take a short recess at this point. I'll review the videotape."

"Thank you," the defense attorney said.

Judge Murphy banged his gavel and called the recess, during which Sisti made a motion for a mistrial in the case against his client. After reviewing the tape, the judge determined that Laplante hadn't made a hand signal after all, and he denied the motion for a mistrial.

One of the final witnesses for the prosecution was New Hampshire State Police sergeant David Kelley, who'd arrested Seth Bader after informing him that his ex-wife's body had been found in the grave site in Waterboro, Maine. During his direct examination, Kelley recounted Seth's indifference upon hearing the news of the body's discovery—and his request for a candy bar after being told he was under arrest.

Under cross-examination, Kelley was skewered by Mark Sisti, who called into question his interrogation techniques and got him to make some damning admissions about the prosecution's case.

"Did you have a shred of evidence to link Seth Bader to Waterboro, Maine?"

"No, I did not, but other evidence did exist."

Kelley gave similar answers when asked if any physical evidence tied Seth to the gun barrel found in Waterboro, and whether police had turned up any receipts showing Seth had ever purchased either a .22 caliber barrel or a Thompson Contender.

Sisti used the remainder of his cross of Kelley to point out the lack of physical evidence in the state's case against his client. Sisti called it the "Immaculate Crime Scene."

No blood had been found on the floor, on the walls, or in Seth's Jeep. He turned to the jury each time he got Kelley to admit there was no evidence of a murder having been committed in Seth Bader's house. This would prove to be the key to their case, Sisti told the jury, before thanking the sergeant for his assistance.

Sergeant David Kelley, who was meant to be a key closing witness for the prosecution, had unwittingly become a spokesperson for the defense.

Seth Bader's defense team opened their case on Thursday, April 30, 1998. They played tapes of telephone conversations between Seth and Vicki, as well as police videos they said proved Seth had tried to warn authorities about Mary Jean Martin. They were certain that much would become clear about their case when the jury finally saw Mary Jean in person.

For the defense, the entire trial was leading up to that moment. Of course, Mary Jean, still in peril of further indictment, would never willingly discuss her true involvement in Vicki Bader's death. She'd likely take the stand and plead the Fifth Amendment. Sisti and Twomey hoped this piece of legal theater would be their coup de grâce. They believed the jury would see each of her assertions of the Fifth as an admission of guilt and conclude the true masterminds of this crime were the femme fatale and her lying, cold-blooded teenage lover.

* * *

The normally staid New Hampshire press corps came to life when Mary Jean Martin pulled into the courthouse parking lot in her flashy red Trans Am. Flashbulbs and questions exploded in equal measure as she approached the courtroom.

Wearing a tight black dress with a plunging neckline, Mary Jean delivered every bit on the promise of her portrayal during the trial. Her overly processed blond hair framed a pale face nearly devoid of makeup, save a generous portion of black eyeliner on both her top and bottom lids.

Before Mary Jean could take the stand, her attorney requested to be heard on a final motion. Richard Foley argued that since his client was taking the Fifth, she didn't need to do it in open court in front of the jury. Prosecutors Kacavas and Laplante agreed. They said there was nothing in New Hampshire requiring the witness to appear before the jury simply to take the Fifth.

Sisti and Twomey argued staunchly to compel Mary Jean to appear in the presence of the jury. They needed her appearance to plant reasonable doubt in the minds of jurors. But Judge Murphy ruled that if Mary Jean was not going to be offering admissible evidence, then her testimony could be taken outside of the jury's presence.

Taking her place on the witness stand, Mary Jean was first questioned by the defense. Paul Twomey asked if she planned to continue to assert her Fifth Amendment privileges if asked under oath about her involvement in Vicki Bader's murder.

"Yes, I would."

Twomey turned toward the bench. "I would move that the witness be compelled, Your Honor."

"That request is denied. The court rules that she has a potential for criminal charges being reasserted against her in the death of Vicki Bader."

Mary Jean Martin was then excused from the proceeding without the jury ever laying eyes on her.

When Mary Jean exited Rockingham Superior Court, the press was waiting for her, notepads and cameras in hand. Throughout the trial she'd been portrayed as a gold-digging temptress, and now here she was in the flesh, holding an impromptu press conference as she walked back to her car.

"Did you see your ex-fiancé in there?" a reporter shouted.

Mary Jean said she had. "He winked at me. It was kind of revolting. Any man who's tried to destroy my life doesn't deserve to wink at me."

"What are you going to do next, Mary Jean?"

"I want to get on with my life, go home, raise my dogs . . . and bring up my daughter."

Mary Jean opened the door of her flame red Trans Am.

"My stomach turns and lurches at the sight of that man," she said.

"Will you tell your story one day?"

Mary Jean got in her car and started the ignition before rolling down the window to answer the question.

"I already told the police everything."

With that, Mary Jean Martin hit the gas and sped from the courthouse parking lot.

Without Mary Jean, the defense only had one other witness to present, Patricia Camara, a friend of Mary Jean's who testified that MJ had told her she and Joe had talked about killing Vicki while they had sex.

During her cross-examination, Camara revealed that she was a tenant of Seth Bader's, paying $167 a month for a $600 condominium in Exeter, the rest of the rent being subsidized under the Section 8 federal housing program. Camara also said she recalled Joey Bader saying that "they" had killed Vicki Bader, but she did not know who "they" were. After her testimony concluded, the final witness in the trial was excused from the courtroom.

Under strict orders from Judge Murphy, Mary Jean Martin's absence from the trial was not explained to the jury at all.

THIRTY-ONE

The Closers

Mark Sisti didn't close his case by proclaiming his client, Seth Bader, a good person. Nor did he close it by proclaiming his client the kind of patsy who deserved anyone's sympathy.

"What he really is, is a chump," Sisti told the jury.

"Seth is portrayed by the prosecution as a vicious killer . . . just a self-absorbed killing machine. The bottom line is you've heard tapes and you've seen what Seth really is. What he really is, is a dumping ground for these people. What he really is, is some kind of a money machine, an ATM on feet. He's a sap, is what he is. And no matter how the prosecution wants to paint him . . . that they want to make him a sophisticated, intelligent, planning, premeditated criminal defense attorney. Well, that can't be."

Sisti told the jury that Seth Bader was completely innocent of the charges against him and that he had had no part in the conspiracy or in the killing of his ex-wife. Again, Sisti placed the blame squarely on Mary Jean Martin, Joe Bader, and Sandro Stuto, characterizing the latter pair as intertwined, serpentine liars that the prosecution had been stuck with to build the foundation of its case against Seth. He shook his head in mock sympathy for the state.

"They were dealt a lousy deck. It's like being dealt five jokers."

Sisti continued, saying that Sandro Stuto and Joe Bader were "the two guys that, frankly, are the very foundation of this building that they're attempting to put up before you right now. And what they have done with Stuto and Bader is essentially found the worst building site in the country, probably a swampy, crummy land. They have put their forms down that they're supposed to be pouring concrete into, and instead of concrete, they dumped a bunch of Jell-O in there. That's what you're stuck with, okay? And that's what they're stuck with."

Sisti then recounted the defense's claims of a sexual affair between Mary Jean and Joe, and he listed inconsistencies in the various timelines the conspirators had laid out. His closing excoriated the characters of everyone he said was really responsible for Vicki Bader's death, a list that didn't include his client. At the end, Sisti came back to what he said the case was really about: evidence, but also character. Namely, the character of Seth Bader, and that of each of his accusers.

"This guy over here," Sisti said, pointing to Seth, "is the odd man out. He was the odd man out from the beginning of this trial until this morning. He's the guy on the hot seat. He's the key to the jailhouse door. He's the ATM machine on feet. That's what he is. And when you sit back and you know about the people that are pals with each other down in Massachusetts, and you know about Joe Bader, and you know about the absolute lack of physical evidence in each one of these critical locations, maybe that light should come on. Because it's *got* to come on."

Sisti pointed to Laplante and Kacavas at the prosecution's table.

"*They* want to play the game of innuendo. The game of innuendo is over. The game of speculation is over. You can't come in here and assume things. That's not what we do in this courthouse. You have a duty. And that duty is to come back with not-guilty verdicts.

"Weeks ago I told you *this* is where we wanted to be to try this case." Sisti gestured to the chambers that surrounded them, then pointed to the door at the back of the courtroom.

"We don't want to be *out there*. We want to be here, where there's *rules*, where there's *fair* people sitting, and where they've got to prove stuff with *evidence*. *Here's* where we want to be. We want to be able to cross-examine psychos. We want to be able to peel off the layers of the onion. And we don't want to be a people that coddles those maniacs like Joe Bader.

"I'm not gonna ask you for favors. Seth's not gonna ask you for favors. Paul's not gonna ask you for favors. But do yourself a favor. Look as closely at this case as you would if you were examining the pipe bomb . . . Folks, they truly have nothing here. It's been a long case, but it lacked a few things. It lacked proof beyond a reasonable doubt. It lacked plausibility. And thank God we have a jury."

Sisti thanked the panel and sat down, closing the defense's case in the murder trial of Seth Bader.

John Kacavas approached his closing arguments very much as the straight-talking man he was. If Sisti had a reputation for rhetoric, Kacavas's was built on clear reiteration of the prosecution's core message: the defendant is guilty, and here is why you should convict.

Kacavas stood in front of the evidence table, facing the jury and holding a pistol in a gloved hand.

"On August 24, 1996, that defendant [Seth Bader] used this gun to shoot Vicki Bader in the head. Vicki Bader's life ended on that Saturday. But the beginning of the end for Vicki Bader started about two years before, when that defendant met Mary Jean Martin. Because together, that defendant and Mary Jean Martin were a deadly combination."

Kacavas set down the gun and removed his gloves. He reminded the jury that they had not had the opportunity to meet Mary Jean Martin in court.

"But you did hear about her. If there's one thing you know for sure about Mary Jean Martin, she's a gold digger, money-grubber, and in that defendant, Mary Jean Martin found a pot of gold, because when she met that defendant in June of 1994, she saw a big house in Stratham, she saw that he owned half of Vicki's house in Exeter, she saw condominiums all over the place, she saw furs he inherited, she saw a valuable violin he inherited, she saw a piano, she saw . . ."

"Your Honor, objection." Paul Twomey was on his feet.

"Approach please." The judge looked none too pleased.

Twomey stood at the bench with Laplante. He argued that the furs, property, and violin were not in evidence, and that further, there was no evidence that Mary Jean Martin had been aware of those things. Kacavas shook his head.

"No, they have. Heidi Boyack testified to each and every one of those things."

The judge agreed, overruling Twomey's objection. Kacavas continued.

"As I was saying, Mary Jean Martin saw *all* these things, furs, a violin, a piano, huge amounts of cash that the defendant carried, stocks, bonds. And Mary Jean Martin wanted that. She wanted the defendant's money. That's the kind of person Mary Jean Martin is. What Mary Jean Martin wanted, Mary Jean Martin got, because for the defendant, Mary Jean Martin was an obsession."

Kacavas again approached the evidence table, where a black tape recorder was set up.

"Vicki Bader knew. She knew how dangerous the defendant's obsession was. That's why she made this tape."

The prosecutor pressed the play button, and the jury heard the conversation between Seth Bader and his ex-wife in which he'd told her about his obsession with his new girlfriend. He hit stop after Seth was heard saying, "Mary Jean is more than a relationship. Mary Jean is an addiction. I am addicted to Mary Jean."

Kacavas implored the jury to listen again to the tapes of the recorded phone calls between Seth and Vicki, citing them as critical evidence of Seth's motive in the murder.

"What Mary Jean Martin wanted, Mary Jean Martin got, because on August 24, 1996, on that Saturday afternoon, that beast over there shot his ex-wife, the mother of his son, in the back of the head while his three-year-old son waited out by the front door of the house. And when that beast and his teenage son, Joseph Bader, finished dumping Vicki's body in a shallow grave in the woods of Maine, Mary Jean Martin got what she wanted. And so did the defendant. The defendant got what he wanted, too.

"Ladies and gentlemen, if you look at the last two years of Vicki Bader's life, you *know* who caused her death, that deadly combination right there, Seth Bader and Mary Jean Martin. But they want you to believe that Mary Jean Martin and *Joe* Bader did this. It doesn't make any sense. But that's what they want you to believe.

"The defendant, when he was arrested on April 12, 1997, said, 'I expect to be acquitted.' He expects to fool you. He expected to manipulate you, like he manipulated

Vicki, like he manipulated the court process, like he manipulated everything that crossed his path all his life. But don't be fooled, don't be manipulated, don't do what he expects. Do justice. Find him guilty as charged."

The jury in the case of *State of New Hampshire v. Seth Bader* didn't come to verdict hastily. They began deliberations on Tuesday, May 5, 1998. On Thursday, May 7, the jury took an early leave, adjourning deliberations an hour early. On Friday, deliberations resumed, and on that afternoon, word came in that a verdict had finally been reached.

At 3:00 P.M., Judge Walter Murphy banged his gavel to establish order in the court. He confirmed with the jury foreman that a verdict was indeed in hand.

"Motion to poll the jury," came the request from the defense table. The attorneys wanted to make each juror stand up and say his or her decision out loud.

"Granted," Murphy said.

One by one, the jurors in the case were asked to affirm their decision. One by one, each of the twelve men and women repeated the same word.

"Guilty."

Epilogue

Vicki's mother, Lois Stewart, sat in the courtroom, as she had every day of the trial. She placed her hand over her mouth when the verdict was read, and then wept openly, the arm of Vicki's brother John Buzby wrapped around her shoulders.

Judge Walter Murphy then sentenced Seth Bader to a mandatory life sentence at the New Hampshire State Prison for Men. Bader was escorted out of the courtroom by sheriffs after speaking briefly with his lawyers.

As the jury filed out of the courtroom, one woman on the panel cried openly.

Prosecutors John Kacavas and Joe Laplante approached Lois Stewart, who thanked them for their efforts. When asked by a reporter what she would say to Seth, Lois declared, "Hold on for as long as you can, because there's a special place in hell reserved for you."

On their way out of the courtroom, Assistant Attorney General Laplante stopped briefly to talk to the press. "At this point, we just hope that these verdicts give some small measure of comfort to the family."

Defense attorney Mark Sisti expressed his client's disappointment to the gathered media.

"We were very, very optimistic," the lawyer said. He then told the press that during jury deliberations, Judge Murphy had denied a request by two jurors for more information from the trial. The jurors were weeping, he said, begging the bailiffs to let them talk to Murphy. What they were worked up about was not known. After the jury left the courtroom, Paul Twomey quickly filed a petition to have the jurors questioned individually about potential misconduct during deliberations.

Seth Bader expressed little emotion at the jury's decision. In the days after his conviction, he granted several interviews to television and newspaper outlets to proclaim his innocence. "There's an old joke that says the operation was successful but the patient died. That's kind of what happened at the trial. The trial was successful, but the wrong person was convicted."

On June 24, 1998, Judge Murphy convened a one-day hearing that would decide the fates of both Mary Jean Martin and her prosecutors.

Mary Jean's attorney, Richard Foley, grilled Assistant Attorney Generals Joe Laplante, John Kacavas, and Michael Ramsdell about the flawed indictment on conspiracy to commit murder. Foley argued that the state had played fast and loose with the evidence and had unconstitutionally used Mary Jean's immunized statements against her. Foley wanted his client to go free and the prosecutors to be charged with misconduct.

Ramsdell and Laplante were adamant that the indictment, such as it was, had been obtained legally and properly. Only Kacavas expressed some misgivings about the process. Ramsdell—by then in private practice—told the judge he believed that Mary Jean's statements had been fair game because she had violated her immunity deal. Ramsdell said, in his mind, when she failed the polygraph on May 7, 1997, it voided her agreement with the state.

Judge Murphy made two rulings. The first was that there was no finding of prosecutorial misconduct. If he ruled otherwise, it would have been a terrible stain on the careers of the three men and the attorney general's office. Murphy had been convinced by Ramsdell's testimony that there had been no bad intent on the state's part.

The second ruling was just as significant. Murphy ruled that the conspiracy indictment against Mary Jean Martin would be dismissed *without* prejudice. It preserved the state's right to refile the charges against her in the future. Considering the hand they were dealt, it was the best all-around outcome for the state.

Lois Stewart waited patiently for the attorney general's

office to make a move, yet they never did. In 2001, Lois made a very public visit to the New Hampshire Attorney General to request he reinvestigate Mary Jean. Another new prosecutor was assigned to the case file, but nothing came of it. Lois was later quoted in a newspaper article saying, "She's walking around enjoying her life. I feel she got away with murder."

Although past and present attorneys (from both sides of the case) are mum about why the state has failed to proceed against Mary Jean, it's not hard to deduce why a new indictment has yet to come down. It's called the "Fruit of the Poisonous Tree." So much of the evidence against Mary Jean is intertwined with facts and statements that are inadmissible against her, it's nearly impossible to separate them all. A charge based on the currently known facts filed against Mary Jean would be subject to numerous legal challenges before trial and would rely heavily on the testimony of convicted criminals. Without the cooperation of Seth Bader himself, proving Mary Jean was on the inside of the conspiracy would be tough sledding.

It's important to note that, as dubious as her claims might seem—that she didn't take part in the conspiracy, that she didn't ask people to slash tires or shoot windows, that she didn't really know what all the money being passed back and forth was for, that she didn't sell Vicki's jewelry in the pool hall, that she didn't do anything improper while working for Aetna, that she didn't steal prescription pads or illegally possess prescription medications, that she didn't solicit anyone for murder, that she didn't know who built the pipe bomb or how it got into the mailbox, and that she didn't know Vicki's life was in danger when she left Seth's house on August 24, 1996—those are her claims nonetheless. Mary Jean Martin is innocent until proven guilty by a court of law.

At last check, Mary Jean was living in Central Florida, still taking care of dogs. She did not respond to requests for comment for this book.

In 1997, Exeter police officers Richard Kane and Kimberly Roberts were cited for heroism after the partners swam the icy Squamscott River to rescue a motorist who had spun out, landed in the water, and become trapped on the roof of her car.

Today, Richard Kane is the police chief of Exeter. He says the Bader case was a particularly difficult one. If he could go back, Chief Kane says he would have immediately taken Seth Bader up on his offer to examine his basement, instead of waiting for weeks, long after Bader had the time to remove any evidence that connected him to the pipe bomb.

Kane's former partner, Detective Kimberly Roberts, left the Exeter Police Department and is now an instructor at the New Hampshire Police Standards and Training Council Academy, teaching the next generation of law enforcement professionals. Captain Roberts specializes in teaching background investigation, evidence collection, and fingerprinting.

*   *   *

Sergeant James Richard Kelly retired from the New Hampshire State Police in 2000 and became an airline pilot based in Portsmouth, New Hampshire. When the airline he worked for folded, Kelly got a job with the TSA as an assistant director of security.

Kelly says that the most satisfying moment of the Seth Bader trial for him was when, after months of publicly denying his involvement in Vicki's murder, Seth told his fellow inmates at the county jail that he had "underestimated the tenacity of the New Hampshire State Police."

Kelly thinks the cast of characters in the case was among the most colorful he'd ever come across. "Those two thugs from Boston," he says, meaning Stuto and Caradonna, "talk about 'Frick and Frack.'"

The former detective has one lasting thought about the defendant. When the truth came out, he was actually surprised it was Seth who'd pulled the trigger—Kelly hadn't thought the man would have been brave enough to do it himself.

On August 14, 1998, Sandro Stuto was sentenced to five to fourteen years in the New Hampshire State Prison for his role in the torment of Vicki Bader. He was released in May 2003, after serving nearly five years.

After his release, Stuto was deported to Italy.

* * *

On December 2, 1998, Sebastian Caradonna pleaded guilty to lesser charges in connection with the pipe bomb incident. The plea required him to serve up to four years behind bars. Part of the deal included his agreeing to testify against Mary Jean Martin at her eventual trial, if she were ever indicted.

What is unclear is why the defense never called him to testify at Seth Bader's trial. The prosecution presumably felt it had enough witnesses without calling Caradonna, whose evasiveness might have undermined his credibility at trial. Perhaps the defense felt that Caradonna would have been a hostile witness, having already accepted a deal from the state. It was only years later that, under closer scrutiny of his statements, Seth's legal team realized that Caradonna said he only dealt with Mary Jean and didn't implicate Seth directly.

Prosecutor Joseph Laplante left the New Hampshire Attorney General's office in late 1998 and took a job with the U.S. Department of Justice, investigating campaign finance irregularities. He commuted back and forth between New Hampshire and Washington, insisting on being home for weekends with his growing family. After two years, he was reassigned to the U.S. Attorney's office in Boston prosecuting major crimes, then as the first assistant to the U.S. Attorney in Concord, New Hampshire.

In 2007, Laplante was nominated by President George

W. Bush to become a U.S. district court judge. He was unanimously confirmed by the U.S. Senate.

Because of his federal judgeship, Laplante is a little more reclusive today. He's had to resign from some of the civic organizations he previously supported, but he still enjoys a good boxing match.

Laplante says he still feels for Joseph Bader, describing him as a "pawn," and says he would have loved to get a crack at cross-examining Seth Bader.

"Seth is a textbook narcissist," he asserts.

Laplante maintains the Bader case was one of his career's most memorable trials. Laplante, although careful with his words, implies a belief that not everyone responsible for Vicki's death received justice.

Assistant Attorney General John Kacavas again followed his friend Joe Laplante to a new job; for several years, he, too, commuted weekly to Washington, D.C., as well as to Los Angeles as a member of the Campaign Finance Task Force.

In 2000, Kacavas was elected to the New Hampshire House of Representatives. In 2002, he was the Democratic nominee in a special runoff election for a seat on the governor's Executive Council (the incumbent had resigned to become the next U.S. Attorney from New Hampshire), but he lost the bid.

Kacavas opened his own law practice, which became quite successful. He even took on his former Homicide Unit boss, Michael Ramsdell, as a partner in the firm. In

2009, Kacavas was nominated by President Barack Obama to become the new U.S. Attorney for New Hampshire.

Now that his staff presents cases before Judge Laplante, Kacavas and the judge have had to bow out of their weekly poker game and can no longer socialize. The only time they get to spend time together is when they are both asked to travel and speak at seminars with judicial officials from emerging nations, such as Iraq or Afghanistan.

Unlike Laplante, Kacavas has a more critical retrospective view of Joseph Bader. At the time of the trial, he'd just finished prosecuting a case in which two teenage brothers murdered their parents and stashed the bodies in an attic. Kacavas has no doubt that Seth manipulated Joe into the things he did, but the former prosecutor is no Pollyanna. He has seen the violence that young men can do and doesn't consider them innocent.

Not long after Vicki Bader first disappeared, her attorney Heidi Boyack left private practice and began working for the New Hampshire court system. She says she found testifying at Vicki Bader's murder trial very cathartic. She could never understand why people believed Seth Bader over her client. The police had failed Vicki; the courts had failed her.

The wife of Boyack's ex-partner John Lewis attended the trial to hear Boyack testify. "Is *that* why you left private practice?" she'd asked afterward.

Boyack hadn't realized until that moment that it was true.

In 2003, Heidi Boyack's high school sweetheart looked her up on the Internet and they rekindled their relationship. They married, and she moved to be with him in Minnesota. Boyack now works for the Minnesota state courts.

Dr. Yvonne Vissing, the original guardian ad litem in the case, said her experience with the Baders was so disappointing that she never took another GAL case in New Hampshire again. Today, she continues her work in academia.

Seth Bader's attorney Barbara Taylor was sanctioned by the Professional Conduct Committee (PCC) for comments attributed to her in an interview she gave to the *Portsmouth Herald* after Seth Bader's conviction. Taylor was quoted as saying the jury's verdict was correct and that she thought Seth had been dishonest with her during the time she represented him in various civil cases, including a wrongful death suit filed against him by his ex-wife's family.

The complaint was filed by a Portsmouth attorney who thought the statements were unethical. Seth Bader also filed a complaint with the PCC, saying Taylor's statements harmed his chances at appeal.

Taylor said her quotes were inaccurate and taken out of context; however, she did admit to saying she had been "burned" while working on the Bader case. Ultimately, the PCC issued her a letter of reprimand.

"It wasn't one of the better periods of my life, but I did get through it, mainly because I also remembered that people have very short memories. That held true of the Bader case," Taylor says. Today, she is retired from practicing law.

James Boffetti, Joe Bader's attorney, left the public defender's office and joined the attorney general's office in the 2000s. As a prosecutor, he felt he was continuing his priestly mission as a fighter for social justice. He rose through the ranks to become senior assistant attorney general, prosecuted many homicide cases and public integrity investigations, and now serves as the chief of the Consumer Protection and Antitrust Bureau.

When asked about the Bader trial, Boffetti said, "I can say that trial remains one of the most significant trials of my career and that I found Joe Bader to be an exceptional young man, even given how he himself was a victim of Seth's violence, cruelty, and manipulation."

Mark Sisti continues to practice criminal defense and is still considered one of New Hampshire's finest attorneys.

After the Bader trial, Sisti says he grew to have deep respect and affection for Joe Laplante and John Kacavas, a feeling that continued when he faced them in later homicide trials. He and Paul Twomey spent the week of jury deliberations waiting alone with the prosecutors and had some deep discussions about the law. Despite their being rivals at the bar, Kacavas himself later commented that those conversations were some of the most important in his growth as a jurist.

Still, Sisti believes there was plenty of reasonable doubt in the case of *State v. Bader*. The lack of physical evidence, the "immaculate crime scene" where not a speck of blood could be uncovered, should have been enough to hang most juries, he says.

The state relied heavily on the testimony of people he believed to be shady characters, like Sandro Stuto and Joe Bader. And, he adds, Mary Jean Martin's role in Vicki Bader's death has never been properly explored.

Over the years, Sisti's partner Paul Twomey became more involved in politics and election law. He represented Democrats, Republicans, and Libertarians in different ballot disputes. He championed a lawsuit against the Republican Party for their effort to jam the phone banks of New Hampshire Democratic get-out-the-vote efforts on Election Day in 2002. Four operatives, including the New England regional director for the 2000 Bush-Cheney campaign, went to jail in that case. The legal fees and penalties left the New Hampshire Republican Party nearly bankrupt, with less than $800 in their war chest at the beginning of the 2006 races.

In an amicable parting, Paul Twomey eventually left the law practice he built with Sisti to open a new firm. He had handled more than two hundred murder trials in his career, and he says all of them were heart wrenching, even the ones he won. Now, Twomey has a caseload of drug and DWI arrests, as well as election disputes.

"My only victim these days," Twomey says, "is the state."

Twomey remains deeply troubled by the Bader case. He is a true believer that Stuto, Mary Jean, and the others set Seth up for the murder in hopes of getting his money. Twomey still ponders whether Seth actually got a fair trial.

In December 2010, Twomey approached the newly formed New Hampshire Cold Case Unit and requested they reopen the Bader case to look at other suspects.

Lois Stewart still lives on Long Island, New York, in the house that Vicki grew up in. Her older son, John, inherited his father's bad heart and passed away in the years following Vicki's trial, but her other son Jim and his family have been a close support system.

The civil suit lingered on, even after Heidi Boyack left private practice and her partner John Lewis took a seat on the bench with the Rockingham Superior Court. The firm had morphed into Borofsky, Amodeo-Vickery & Bandazian, and Stephen Borofsky headed up the wrongful death suit. When the case was finally heard in 2004, Seth refused to sit in the courtroom for the trial.

After all the evidence was presented, the judge found that Seth's actions were "wanton, malicious, and/or oppressive" and had caused his ex-wife to "suffer to an unimaginable degree." The estate of Vicki Bader was awarded $4.4 million.

Although Seth's assets did not total that amount, they were still considered expansive. They included all of the real estate, the Steinway piano, and the Guadagnini violin. The $400,000 musical instrument has been the focus of mystery, as certain parties claim not to know its whereabouts, with other legal firms claiming to have secured it in lieu of pay.

The money is dedicated to Vicki's heirs: Joe, Matt, and Sam. Seth continued to stall and obfuscate, but by late 2010, Seth finally conceded to selling off some of his property to pay the debt.

Lois says she wrote a letter to Seth in prison, one she hoped would get out all the anger and sadness he caused her. She asked that he not respond to her, and he has not.

Lois remains very protective of the boys, but especially Sam. In the years following his mother's murder, Sam was adopted by a new family and changed his name. According to Lois, Sam has tried hard to have a normal life despite his knowledge of his troubling family history.

To this day, Lois says she feels sorry for Joseph Bader. She recognizes Seth Bader put him in an impossible situation. "Still," she says, "I know Joe for who he is."

Lois says Joe made a surprise appearance at the end of the civil trial. When someone asked the young man why he had come, he reportedly said, "I came for Lois." But she found his answer to be insincere. Lois believes the only reason Joe came was to see if he would be getting any money.

*   *   *

Matthew Bader declined to be interviewed for this book.

In the minds of most trial watchers, Joe Bader will perpetually remain a troubled fifteen-year-old boy. But Joseph Bader grew up, kept his last name, and started his life all over again.

Joseph admits that his feelings for Vicki changed after her suicide attempts. In correspondence regarding this story, he wrote:

"Up to this time in my childhood, I had been abandoned and betrayed by just about anyone I had ever come to depend on or trust, and her suicide attempts really hurt me on that level. Add to that all of the other turmoil in my life at the time and the fact that Seth intentionally used those feelings to control and manipulate me, and I don't think anyone could honestly say they had a clear sense of their feelings."

Despite the lack of emotion he may have demonstrated at the time, Joseph Bader says the consequences of August 24, 1996, continue to be with him every day of his life.

"These events are woven into the fabric of my life in such a way that they affect everything I do and think," he wrote. "I am the type of person that tries to learn from everything, and these events were an education in psychology in many ways. Looking back, I learned a lot about fear, manipulation, deception, and greed; but I also learned a lot about love, human nature, and trying to make things right, no matter what the cost. The events in our lives shape us in ways we don't usually think about on a conscious level, but they always provide lessons, if we look for them."

Authors' Note

When we wrote to Seth Bader at the New Hampshire State Prison for Men, the prospects for obtaining his cooperation seemed doubtful at best. In the years since his conviction, Seth Bader has fiercely proclaimed his innocence at every opportunity. He continues to espouse the theory—despite the lack of evidence—that Mary Jean Martin seduced Joe in order to get the teenager to murder Vicki Bader. The motive was money, Seth insists, and framing him for the killing would have liberated all of Vicki's and Seth's assets for MJ and Joe to live on.

Seth continued to use Sisti and Twomey for some of his early appeals, but he has since retained the services of a Massachusetts lawyer. It's clear that Seth, however, continues to mastermind the strategy and arguments of his case today.

First approached about this book in February 2010, Seth agreed to accept written questions and answer in kind, but he made his own rules about what he would reveal about his story.

> There is a lot I will not discuss. I do not bare my soul to strangers. Nor will I rub salt into Vicki's family's wounds. And some of the facts may not be believed coming from me; better you talk to independent sources.

Seth was told that his cooperation for this book would not change the main facts of the story—that he was convicted in 1998 of murdering his ex-wife—but that it would help give a more rounded, more human portrayal of himself and his story. Seth at first seemed uninterested in the way people view him today. But after writing and mailing a six-page letter describing his state of mind, Seth wrote and mailed a second letter on the same day. It was one page long and we can only assume he was compelled to write it suddenly and urgently.

> Just an added thought . . . If I say I am innocent, I come across as being in denial. If I criticize anyone connected to the case, I come across as bitter or whining. If I am calm, I come across as cold-blooded. No matter what I say, I make myself look bad.

Despite this concern, Seth did go on to write several letters responding to five or six questions asked of him at a time. Seth's letters were also full of rich details about his life growing up in Brooklyn and his relationships with his parents and with Mary Jean Martin. He refused to answer specific questions about Vicki and his sons, but over time, he volunteered observations about them.

Despite his efforts not to be too revealing, Seth was at times self-reflective and jovial.

> It is fair to say that I am not the most socially polished person whom God ever put on Earth. This is what comes of being the bookish only child of modestly wealthy and somewhat elderly academics. I do not mean to be overbearing, but I probably seem that way at times . . . I would like to think I have mellowed with age. Form your own opinion.

With every letter, Seth goaded us into retrieving court documents associated with his case and his appeal. Only a handful were available to the public at the time the correspondence began. He kept asking what our knowledge of people like "inmate John Doe" was. They were breadcrumbs he was dropping that he felt no one was picking up fast enough.

> Upon reviewing our correspondence I sense a growing disconnect between what you are asking for and what I am inclined to provide. You seek human-interest material. Are you planning something along the lines of "Inside the Mind of a Vicious Killer Lawyer"? I

hope you instead plan to do some real investigative journalism. If you go down that path you will uncover a story which does not make me a candidate for sainthood but which is quite different from the "official version" presented at my trial.

The evidence Seth presents to demonstrate his innocence includes the three following claims:

- In his interview by state police, Sebastian Caradonna never said he was hired or solicited by Seth Bader. He said the whole terror operation was orchestrated by Mary Jean Martin, who handed out all of the money.
- In May 2001, a county jail inmate (referred to only as "John Doe") said that Sandro Stuto told him before the 1998 trial that Seth had nothing to do with Vicki's murder. Doe claimed Stuto said there was a plot among several people to get insurance and estate money and to frame Seth. Doe said they were "all banging Seth's ex-girlfriend," including Joseph Bader.
- In 2005, after running into Joseph Bader at Hampton Beach, a childhood friend remembered a conversation the two had immediately following Vicki's disappearance in 1996. Kory Almand had been a neighbor and one of Joe's closest friends. Almand remembers teenage Joe talking about how he would "mess around" with Mary Jean, implying they had a sexual relationship. While in Joe's room, he witnessed Joe smash his

pillow with a baseball bat while saying how he wanted to kill Vicki. After she disappeared, Almand and Joe camped in a tent in Seth's yard, and Joe told his friend Vicki was dead and that he had shot her. The goal, he said, was to frame Seth and get his money.

Despite their tantalizing revelations, time and again state and federal prosecutors and judges have put little credence in the claims and have denied Seth's appeals. Why? The authors took a closer look at each of the arguments.

The transcript of Caradonna's police interview does show that the man only spoke of his interactions with Mary Jean, as she was always the alleged go-between. But to say this proves Seth Bader wasn't involved in the plot is not credible. Caradonna was always cagey about the way he phrased the extent of his knowledge and his participation. It's an easy read between the lines to see Caradonna was trying to protect himself during his police interrogation. Though he didn't call him out by name, Seth's role as the puppet master of those negotiations is clear.

"John Doe's" testimony in his affidavit seems sincere. It's very likely he believed he heard Sandro Stuto say the murder was a setup. Stuto, after all, had been bragging to fellow inmates he was a bone breaker, somehow mob-connected, when there's no evidence he actually was. Jailhouse confessions and jailhouse boasting come in equal measure and are difficult to distinguish. Remember,

Seth Bader also freely spouted claims of his culpability while behind bars. So who was bragging and who was confessing: Bader or Stuto? Nevertheless, the claim never rose to the level of "new evidence" sufficient to warrant a new trial.

Lastly, Kory Almand's statement—also sincerely offered—is the most troubling. Did Joe Bader tell his best friend he shot Vicki only days after she disappeared? It's very likely the teenager *said it* (even Lois Stewart thinks Joe might have bragged to his friend about the killing), but unlikely he actually *did it*. Joe often relished his role as the cul-de-sac kid from the concrete jungle. Instead of casting his domineering father in the starring role, Joe was able to take control over both parents in his story. If the plan really was to frame Seth for the killing, the alleged "co-conspirators" missed plenty of opportunities over several months to spring the trap. *Why* Joe would say such a thing—days after dumping Vicki's warm body in the dirt—is a better question for psychologists than criminologists. A chilling statement made, but not nearly enough to set a convicted killer free.

Seth's appeals through both the state and federal courts focused primarily on these recantations as bases for a new trial. Over the past thirteen years, Seth has lost and exhausted all of his appeals, but his lawyer continues to search for novel avenues to get a new trial and eventually win his release.

While many of the items on Seth's list could raise legitimate concerns in a possible future trial, our examination of thousands of police and court documents obtained through a Right to Know request revealed countless factual details about Seth's case. While he would argue that many facts excluded from trial proved his innocence, it could easily be said that there were as many excluded facts that would have further proved Seth guilty.

As is our intention with every story we have the opportunity to tell, we endeavored to present a thoroughly researched and documentable account of what happened during the course of the Bader marriage, the court battle that ensued after the divorce, the timeline of the campaign of terror waged against Vicki Bader, her murder, and the ensuing investigation. Seth Bader's contributions, while illuminating, do not change the fact that he was convicted of the murder of Vicki Bader.

As is invariably the situation when writing about a criminal case, the literary temptation to paint some characters as "good" and others as "evil" is often thwarted by the very real fact that most human beings, even those who have committed the most despicable acts, tend to fall somewhere in between. What makes this story so fascinating isn't just the confusing dichotomies of Seth Bader and his accomplices, but the idea that while many of the evildoers in this tale were, in fact, motivated by greed and a lack of regard for human life, others were plainly manipulated, or simply slaves to their inability to exert reasonable judgment.

Even Seth himself seems to wrestle with the figures involved in his story. It is his belief now, for example, that we would get a real glimpse inside of Vicki Bader's mind if we were to read a memoir describing one woman's struggle with bipolar disorder. This compassionate point of view is in stark contrast to the man we met in so many police reports and court documents, a man who portrayed his ex-wife as "crazy" and "unstable," without any acknowledgment that she might have been suffering from a potentially treatable medical disorder.

Life at the New Hampshire State Prison for Men is a productive one for Seth. At the time of this writing, he works as a clerk in the Industries shop, where inmates learn trades and produce furniture and other products to sell at the prison store across the road. He continues to maintain a law practice of sorts, both working on his own case and, according to insiders within the New Hampshire court system, writing copious briefs for his fellow inmates on a variety of matters.

Seth also teaches classes relating to legal issues in the prison, and he mailed to us the notes he planned to use for a lecture. The title of the class was "Whose Right to Bear What Arms?—Law, History, Movement Conservatives, and the Second Amendment."

Still, it is clear that Seth Bader's intellectual productivity in prison is designed to maintain his mental acuity for his primary mission—to win a new trial that will reverse his murder conviction. And he is very hopeful that he will succeed in that effort in the not-too-distant future; so hopeful, in fact, that he suggested we might put off the publication of this book until such time as he makes his case.

> Probably this spring I will be filing a new habeas corpus petition in Merrimack County Superior Court. That petition will include a great deal of documentary evidence, both old and new. Would it be better to hold off with this project until you see those documents? Some will be old news, included for content. At least one will be a startling new matter.

There is no doubt that any presentation made by Seth Bader in court will not only retread old facts, but will also include startling revelations. Whether those revelations will be helpful to his appeal is another matter. Seth's legal creativity and tenacity were never in question to us or to the investigators and prosecutors involved in his case. Seth is never at a loss for new revelations. But those revelations are often presented despite factual evidence to the contrary, and they don't tend to add much weight to his version of history.

Prosecutors Joseph Laplante and John Kacavas portrayed Seth Bader as a man motivated by money, a sore loser who would not admit defeat to his ex-wife on any battlefield. Defense attorneys Mark Sisti and Paul Twomey portrayed Seth as a patsy, taken advantage of by unscrupulous people interested only in his wallet. Both portrayals are accurate; in fact, they overlap. It seems that motivated by his own lust and desire to be loved, Seth would go to any lengths to maintain his relationship with Mary Jean, even commit murder. His ego would not allow him to lose to his ex-wife, to pay her any amount of money, but the loss of the cash itself was only important as it depleted his ability to pacify his new fiancée with dinners, flowers, and jewelry. How else could one explain Seth's desperate offer to concede everything he fought Vicki for in court if only she would tell him whatever secrets about Mary Jean she might possess? Not until Vicki was finally gone did the couple concede that their relationship was doomed because of their own shortcomings, not the shortcomings of others.

While the facts about the case presented in this book don't discount Seth Bader's talents when it comes to framing his version of events, our story does defer to the overwhelming opinions of those objective individuals who were brought into the case at so many points during the investigation, from beat cops to state police detectives, from babysitters to court-appointed guardians, from divorce attorneys to lead prosecutors for the state.

In their eyes, and in ours, Seth Bader is serving a sentence that will take far more than one new revelation, no matter how startling, to overturn.